WHEN PROTEST MAKES POLICY

CAWP Series in Gender and American Politics

SERIES EDITORS:

Susan J. Carroll, Rutgers University

Kira Sanbonmatsu, Rutgers University

TITLES IN THE SERIES:

When Protest Makes Policy: How Social Movements Represent Disadvantaged Groups
by S. Laurel Weldon

The Paradox of Gender Equality: How American Women's Groups Gained and Lost Their Public Voice
by Kristin A. Goss

Center for American Women and Politics
Eagleton Institute of Politics
Rutgers University
www.cawp.rutgers.edu

WHEN PROTEST MAKES POLICY

How Social Movements Represent Disadvantaged Groups

S. LAUREL WELDON

THE UNIVERSITY OF MICHIGAN PRESS

ANN ARBOR

First paperback edition 2012

Published in the United States of America by
The University of Michigan Press
Printed and bound by CPI Group (UK) Ltd, Croydon, CR0 4YY

2015 2014 2013 2012 5 4 3 2

A CIP catalog record for this book is available from the British Library.

Library of Congress Cataloging-in-Publication Data

Weldon, S. Laurel.
When protest makes policy : how social movements represent disadvantaged groups / by S. Laurel Weldon.
p. cm. — (CAWP series in gender and American politics)
Includes bibliographical references and index.
ISBN 978-0-472-11748-2 (cloth : alk. paper)
1. Social movements—Political aspects. 2. Feminism—Political aspects. 3. Social movements—Political aspects—United States. 4. Feminism—United States. I. Title.
HM881.W45 2011
303.48'4082—dc22 2010024622

ISBN 978-0-472-02637-1 (e-book)
ISBN 978-0-472-03511-3 (pbk. : alk. paper)

For Aaron, Audrey, and Zed,
with all my love,
and in memory of Iris Marion Young

Contents

Acknowledgments

A book-length project necessarily incurs many debts, so I have many people to thank. First, I thank my colleagues at Purdue University who helped me repeatedly and in many different contexts with this book. Leigh Raymond read most of the chapters, and his enthusiasm for this project shored me up when my confidence lagged. I have also been grateful for his appreciation for a certain local Indian restaurant. Jay McCann is astoundingly generous with his time, excellent advice, and fresh coffee. Suzie Parker made important suggestions about how to think about the Democratic Party in the Southern states in the United States and provided invaluable advice about survey design and analysis. In addition to teaching me to really appreciate a Margarita, Rosalee Clawson read several of these chapters and taught me much about surveys and intersectionality. Bill Shaffer is a great friend and colleague, reading and critiquing just about every chapter in this book at some point and offering suggestions, advice, and beer. Bert Rockman has been a mentor of mine since graduate school, taking time to provide me advice on questions big and small, including many of the chapters and ideas presented in this book. His influence in setting me on the institutional road is no doubt substantial. Bob Bartlett also read every chapter here and provided sage advice about the proposal. Pat Boling gave me expert feedback on many of these chapters as only a fellow scholar of feminist theory and public policy could. Harry Targ provided invaluable expertise on labor organizing and politics. Aaron Hoffman argued with me about nearly everything in this book and nearly drove me crazy by finding things I could improve when I thought I was finished. This made the book much better. Aaron also helped shape the idea for the book and supported my nascent vision of the book when I was not sure it would be of interest. Other Purdue colleagues helped me solve a problem with a particular part of the analysis (Eric Waltenburg and Roger Larocca) or provided important feedback on drafts of chapters and the proposal (Ann Clark, Niambi Carter, and Daniel Aldrich).

I am also lucky to have an extended network of brilliant and creative colleagues in the broader discipline who are unfailingly generous with their time.

Jane Mansbridge provided suggestions on many parts of the project, helping with important refinements in the argument. Karen Beckwith generously provided feedback at key moments. Amy Mazur also talked with me at length about many of these ideas, providing encouragement and feedback. The wide-ranging discussions I have had with Mala Htun have helped me better to articulate many of the ideas in these pages. David Meyer is a reliable source of feedback and enthusiastic support for a more junior colleague; his collegiality is admirable. Melissa Williams has been an inspiration and support for more than a decade.

For helpful discussion, assistance with data or technical matters, or incisive questions about particular issues or chapters, I thank David Alexander, Olga Avdeyeva, Debbie Bahu, Maryann Barakso, Sylvia Bashevkin, Anya Bernstein, Lisa Brush, Lisa Baldez, Amy Caiazza, Suzi Dovi, William Dunn, Rachel Einwohner, Amy Elman, Brian Fuerst, Carol Gould, Bernie Grofman, Ange-Marie Hancock, Susan Hansen, Don Kerchis, Cheryl Kerchis, William Jacoby, Judson Jeffries, Jyl Josephson, Katsuo Nishikawa, Pam Paxton, Andrew Rehfeld, Sue Tolleson Rinehart, Kira Sanbonmatsu, Oxana Shevel, Evelyn Simien, Dorothy Stetson, Dara Strolovitch, Terri Towner, and Larry Weldon. I thank Pamela Lubin and Manjusha Gupte for research assistance. I am also very glad that Maura Bahu and Patrick Jessee, who were undergraduates at Purdue, each worked with me on a chapter of the book. They made the work much more fun than it would otherwise have been, and I learned a great deal from both of them. I thank Lori Norris, Brianne Belliveau, Jackie Strange, and Vicki McKinley for helping with household matters and child care so that I could devote my attention more fully to these pages.

This work has been presented at various stages to the Midwest Political Science Association and the American Political Science Association and at Purdue University (especially at the Public Policy and Political Theory Workshop); the University of Pittsburgh; the University of Toronto (Canada); the University of Victoria (Canada); the University of California, Irvine; and Georgetown University. I thank the people who participated in those sessions for their helpful comments and questions. Two of these chapters were published in journals (the *Journal of Politics* and *Political Research Quarterly*), and the process of review improved those chapters and helped me to think about this project. I thank the Institute for Women's Policy Research (especially Amy Caiazza) and the Center for American Women and Politics for making so much valuable data available.

I thank Melody Herr at University of Michigan Press for her support for this work and for her attention to detail. Anonymous reviewers at the University of Michigan Press, as well as Susan Carroll and Kira Sanbonmatsu, series editors, provided important suggestions and comments on the manuscript.

Having received all this help and support from such a wide range of people, it would be shocking if errors remained in the text. Indeed, at this point, I can hardly be blamed for such errors, and I suggest that any problems be laid squarely at the feet of one of the aforementioned colleagues.

We all know books require emotional as well as intellectual resources, and in my case, my friends and family so often shored me up, made me laugh, or helped out with my kids that I feel lucky to have such a big group to thank. Laura Barker and Cathy Flynn picked me up from a distance when I needed a hand. I thank Leigh, Teresa, Ximena, and Chris for being our Lafayette "family" and making our life here fuller of love, laughter, and care. Thanks also go to my exceptionally wonderful family: to my mother for being an inspiration and unflagging support, not to mention a source of great jokes; to my father for encouraging me and standing behind me every step of the way (and for helping out with free statistical advice sometimes); to my brother (Kaljo) and sisters (Christine, Allison, and Katie) for making my family so much richer and for being a good uncle or auntie when their sister needed a little help with child care. My mother's partner, Don Walker, has always been there for me; my father's wife, Jill Weldon, has also been a great support. Great big thanks go to my family-in-law: no one could ask for more love and support than I have been lucky enough to enjoy from the Hoffmans.

I am sustained by my loving husband and children, and I dedicate this book to them. I thank my amazing children, Zed and Audrey, for being themselves. Words cannot express my debt, intellectual and personal, to my wonderful partner, Aaron Hoffman, but I am foolish enough to try in the brief space available here. He is the best partner anyone could possibly imagine, and he has given generously of his time to offer feedback on the book. He is a wonderful father to our children. He cooks delicious meals and picks out fabulous wines. He makes me laugh and makes my life fun.

Finally, as I was writing this book, my friend and mentor (and former dissertation advisor) Iris Young passed away. I am sorry she will not get to see this book. I hope this book contributes, in its own small way, to furthering her legacy of pressing for both social-structural analysis and attention to the ways power and difference are entwined. I also dedicate this book to her memory.

Introduction: Movements, Marginalization, and Representation

In the aftermath of the 1999 "Battle in Seattle," when more than 50,000 people gathered in Seattle to protest globalization and the World Trade Organization (WTO), protesters claimed success in representing the marginalized and disenfranchised of the world. Indeed, activists of all stripes see themselves as "representatives," giving voice to perspectives that would otherwise be excluded.[1] By providing better representation of historically disadvantaged groups, social movements further inclusion, produce greater trust in government, and reduce social conflict (Mansbridge 1999; Williams 1998; Wolbrecht and Hero 2005; Costain 2005). But social movements are frequently criticized for overrepresenting the privileged and lacking democratic accountability.[2] Moreover, critics allege that movements deepen exclusion and marginalization when protest tactics disrupt deliberation, prevent compromise, and emphasize differences over commonalities, fragmenting the polity into separate "identities" or "special interests."[3] Given these concerns, what are we to make of social movement claims to represent or "speak for" the excluded? Do social movements offer a pathway to a more inclusive democracy or toward a more polarized, fragmented, elite-dominated polity?

Examining a variety of public policies, I show in this book that social movements are important avenues of political representation, especially for excluded and disadvantaged groups in established democracies. Social movements, I find, constitute a critical avenue of policy influence for women, workers, and women of color, an avenue often more important than political parties, interest groups, or electing group members to government office (descriptive representation). Indeed, movements are so important that we ought to further such mobilization wherever we can. I propose the ideal of the *advocacy state* as a guide to deepening inclusive democracy. Such a state is aimed at furthering the mobilization of disadvantaged groups both within the formal institutions of government and in civil society.

Social movements enable representation and inclusion by facilitating the articulation of group consciousness, by organizing and mobilizing the very groups to be represented. Disadvantaged groups define themselves and identify their priorities through such movements.[4] Without social movements, there are no constituencies or group perspectives to be represented. Furthermore, through a variety of activities and agents (movement organizations, intellectuals, publications, theater, protests, etc.), movements articulate and diffuse to the broader citizenry alternative, otherwise marginalized perspectives on political issues, enriching deliberation about policy issues (Mansbridge and Flaster 2007; Fraser 1995; Young 2000).

Mobilization of socially and economically disadvantaged groups is more easily undertaken in the informal, fluid world of social movements, because formal institutions tend to disempower and exclude these groups. The "entry costs" are lower for social movement mobilization than for other types of political mobilization. Moreover, social movements can be very influential. In fact, the research presented in this book shows that social movements can be more effective avenues of policy influence than electing larger numbers of women or minorities to political office, voting, traditional lobby groups, or political parties. They also enhance the effectiveness of these other mechanisms of representation.

Empirical and theoretical studies of democratic representation, even those focused on representation for disadvantaged groups, have mostly overlooked this important contribution to democracy. The literature on representation for marginalized groups has traditionally focused on the value of descriptive representation in the legislature.[5] This is an important area of research, to be sure, but an overemphasis on descriptive representation in the legislature leaves other important avenues for representation unexamined, ignores the way different avenues of representation interact, and results in a tendency to overlook the institutional context (Weldon 2002; Childs 2006; Mansbridge 2003; Poggione 2004; Wolbrecht and Hero 2005). Indeed, an emerging literature is revealing the complexities involved in processes of representation. For example, social movements and government agencies can be mechanisms of representation for marginalized groups, and there are politically important links between feminist organizations and legislators.[6] This is not to suggest that the literature on descriptive representation in the legislature claims that electing women or people of color is the only way to obtain policy change (no scholar says such a thing); rather, the point is that descriptive representation in other places and other mechanisms of substantive representation have been understudied in relation to their importance in securing policy change of significance for marginalized groups.

The main empirical literature focusing on the political significance of social movements (political sociology) tends to focus on questions relating to the causes of social mobilization, their success or failure in maintaining mobilization, or perhaps their ability to obtain particular policy goals; democracy tends not to be a "dependent variable" for sociologists.[7] As a result, few scholars of social movements have assessed these movements in terms of their potential contribution to democracy, especially for marginalized groups. Democratic theorists, meanwhile, have mostly overlooked or devalued the *representative* role of social movements. Although many political theorists assign an important role to social movements, they mostly see movements as providing an avenue for or model of *participatory* democracy.[8] Some theorists see the very existence of social movements as providing a *critique* of representative democracy (Kitschelt 1993).

There is a growing recognition of the important connections between participation and representation (Young 2000). In this instance, thinking of social movements as offering avenues of representation as well as participation suggests new ways to value these organizations and new ways to promote democracy. Instead of criticizing social movement organizations for focusing on representation rather than participation (e.g., Acker 1995; Putnam 2000), scholars should focus on which types of movement organizations or institutions provide which democratic functions (Edwards et al. 2001). Indeed, moving beyond the traditional pluralist focus on representation through a system of interest groups (Dahl 1962; Truman 1951; Walker 1991), contemporary theorists of representation have come to emphasize civil society actors such as voluntary associations as a critical avenue of democratic representation (Cohen and Rogers 1992; Warren 2001). Drawing on this work, I propose that the democratic ideal requires an "advocacy state" that both includes agencies designed to promote marginalized groups (e.g., women's policy machineries) and also encourages autonomous organizing by these groups in civil society. As a way of showing the practicability of the ideal, I offer concrete examples of real policies that encourage autonomous organizing by marginalized groups. These arguments point to new ways to improve and deepen democracy and further inclusion of the most marginalized segments of society.

The Plan of This Book

In the rest of this introduction, I outline the conceptual bases for arguing that social movements provide democratic representation, despite the absence (much of the time) of formal mechanisms of authorization and accountability that many see as the sine qua non of democratic representation. I use this argument to outline the advocacy state as an ideal: this is the idea that democratic states ought to foster the self-organization and mobilization of disadvantaged groups within and outside of state structures. In the chapters of this book, I provide further elaboration of and empirical support for these points, using a variety of primary sources (interviews, surveys) and secondary ones (existing data sets, newspaper articles, other published works).[9] Drawing on a series of analyses of women's movements and labor movements both in the United States and in established democracies more generally, I aim to show that social movements provide a vital form of democratic political representation, through both conventional and newer avenues of political expression. I supplement the cross-sectional, statistical analyses of multiple countries or states at a single point in time with case evidence from Canada, the United States, Norway, or other established democracies, to illustrate the dynamic relation between protest and policy over time.[10]

Social movements organize political mobilization through traditional lobby or interest groups, voter registration and education initiatives, and leadership institutes. They also work through the everyday politics of language change, institutional reforms, consumer boycotts, street theater, cultural criticism, and grassroots efforts to promote broader social change (Mansbridge 1995; Mansbridge and Flaster 2007; Rochon 1998; Beckwith 2007; Katzenstein 1998). Through these efforts, social movements *create* the constituencies and corresponding group perspectives that can be represented, a critical (if often overlooked) aspect of the process of representation (Williams 1998; Young 2000). More generally, social movements create and revitalize democratic civil society and fundamentally shape the architecture and operations of political institutions. These ongoing interactions between the state and civil society can have lasting impact far beyond the particular movement in question (Meyer 2003; Meyer et al. 2005; Costain and McFarland 1998).

At the same time, however, analysts have raised a number of concerns about social movements that bear directly on this argument about social movements as democratic representatives. The first, most practical concern is whether social movements actually have any lasting influence. Some posit that resilient social structures such as patriarchy, capitalism, white privilege, or other structures that work through the coercive power of the state obstruct efforts to transform policy outcomes (Bell 1987; MacKinnon 1989; Abramovitz 1992). Others argue that direct influence through formal electoral avenues of representation is the most direct, effective way to influence policy, contending that it is elected officials who set the agenda (Haider-Markel et al. 2000; Kingdon 1984; Spill et al. 2001). In chapters 1, 2, and 3, I seek to establish that for women and for workers, social movements can be more effective avenues of influence than traditional legislative representation and can prompt policy changes that matter a great deal to the everyday lives of these groups. These chapters examine movements and policies cross-nationally and in the United States.

Another concern focuses on the internal politics of social movements, pointing to evidence that movements best represent privileged groups and do a poorer job of "speaking for" the marginalized. I address this question in chapters 4 and 5, pointing out that while they are not perfect, social movements are still the best avenues of representation for disadvantaged groups, especially for groups, such as women of color, who tend to "fall through the cracks" of more generally focused organizations and institutions. Indeed, I show that women's movements are critical for policy developments that promote the distinctive interests of women of color. Women's movements do a better job of representing all women, though, when disadvantaged subgroups of women can organize themselves separately.

In chapter 5, I aim to provide evidence about the tripartite relationship between (1) the constituency "women" and various subgroups of women (women of color, working-class women, professional women, lesbians); (2) women's organizations; and (3) the public sphere (media and policy-making). The chapter presents a more detailed look at local women's organizations and their access to the media in the U.S. city of Chicago. I find that women's organizations, taken together, do a better job of representing the diversity of women—both descriptively and substantively—than do formally representative organizations such as legislatures and political parties. This suggests that social movements taken as a whole (but not necessarily any particular activists or organizations) are more representative of the diversity of social groups and attend more to diverse interests than previous research suggests. In addition, different sorts of organizations perform different democratic functions.

In chapter 6, I draw on the preceding analyses to suggest some ways to improve representation by social movements and to create a more inclusive democracy. I argue that states should actively encourage and foster the development of social movements and provide opportunities for activist participation in policy-making processes. Given the structured inequalities present in all contemporary and foreseeable democracies, the ideal democratic state would have to be an advocacy state, one that fostered independent movements especially of the most marginalized.

There are at least two reasons that scholars might be skeptical that such an advocacy state would work. First, some argue that inclusion of social movements in the state too often results in a depletion of civil society and a weakening of democracy (Dryzek et al. 2003). However, I contend that the risk of cooptation and depoliticization occurs not when social movements participate in policy-making processes (through public consultation, lobbying, bargaining, etc.) but, rather, when social movements are entirely absorbed by the state. When all the major social movement organizations and institutions are inside the state and there are few autonomous organizations, activists risk losing the leverage they gain from a broader base of public support. But it is possible for state policy to encourage strong, autonomous social movements without compromising movement autonomy, as I show in this introduction and in chapter 6. Moreover, if a dual strategy of organizing inside *and* outside the state is pursued, the dangers of depletion are far smaller, and the potential payoff in terms of the representation of otherwise excluded groups is tremendous.[11]

A second possible objection to an advocacy state focuses on whether it is possible, in practice, to distinguish systematically disadvantaged social groups from those that are not so disadvantaged. Although many scholars are skeptical that government policies can effectively discern disadvantaged groups, scholarly discussions tend to ignore the many examples of such policies that work reasonably well in practice. I offer the Court Challenges Program of Canada and the Disadvantaged Business Enterprise Program of the U.S. Department of Transportation as examples of programs that effectively targeted disadvantaged groups and facilitated their political mobilization.

Let us turn, now, to considering the conceptual bases for arguing that social movements can provide a kind of democratic representation, despite the absence (much of the time) of formal mechanisms of authorization and accountability.

Social Movements, Marginalization, and Representation

Substantive representation is partly a process of agenda setting, or prioritizing problems (Jones and Baumgartner 2005). Asking whether governments reflect the priorities of citizens is one way of getting at this sort of representation. Of course, the sets of priorities of citizens—indeed, the view of the appropriate role of the state—vary systematically by group. For example, a large body of scholarship shows systematic differences between women and men in public opinion and voting behavior both in the United States and cross-nationally.

Numerous studies establish the relationship between race and ethnicity and public opinion, both in the United States and cross-nationally. It is well established that class affects political attitudes, and in some contexts, religion is also an important factor. Political attitudes vary systematically across subgroups as well (i.e., Latinos v. Latinas, African American men v. white men, Latinas v. white women, etc.).[12] The distinctive attitudes and priorities associated with each social group can be thought of as a sort of group perspective (I describe this idea more fully in chapter 1). To assess how well particular groups are represented, we can ask whether their attitudes and views are articulated as part of the political process and whether these priorities are reflected in policy agendas and outcomes.

Comparing policy issue agendas to group agendas or perspectives to examine the degree of correspondence or disjuncture can be done at either an individual or collective level, by asking whether the priorities of this individual or legislative body or organization reflect the priorities of this particular group. So we can think of representation as a systemic or macropolitical process, asking how well this particular political system represents citizens. Such an approach, however, has rarely been undertaken at the macro or systemic level (Baumgartner and Jones 2005; Costain 1994).

This analytic approach is especially valuable for studying the representation of systematically disadvantaged groups, sometimes called "marginalized." Although there are many differences across marginalized groups defined by race/ethnicity, gender, class, sexuality, and the like, they share the characteristic of being disadvantaged in multiple arenas (social, economic, political), of having an experience or group history of formal exclusion from public life (and sometimes economic and social exclusions as well), and of being defined by characteristics that are relatively immutable (Williams 1998). Note that pointing to the disadvantaged position of these groups need not imply that the form and degree of disadvantage are the same (Cohen 1999, chap. 2). The argument I advance here does suggest, however, that similar measures will improve representation for groups suffering a wide variety of forms of disadvantage (for a contrasting view, see Htun 2004).

If groups have distinct perspectives and concerns, substantive representation for those groups can be evaluated by examining the extent to which these views influence public discussion of policy issues and, ultimately, policy outcomes themselves (Jacobs and Shapiro 1994). To do so, however, we must be clear about what counts as a group perspective and how such a perspective might influence public debate and policy. Much social science research demonstrates considerable variation across and within the groups I discuss here, in terms of their priorities, concerns, and so on. Despite this heterogeneity, however, groups can be thought of as being characterized by distinctive points of view. One way to square this seeming contradiction is to note that group perspectives are characteristics of groups, not individuals. A group perspective may not find itself perfectly instantiated in any particular individual, although the vast majority in a group will share some set of overlapping concerns. Moreover, a group perspective emerges in interactive contexts, where members of the group discuss their status or fate with each other. This process brings to the foreground aspects of individual experience that are shared with other group members; it also highlights those aspects of experience that are different from other group members. In such contexts, group members discuss those elements of social or political life that loom large in their experience (police brutality, discrimination, etc.), although it is unlikely that they agree on the specific actions that individuals or collectivities ought to take to address these concerns. This set of issues can be thought of as being a group perspective even if the group is not unified in terms of ideology or interests in every case (I say more about this idea in chapter 1).

Avenues of Social Group Representation

How are group perspectives best articulated in established democracies? If we examine the question of representation at the macro level, we can examine a variety of mechanisms for the articulation of social group perspective, explore the relationships between them, and ask which ones (or which combinations) seem to have the most influence on deliberative processes and policy outcomes. Although descriptive representation is often valued for its symbolic effects (i.e., contributing to the social construction of groups as, e.g., powerful or powerless) and for legitimating government decisions, it is also thought to have substantive effects. Indeed, it is perhaps the single most examined avenue of substantive representation in the literature. Other possible avenues of influence for marginalized groups include political parties, interest groups, and social movements. In this section, I discuss the advantages and disadvantages of each avenue of representation and theorize the relationship between them. I contend both that social movement representation is the most effective avenue for marginalized groups and that it also improves representation by traditional, intralegislative means (descriptive representation in legislatures and political parties).

DESCRIPTIVE REPRESENTATION IN PUBLIC OFFICE

Much of the literature on the political representation of marginalized groups focuses on women and minorities in public office, asking whether or under what circumstances legislators or bureaucrats from these groups differ from those of other ascriptive groups in terms of their policy priorities, ideology, or style (Weldon 2002b). This literature importantly illustrates why it matters that women and minorities are present among the representatives of a diverse democratic public. The presence of members of such groups (1) increases trust in government, political mobilization, and participation by marginalized groups; (2) increases the likelihood that a more diverse set of interests and experiences will be articulated during policy deliberations; and (3) undermines the social construction of marginalized groups as incapable of leadership (Mansbridge 1999; Williams 1998; Swers 2002; Thomas 1994). While valuable, however, this literature is overly focused on only one dimension of the process of political representation: intralegislative representation as accomplished by individual legislators. But representation is a multidimensional process, and important aspects of the representative process are obscured by this focus on intralegislative representation. Institutions that mediate between social groups and formal political processes (parties, interest groups, social movements, etc.) are a critical aspect of this relationship. In terms of influence on policy outcomes (one of the most concrete manifestations of effective representation), extralegislative avenues of representation can be the most important ones.

POLITICAL PARTIES

Political parties are "mediating institutions" that potentially link marginalized groups to democratic political processes (Wolbrecht and Hero 2005). Some scholars have argued that party competition advances inclusion, as parties who fail to respond to excluded social groups will be at an electoral disadvantage (Key 1949; Dahl 1962). Multiparty systems better enable links with particular social groups, such as class and religious groups (Powell 1982; but see Chhibber and Nooruddin 2004). Further, research on women and politics suggests that left political parties are more likely to increase women's descriptive representation and, at least sometimes, appear to be more favorable to advancing women's substantive representation as well (Mazur 2002). However, it is clear that for some issues important to women (violence against women, reproductive rights), left or right party ideology is a poor guide to whether the party will support women's interests (Weldon 2002; Elman 1996). Indeed, Frymer (2005) points out that party competition has not advanced representation for African Americans in the United States, and Sanbonmatsu (2002) shows that the importance and alignment of parties varies across issues. Leighley (2005) argues that since parties are strategic actors, they aim at mobilizing supporters and are not necessarily the equalizing, inclusion-promoting institutions they are sometimes thought to be. Leighley emphasizes the importance of studying the relationship between parties and other mobilizing groups (e.g., voluntary associations) as critical for sorting out the complex relationship between parties and inclusion.

Parties are most likely to advance substantive representation when they are pressured by organizations independent of the parties themselves. Strong links between political parties and organizations of marginalized groups are likely to advance substantive representation, but it is important that marginalized constituencies maintain an independent organizational base outside the political party (Weldon 2002; Wolbrecht 2000). This can be seen most clearly in the case of strong social movements of marginalized groups that are transformed into dedicated political parties, as in the Icelandic women's party or in the case of parties that focus on particular ethnic or racial groups, like the Bloc Québécois in Canada. When such movements are completely subsumed in the party system, their mobilizing potential decreases, their links to marginalized constituencies weaken, and substantive representation is decreased. Extralegislative avenues offer the most mobilization potential and political leverage on existing political parties, regardless of the number of parties.

INTEREST GROUPS AND VOLUNTARY ASSOCIATIONS

Theorizing civil society groups as critical for representation has a long history. Classical pluralism portrayed the interest group system as a place for marginalized groups to counter their numerical disadvantage in a "one person, one vote" system. Here, such groups could organize on those issues most important to them, motivated by the intensity of their concern for the issue. Recently, there has been a resurgence in interest in civil society and voluntary associations in general, including their potential representative role (Skocpol 2005; Warren 2001; Strolovitch 2006). Voluntary associations might have the potential to equalize representation, since time and commitment are more equally distributed and less fungible than money (Warren 2001, 84). However, at least in the United States, these associations may also exacerbate inequalities. Such associations multiply the influence of those who already have resources, so they tend to be more effective advocates for their most advantaged constituents (Skocpol 2005; Strolovitch 2006).

Interest groups or pressure groups are "generally defined as organizations, separate from government though often in close partnership with government, which attempt to influence public policy. As such, interest groups provide the institutionalized linkage between government or the state and the major sectors of society"(Wilson 1990, 1). Not all voluntary associations are interest groups. Indeed, social movement organizations and what Walker calls "citizen groups" exhibit striking differences with interest groups in terms of the tactics and purposes of the organization (Walker 1990; Weldon 2002).

Warren (2001) argues that in order for voluntary associations to promote representation, these organizations must have democratic internal structures (see also Chambers and Kymlicka 2003). Putnam (2000) argues that the largest and most influential social movements are merely "chequebook" organizations that have little connection to the constituents. Skocpol (2005) criticizes contemporary voluntary organizations for moving away from a federated structure (where national organizations retained fairly close connections with state chapters) to one where such connections are weak or nonexistent. Fisher (2006) criticizes contemporary progressive social movement organizations for "outsourcing politics" by hiring canvassing firms (e.g., the People's Project) to do their fund-raising for them, instead of relying on (and maintaining) a grassroots infrastructure that better connects to members.

In the case of voluntary organizations representing marginalized groups, these concerns about internal democracy and grassroots connections may be overdrawn. I argue later in this introduction that the *voluntary* nature of these associations means that such mechanisms for internal democracy are less important for representation than has generally been assumed. This is especially the case for social movement organizations representing marginalized groups, one kind of voluntary organization, that have other bases of legitimacy that provide the basis for a kind of democratic representation.

SOCIAL MOVEMENTS

Social movements are a third type of mediating institution that potentially improves substantive representation for marginalized groups (Wolbrecht and Hero 2005). A social movement is a form of political organization in which membership and action is based on a shared sense of purpose and/or identity, aimed at changing social practices or prevailing power relations (McBride and

Mazur 2008; Meyer et al. 2005; Tarrow 1998). These efforts to create social change mean that social movements are nearly always confrontational in some way, combating some opponent, most often an established authority or elite (Tarrow 1998; Meyer et al. 2005). Movements are distinguished from the individual acts of contention by which they are constituted by the sustained nature of the mobilization.

Social movements employ a wide variety of political tools and tactics that run the gamut from conventional pressure group tactics such as lobbying to protest, street theater, cultural events, and alternative living arrangements. Some of these activities may seem to have a tangential connection to formal, institutional politics, being much broader in scope. Indeed, as Bashevkin (1996, 139) notes, "parties attempt to win power, interest groups try to influence government decision-makers, and social movements work to 'change the world.'" But the very breadth of social movement goals and the variety of tactics is their strength, especially when it comes to representing marginalized groups. Connections between diverse organizational forms provide important liaisons to and influences on formal politics that are easily missed. Indeed, social movements underpin other mechanisms of representation, such as descriptive representation, parties, and interest groups, in important ways, magnifying their impact and making them more effective mobilizers and advocates for marginalized groups. Social movements form the constituencies and produce the distinctive group perspectives that we hope to see reflected in democratic processes. Without social movements, there would, in a sense, be nothing to represent.

Elaborating the Mechanisms of Social Movement Representation

In this section, I elaborate the mechanisms by which social movements provide democratic representation for marginalized constituencies, focusing on (1) constituency formation, (2) the development of counterpublics and group perspectives, and (3) the diffusion of group perspectives and their injection into policy deliberations.

SOCIAL MOVEMENTS AND CONSTITUENCY FORMATION

Theorists of representation for marginalized groups stress that constituency formation is a critical part of group representation. Williams (1998) argues that self-conscious group identification and mobilization is an important precondition for effective representation for marginalized groups; Mansbridge (1999) argues that descriptive representation is especially important in some cases as a way of compensating for "uncrystallized" interests. This suggests that for issues that have been politicized and in cases when group members are well aware of their importance, descriptive representation might have less impact (e.g., in the area of abortion). So arguments for descriptive representation for marginalized groups implicitly or explicitly acknowledge that developing group consciousness and political mobilization is critical to an effective process of representation. They also acknowledge that the effectiveness of descriptive representation and electoral processes of representation is related to this broader mobilization.

Indeed, the very idea of representation assumes that there is some entity to be represented, a constituency of some kind. The criticism that women and minorities or any other group are unrepresented by government turns on the assumption that there are broader constituencies to which these categories correspond. But this assumption needs further examination. As Warren (2001, 84) remarks, "Class situation or other sociological commonalities are not sufficient for unity and action" (see also Weir 1992). The category "women," for example, names a complex social group that is internally riven by conflicting interests and identities. Indeed, some scholars argue that efforts to examine women's representation rely on the pernicious fiction that there is such a group, arguing that women cannot be represented *as women:* there are too many differences and divisions among women to claim that all women share any interests or have a common experience, identity, or bond of solidarity.[13] If women are so different, what can it mean to represent women as women? Moreover, no formal process links particular representatives to this diverse, diffuse group. What ground can there be for seeing such a diverse, diffuse social collective as a "constituency"?

In the absence of self-identification as a constituency, arguments about representing such a group in a democratic context smack of vanguardism (Williams 1998). But even diverse, diffuse social groups manage to mobilize and organize themselves into political entities. Social movements are critical to such processes of mobilization. When they mobilize in social movements, marginalized groups create organizations where they can squarely confront inequality, discussing and analyzing common problems and issues among themselves. This collection of organizations, this oppositional community, can be thought of as a "counterpublic," a public comprised of those belonging to the marginalized group (Fraser 1992, 1995; Young 2000; Mansbridge 2001). Social movements, then, create counterpublics of marginalized groups (Fuentes and Gunder Frank 1989; Weldon 2002).

In this sense, there is no meaningful constituency of a marginalized group without a social movement to delineate it, to create a group consciousness or make an aspect of identity salient. Social movements create the sense that those in the movement have a linked fate, a future tied to that of other members of their group (Dawson 1992). Moreover, a constituency needs an oppositional consciousness. Many marginalized groups have a subordinating group consciousness, but it is not necessarily one that supports their actions as a political group for emancipatory purposes. The definition of an oppositional consciousness requires struggle as activists form oppositional communities, pulling together strands of collective memory and tradition that support struggle against oppression (Morris and Braine 2001). As Mansbridge (2001, 1) puts it:

> Members of a group that others have traditionally treated as subordinate or deviant have an oppositional consciousness when they claim their previously subordinate identity as a positive identification, identify injustices done to their group, demand changes in the polity, economy or society to rectify those injustices, and see other members of their group as sharing an interest in rectifying those injustices.

Oppositional communities or counterpublics offer spaces where marginalized groups can discuss their status among themselves and develop such an oppositional consciousness, discussing the issues and problems that concern them.

COUNTERPUBLICS AND GROUP PERSPECTIVE

The set of issues discussed in a marginalized community can be thought of as a group perspective, an agenda of issues that confront those occupying a particular social position, sometimes stemming from shared interests but sometimes merely reflecting shared areas of contention (Young 1994, 2000). These issues may be raised in discussions of policy, or they may be raised in cultural productions, at social events, and so on. A group perspective is an element of oppositional consciousness, an "empowering mental state that prepares members of an oppressed group to act to undermine, reform or overthrow a system of human domination. It is usually fueled by righteous anger over injustices done to the group and prompted by personal indignities and harms suffered through one's group membership" (Mansbridge 2001, 4–5).

Although there are many differences within marginalized social groups, such groups can be understood as being similarly positioned by social structures. For example, women may respond to barriers or opportunities differently, but they are confronted with similar choices and obstacles. Aspects of femininity shape women's experiences of work, family, sexuality, and community, albeit differently. Such a shared positioning does not suggest a shared identity or shared experience, but it does suggest that some of the same issues and concerns shape the experience of all women. This perspective, or list of issues, is a product of collective discussions among diverse women. Perspectives are articulated as groups self-organize; they reside in groups, not individuals (Young 1994, 2000).

The idea that groups share a perspective does not suggest unanimous agreement with particular policy positions, nor does it suggest that the shared agenda of issues exhausts the issues important to the members of the group. Rather, this idea suggests that certain issues confront group members in their shared social location *as members* of that particular group. Thus, the system of organizations forms a sort of community or public that creates a group perspective that can be represented in democratic deliberations. This "articulation function" is important for the political representation of these groups: it means there is something that can be represented by elected officials, social movement leaders, and others who aim to speak for the group.

So it is possible to think about activist organizations as representing a social group without assuming, in an essentialist way, that all women share some fundamental essence or nature as women or that there are no significant differences and inequalities among women. For example, claiming that women's organizations represent women as women does not imply that women share an identity or that they share all their interests as women. It merely suggests that women confront some similar issues as women. The system or set of women's organizations can be thought of as a mechanism for articulating women's perspective. While individual women's groups tend to be homogeneous in some way, reflecting the social network on which they are based, the set of women's organizations as a system is more diverse. There is considerable ideological, racial, class, and other diversity across women's groups, but they focus on a set of overlapping issues that can be thought of as reflecting the social position of women. When women's groups raise these issues for discussion, they provide some representation for women. Again, this account focuses on women's organizations *taken as a group*. It does not claim that any particular organization represents or could represent all women.

SOCIAL PERSPECTIVES AND POLICY AGENDAS

The preceding perspectives sometimes penetrate the broader public discussions of policy issues. This matters because these discussions are an important part of the policy-making process. Civil society, or the public sphere, is a sort of "policy primeval soup," where ideas of all kinds are sloshed together (Kingdon 1984, 116). It is like a transmission belt, bringing ideas from citizens to government; issues are taken up from public opinion and absorbed into the government agenda (Young 2002; Kingdon 1984; Chambers and Kymlicka 2002).[14] Indeed, without an active citizenry, many scholars argue, the formal processes of democracy, such as elections, are little more than empty shells, vulnerable to reverting to autocratic forms of rule (Norris 2002). Being able to influence public discussion is thus an important, albeit indirect, avenue for policy influence. Indeed, Berry's (1999) study of the influence of citizen groups in the United States concludes:

> Citizen groups are "heard" in many important ways in the policymaking process. They are singularly impressive in their rate of participation before congressional committees, in their disproportionate share of network news stories featuring interest group opinions, and in their ability to get newspapers to report on research they have sponsored. (391)

Civil society consists of both counterpublics and dominant publics. Dominant publics address the broader community in a seemingly open way, but access and representation in these publics tend to favor socially, politically, and economically privileged groups (Berry 1999; Schlozman et al. 1999; Walker 1991; Strolovitch 2006). As E. E. Schattschneider (1960) famously remarked, "The flaw in the pluralist heaven is that the heavenly chorus sings with a strong upper-class accent" (cited in Putnam 2000, 340). "Counterpublics" of marginalized groups are so-called because they form in reaction to their exclusion from and/or oppression in dominant publics.[15]

Seeing civil society as an arena in which it may be possible to use argument, persuasion, and shame to counter raw coercive power suggests that relatively powerless groups may be able to exercise some influence there. In civil society, the excluded and stigmatized can group together to demand recognition of their dignity and humanity, of their capabilities and worth (Young 2000; Fraser 1992). While established political parties and political institutions seem resistant to change and difficult to penetrate, the boundaries of civil society are more fluid, and forms of organization are more varied. The entry costs are lower. In this sense, civil society is more accessible than electoral politics. This additional accessibility is particularly important in providing openings to intersectionally marginalized groups, for whom the barriers for entry into formal politics are even greater.

At least sometimes, it seems that marginalized communities are able to draw public attention to the issues of concern to them. In 2006, hundreds of thousands of immigrant workers in the United States organized coordinated work stoppages and marches on May 1 in order to influence the debate on immigration law reform (Preston 2007). Similarly, social movement activists drew attention to criticisms of globalization through protests against the International Monetary Fund and the World Bank, especially the "Battle in Seattle." Activists continue to seek to disrupt international economic summits to present issues of labor rights, human rights, environmental protection, and the like. When the perspectives of marginalized groups are attended to in dominant publics, a form of political representation has been accomplished.[16]

Objections to Movements as Avenues of Democratic Representation

There are at least three objections to seeing social movements as avenues of democratic representation. The first objection, which concedes that social movements provide representation, argues that it is not a democratic form of representation. The second objection concerns inequalities within social movements, arguing that social movements do not represent the most marginalized and disadvantaged groups of people. The third objection claims that social movements have become less participatory as protest has become mainstream, professionalized, or co-opted by corporate interests. I consider each of these objections in this section.

ARE SOCIAL MOVEMENTS DEMOCRATIC REPRESENTATIVES?

Some who grant that the process of articulation of group perspectives in public debate is a form of representation may contest the idea that this is a form of *democratic* representation, or that it contributes to democracy. Andrew Rehfeld (2006), for example, has argued that we need a broader account of representation that captures the many nondemocratic forms of representation.

Specifically democratic representation, on this view, is distinguished by its procedural legitimacy (Phillips 1995; Williams 1998; Warren 2001; Rehfeld 2006). Large bureaucratic, national organizations are very influential, but they seem to have little connection to the grass roots (Putnam 2000; Skocpol 1999, 2003). Activists are not elected. In the absence of formal procedures, what ties activists to their constituents? Even if those involved in these organizations were extremely active and able to keep organizational leaders on a short leash, small numbers of people actively participate in these movements compared to the constituencies they are supposed to represent. How can we see these organizations as speaking for a larger group of people with whom they have little interaction?

One part of the answer to this question has to do with the limits of traditional electoral modes of democratic representation, especially for marginalized groups. For example, elected representatives also have relations with small numbers of constituents compared to the whole group that they purport to represent, even whole caucuses of legislators. For example, many women have not voted for any of the women in the women's caucus and cannot be said to hold them accountable. So part of the problem is that we do not have any electoral mechanism by which women, as women, may hold their representatives accountable (Phillips 1995; Williams 1998).

One response might be to suggest institutional reforms to make electoral politics more responsive to marginalized groups (Mansbridge 2005). This, however, is harder than it sounds (Williams 1998; Phillips 1995). Many institutional reforms that have been proposed to improve the voice of marginalized groups in politics have shortcomings themselves. For example, efforts to redefine electoral districts in the United States to provide more African American representation (in descriptive terms) have had the unintended consequence of making formerly mixed districts more homogeneous and have consequently elected representatives who are less likely to listen and be receptive to African American concerns than they might have been in the past when they represented a coalition of groups (Lublin 1999). Of course, redistricting does not do much for women, who are scattered throughout the population (Htun 2005). On the one hand, single-member plurality electoral systems (so-called winner-take-all systems) make it more difficult for minority groups and women to gain a foothold (Welch and Studlar 1990; Matland 1993; Rule and Zimmermann 1994). On the other hand, proportional representation empowers not only marginalized subgroups but also advantaged minorities and reactionaries who wish to preserve the status quo, and it still does nothing to ensure that women representatives are accountable to women. Scholars have been concerned that constitutional measures to ensure the representation of minority groups (e.g., consociationalism or other systems of group representation) unnecessarily freeze social relations, making them too rigid a solution to a complex, shifting problem (Phillips 1995; Williams 1998). Quotas have increased descriptive representation somewhat (Tripp and Kang 2007; Mansbridge 2005), but it is not at all clear that they improve substantive representation. In countries with party lists, parties can be careful to place only women who are "party hacks" in the coveted positions at the top of the list where they are more likely to be elected. (The concern here, of course, is not that only women can be party hacks but that if they are expected to toe the party line, they will not challenge the party to change its platform on women [Jacquette 1997; Elman 1996; Bashevkin 1985].) Some scholars point out that outcome-oriented quotas improperly interfere with electoral choice, reflecting authoritarian tendencies and perhaps explaining the greater popularity of these measures in authoritarian contexts (Htun forthcoming; see also Tripp and Kang 2007).

Moreover, if we focus only on such formal rules of authorization and accountability, we have no way to describe the problems that marginalized groups confront as they seek to express themselves in democratic deliberations (Williams 1998). Although they are formally included in democratic electoral processes, facially neutral procedures may mask substantively biased processes (Williams 1998; Young 1990). Social norms, deep social inequality, discrimination, and the organization of institutions may mitigate against the articulation and appreciation of the distinctive perspectives and experiences of marginalized groups (Young 1990, 2000; Mansbridge 1999, 2005; Weldon 2002). For example, the norm that women take primary responsibility for child care undermines sexual equality in the workplace and interferes with women's chances of successful leadership in general (Gornick and Meyers 2007) and in electoral politics in particular (Mansbridge 2005). These norms maintain sexual inequality even where facially neutral policies persist. Similarly, past policies undermining African American household wealth also continue to contribute to economic inequality and unequal access to public office—again, even when formal bars have been struck down (Mansbridge 2005; Katznelson 2005). Cultural norms that privilege the forms of communication and substantive concerns of dominant groups as more legitimate make it difficult for marginalized groups to have a voice even when they manage to be present (Young 2000). Institutions tend to be organized around the concerns and issues of historically dominant groups, creating an additional barrier to institutional responsiveness to new sets of concerns or issues not encompassed by these categories (Weldon 2002b).

These informal obstacles mean that the policy-making process as a whole is biased against the expression of the perspectives or interests of the marginalized group, presenting barriers to equal or fair representation for members of marginalized groups (Williams 1998; Young 2000; Weldon 2002). This is not just a problem of representation more generally but a problem for democracy, because these informal biases undermine the political equality of citizens. We need an understanding of democratic representation that gets at this problem of inequality.[17]

As noted, democratic representation has not always been equated with electoral processes. Scholars of representation have long recognized civil society as an arena in which political representation can occur. Classical pluralism pointed to the interest group system as an arena that complemented representation through formal electoral processes. Minorities with intense preferences could mobilize in civil society to overcome their numerical disadvantage in majority-rule systems (Dahl 1962; Truman 1951). Warren (2001, 84) similarly notes that representation in associations has the potential to equalize representation, since "in principle, associations can level the playing field, organizing pressure and votes in ways that can compete with money." On this model of democratic representation, citizens may organize themselves into constituencies by forming voluntary associations to reflect their shared interests or concerns (Williams 1998). As long as everyone has an equal opportunity to join or form such groups, each citizen is still being treated equally.

The representative effects of associations depend on the organization's "ability to communicate interests, norms and identities of members to public officials" (Warren 2001, 84). In electoral forms of representation, constituencies are formally defined by governments (on the basis of geography, ethnicity, or the like), but for informal, voluntary representation, relations of authorization and accountability are largely the product of the formation of associations themselves. The vitality and influence—and sometimes the very existence—of voluntary associations depends on the perception of members that their interests and concerns are being taken into account. If members become sufficiently disenchanted, they will quit the organization and perhaps join or form a competing association. This mechanism certainly is not perfect or precise. For example, it has taken a long time for the Women's Christian Temperance Union (WCTU)—an antialcohol organization in the United

States—to fall into obsolescence. But the same must be said for electoral mechanisms of authorization and accountability. They are very crude mechanisms indeed for communicating views or enforcing mandates on the multiple and competing agenda items that representatives must address (Lindblom and Woodhouse 1993). So the voluntary nature of social movement activism and participation, particularly for smaller groups, renders some of the issues about authorization and accountability less pressing. In addition, more formal processes of representation can, by their very nature, be less accessible—the bureaucratic, formal nature of such processes can make them less accessible to some and can privilege those who are more literate in the language and procedures of bureaucracy.

This is not to say that informal organizations are necessarily more democratic. Nor would I contest the argument that formal rules holding organizational leaders to account and providing for rank-and-file participation are often preferable, especially for large bureaucratic organizations. The point is that there are some trade-offs between formal mechanisms of accountability and accessibility to the most marginalized. Moreover, there are some mechanisms, however crude or basic, by which constituents may hold organizational elites accountable. Many large, bureaucratic organizations do provide for elections and other means of participation (Barakso 2005; Beckwith 2005b).

In addition, activists are bound by internal mechanisms of accountability, a sort of "internal" or "gyroscopic" basis for accountability (Mansbridge 1995, 1999, 2003). Activists behave as if they were accountable to a broader movement, explaining and justifying their actions to themselves and others. Social movement leaders can persuade their followers by giving an account of their actions, as when Gloria Steinem explained her decision to get married after years of criticizing the institution of marriage. This is also part of the representative relationship. Individual social movement leaders are committed to and engaged with a broader group of activists to whom they feel they must explain themselves (Mansbridge 1995). There are also processes of shaming and claims that are made on activists by others (Young 2000). Indeed, this pressure is sometimes so strong that observers worry that social movement representatives are unable to compromise because they will lose support.

Social movements are more effective at representing marginalized groups not when they have formal rules or electoral processes but when they are characterized by norms of inclusivity. An analysis of the global movement on gender violence shows that the movement foundered and was unable to exert effective influence until it developed norms aimed at including marginalized subgroups. These norms include ensuring descriptive representation within organizations, facilitating self-organization (e.g., caucuses) of disadvantaged groups, and adopting a norm of consensus decision making while institutionalizing dissent. These informal norms strengthen movements at the same time as they improve the representation of marginalized subgroups. Separate organization signals to marginalized subgroups that they have a place within the movement. It also provides a mechanism for ensuring that the diverse concerns and wider range of social knowledge encompassed by any social group are brought under the purview of the movement (Weldon 2006a, 2006b; Mansbridge 2005; see also chapter 4).

Insisting on formal processes of accountability in social movements risks severing democratic theory from contemporary scholarship and political practice on democracy, especially as it pertains to marginalized groups. Scholars interested in how democracies actually work are increasingly interested in civil society. Developments across Eastern Europe have drawn attention to the power of popular protest, of argument, and to the importance of legitimacy; here, citizens bravely organized against autocratic governments to force democratic reforms giving citizens more say in government (Young 2000; Howell and Mulligan 2005). Scholarship on the politics of gender, race, and class in democracies focuses on social movements aiming to advance these groups at least as much as it does on these groups' involvement in formal political processes. Also, political practice often treats social movement activists as if they are the best spokespeople for groups, and citizens from these groups trust such independent groups to be watchdogs vis-à-vis officials—over whom they formally have more influence. In the United States, the NAACP is often treated as a representative of African American interests at least as legitimate as the Congressional Black Caucus, and NOW is seen as speaking for women at least as effectively as the women's caucus in the legislature. Recognizing the democratic representative function of social movements has the advantage of capturing current political practice and scholarship that explicitly or implicitly sees social movements as important to democracy.

DO SOCIAL MOVEMENTS NEGLECT THE MOST MARGINALIZED?

Another objection to seeing social movements as an avenue of democratic representation points to the inequalities in access to social movement organization: people are differentially represented by social movement organizations. As noted, many of the inequities that characterize society at large also shape civil society and social movements. Race inequality is reflected in the fact that

African Americans have less access to social capital than do whites in the United States (Dawson and Cohen 1993). Those who are better off socioeconomically are more likely to participate in a wide variety of civic and political activities than those who are less privileged (Berry 1999; Walker 1991; Schlozman et al. 1999). Those who are most disadvantaged, those at the intersection of axes of marginalization, are even less able to use the avenue of civil society as a means of participating in democratic politics or voicing their opinion. Strolovitch (2007) finds that such organizations are much less likely to advocate for these marginalized subgroups than they are to advocate for more privileged subgroups. Social movements, then, likely do a better job of representing the privileged than they do the disadvantaged segments of the constituencies they claim to represent.

Of course, to say that the members of marginalized groups are differentially represented is not to say that such groups are not represented at all. Indeed, all mechanisms of representation exhibit this pattern of being more accessible to privileged groups. Moreover, albeit imperfect, social movement organizations may offer particular opportunities for the most disadvantaged groups. Social movements employ a wide variety of organizational forms, and many organizations make inclusion of disadvantaged groups a priority. The efforts of these organizations have spawned a number of organizational mechanisms for the representation of marginalized groups (e.g., caucuses) (Weldon 2006a, 2006b). Despite their shortcomings, social movement actors have been the source of pressures for greater inclusiveness.

It is also important to note that movements that are less inclusive are less likely to be successful. Conversely, inclusiveness strengthens social movements and improves policy impact. It seems that decision-making processes that are more inclusive strengthen solidarity and make social movements more influential (Weldon 2006a). In addition, movements in which subgroups are organized in separate caucuses or organizations seem to be more influential in policy discussions (Weldon 2006b). In sum, then, the same exclusions that characterize traditional, electoral representation also characterize social movement representation. But there are mechanisms for mitigating the impact of such exclusions, and those movements that undertake such measures are more likely to affect public discussions and thereby policy outcomes.

We cannot talk about inequality in representation by civil society groups as a problem for democracy and representation unless we think these organizations perform democratic representative functions in the first place. Complaints about differential access to civil society might be evidence of social inequality or of unequal preparation for or access to electoral office, but they are not evidence of differential democratic representation itself. Most scholars criticizing inequality in civil society are not arguing for excluding or eliminating the organizing and influence of civil society groups; rather, they are arguing that differential access to this avenue of policy influence is a problem for democracy because of unequal representation and policy influence. The way to make it more democratic is to level the playing field, not to eliminate these independent efforts to influence policy-making.

ARE CONTEMPORARY MOVEMENTS BECOMING LESS PARTICIPATORY (AND LESS DEMOCRATIC)?

Most theoretical accounts of the role of social movements in democratic politics focus on social movements as opportunities for participation (see note 8 from this Introduction). Social movements do constitute opportunities for and forms of political participation, but they also offer a form of representation. Indeed, democratic theorists are increasingly emphasizing the degree to which these concepts are linked. Young (2000) argues that representation is unavoidable in all but the smallest, most simple contexts (e.g., small committees). Even small communities necessarily employ some kind of representation in decision making, even if it is informal, de facto representation.

Democratic critics of representation should not confuse existing institutions of representative government, which sometimes do alienate citizens unnecessarily, with the *ideal* of representative government, which depends on some degree of participation (Young 2000). Representation cannot work in the context of a completely passive citizenry. The subjects of representation must actively authorize and hold their representatives to account. Seeing representation as an ongoing process, moreover, means that representation is never "finished" (Young 2000; Weldon 1999). Constituents may change their minds, withdraw their support from positions they previously supported, and so on. Young argues that constituent participation in processes of authorization and accountability is critical for democratic representation (see also Warren 2001).

In order to assess the relative importance of these formal mechanisms of authorization and accountability, let us review the reasons for considering them important in the first place. Formal processes of authorization and accountability offer mechanisms by which constituents can ensure that spokespeople or organizations speak for them; they may authorize a group or person to speak for them by endorsing a particular view, and they may withdraw that authorization if they feel the group or person no longer represents them. In this way, constituents ensure a tight link between their own views or preferences and the representative's actions. This helps ensure that representatives provide these constituents with a voice. The core concern here is not the formality of the mechanisms but, rather, their effectiveness.

If we evaluate social movement organizations in terms of whether they are effective in giving constituents a voice, we may have to reconsider the dominant line of criticism of large social movement organizations, which is overly biased toward participation and takes no account of the representative role these organizations play. Consider the following example: A survey of a community-based pro-life group in North Dakota found that although the organization was sending busloads of protestors to Washington, DC, to agitate for laws banning abortion, there was a wide variety of views among the participants in the protest, and some were even pro-choice. A similar survey of a large social movement organization focused on abortion found that members' reported views on abortion varied very little and were nearly perfectly aligned with the formal position of the organization (McCarthy 2007, 1987). Clearly the large-scale social movement organization does a better job of voicing the concerns of constituents than does the small-scale organization. But the scholarly assessment of the value of these groups for democracy has been exactly the opposite.

Why would this be? People get involved in small-scale, face-to-face groups for a variety of reasons, but we know that one important mechanism is preexisting social networks. In the North Dakota case, a pastor of a church was pressuring people to go to DC and participate in the protest. Not participating meant admitting to one's friends and fellow parishioners that one might not share their views, something that can be hard to do (McCarthy 2007, 1987). In the case of the large social movement organization, the very anonymity that might appear as alienation to those looking for increased participation is what helps to ensure the purely voluntary nature of the participation and the authorization of the representative organization that flows from it. People join the organization because they wish to support its stated goals; they quit the organization when it moves too far away from those goals. Since these organizations are nothing without members, they find ways to monitor their support and can be very responsive. Indeed, some scholars have recognized that although traditional, fraternal organizations are on the decline, it is not clear that this is bad for the representation of disadvantaged groups: the proliferation of new social movement organizations in the United States has been very effective at getting the concerns of these groups on the agenda (Berry 1999; Warren 2001, 224).

Of course, this only suggests that these organizations speak for their members. But I have been making a stronger claim, that social movements represent social groups. Note that I here say "social movements," not a particular organization. Few movements of the type discussed here are characterized by only one organization. Contemporary social movements of marginalized groups include a wide variety of organizations, large and small, bureaucratic and informal, narrow and broad. A movement includes all these organizations as a set. While individual organizations may be more or less inclusive, representative, or participatory, the movement as a whole is less likely to lack mechanisms for inclusion, representation, or participation. A group perspective, then, is not the set of issues raised by any one group but, rather, the issue agenda raised by all the movement organizations together. I give an example of what it means for a set of organizations to represent a social group in chapter 5.

If these social movement organizations do provide a mechanism for the articulation of the views of marginalized groups in politics, they become very significant mechanisms for deepening democracy. Ensuring greater inclusion of marginalized groups is one of the great challenges for contemporary democracies. Despite formal integration, many groups remain unequally represented by formal electoral processes, and even the most effective measures that aim to involve more people in formal political processes would have little impact. Even with increased participation, universal, group-neutral processes offer inadequate opportunities for voicing group perspectives, which can cause frustration and alienation. For example, minorities in both the United States and the United Kingdom report higher levels of dissatisfaction and cynicism about political parties than do whites (Kittilson and Tate 2005). The increasing popularity of legislative quotas or reserved seats to increase the descriptive representation of women and ethnic minorities suggests that a broad range of societies are attempting (at least symbolically) to remedy problems of inclusion (Htun 2005). The developing literature suggests that an assumed link between descriptive and substantive representation may be weaker than some have hoped. Substantive representation for disadvantaged groups is a difficult goal to achieve, but social movements may represent the best mechanism we have. In this context, ignoring social movement representation for marginalized groups because of its informal or fluid nature seems foolhardy.

A Macropolitical, Structural Approach to Social Representation

Scholars of representation for marginalized groups point to the systemic, historic nature of the problem of group representation. Problems of group representation do not stem from fleeting differences of opinion or unpopular points of view. Rather, problems for democratic representation arise when groups are disadvantaged across multiple (social, political, economic) arenas, when such disadvantage stems from historical patterns of societal discrimination and oppression (and reflects the persistence of such patterns), and when membership in such systematically disadvantaged groups is experienced as immutable (Williams 1998; Mansbridge 1999; Young 1990, 2000). In other words, group marginalization is a product of social structures that shape processes of representation. Addressing group marginalization, then, requires changing the constellation of social norms and institutions—social structures—that systematically privilege some social groups over others.

Many of the measures that aim to improve political representation for marginalized groups would chip away at such social institutions and norms. For example, measures increasing the physical presence of marginalized groups in public office, such as quotas, may undermine the social construction of these groups as unfit to lead (Mansbridge 1999). Social movements, however, often seek to confront these norms and institutions directly, addressing multiple issues, using multiple tactics, and aiming for policy change as just one facet of broader cultural change (Rochon and Mazmanian 1993; Rochon 1997; Bashevkin 1996; Weldon 2002). In addition to crystallizing interests and articulating issues that matter to particular groups themselves, social movements often affect broader social values and convince those beyond the particular group in question of the justice of their claims. So, in democracies, social movement mobilization can sometimes be effective in changing policy outcomes by creating broad political pressure on legislators even when no members of the group are present.

When members of marginalized groups are present, broader mobilization of the group in social movements can improve the influence of descriptive representatives by providing arguments and political support on which they may draw. Indeed, many studies of policy outcomes important to women, African Americans, and the poor identify protest as a key catalyst for policy change (Piven and Cloward 1993; Weldon 2002; Marx 1998). For these reasons, I would expect that mobilization in social movements provides more concrete payoffs in terms of policy outputs (policy adoption) than does improving descriptive representation through electing or appointing additional members of marginalized groups (although both avenues of representation likely improve representation for marginalized groups). In addition, for more diffuse marginalized groups, where membership is more difficult to ascertain objectively or is more fluid (e.g., groups based on class or sexuality), social movement mobilization is more practical. Thus, there are many reasons for thinking of social movements as critical for the democratic representation of marginalized groups.

If social movements play or could play such an important role in democratic representation, especially for disadvantaged groups, this suggests that democratic states should take an active role in fostering and encouraging independent mobilization by disadvantaged groups. Over the next few chapters, I show how social movements provide substantive representation for women, workers, working women, and women of color in terms of concrete policies. I also compare social movements to other forms of representation.

Conclusion

Democracy necessarily involves more than mere state institutions. Indeed, a vibrant civil society is critical to democracy (Putnam 1993, 2000; Norris 1999; Warren 2001; Dryzek et al. 2003). Social movements create counterpublics where marginalized groups interact to articulate their distinctive perspectives. Activists advance these distinctive perspectives in both intralegislative and extralegislative policy deliberations, such as public hearings, protests, and the like. In doing so, they often alter the government agenda, inserting the issues of importance to marginalized groups into a list of issues from which they would otherwise be excluded.

Because they directly address the social-structural nature of political marginalization, social movements are often more effective in influencing policy than the traditionally sought electoral routes to political influence. Moreover, social movements are more accessible to and representative of intersectionally marginalized groups. The voluntary nature of political association in civil society creates mechanisms of accountability that (albeit crude) ensure that social movements respond to their constituents.

Arguments that social movement organizations are not avenues of democratic representation because they are not held accountable in regular electoral processes depend on an incomplete account of processes of democratic representation. Equating democratic representation with formal electoral processes fails to capture important intuitions about failures of representation, misses the multidimensional nature of representation, obscures critical parts of the representative process, and misconstrues how representative democracies actually work. Noting that social movements provide an avenue of democratic representation, in contrast, helps to illuminate problems of underrepresentation for marginalized groups; reveals the limits of formal, electoral processes of representation; points to the necessity of embedding these processes in a vibrant, active civil society; and suggests new avenues for deepening democracy.

CHAPTER 1

Representing Women in Democratic Policy Processes

In this chapter, I seek to substantiate two key claims in the argument that social movement can represent marginalized groups. First, women's movements influence policy processes in significant ways. Second, in determining policy outcomes, this influence is at least as important (and in some cases more important) as the number of the women in the legislature, and therefore we ought to be examining multiple avenues of representation for women. I also elaborate on the conceptual bases for the argument that social movements represent women in a substantive sense, focusing on the nature of group perspective. I offer an account of group perspective that seeks to reconcile two critical insights in the representation of marginalized groups. On one hand, such groups are diverse and riven by internal conflict, crosscut by social axes of gender, race, class sexuality, and the like. On the other hand, group members sometimes seem to represent the broader group in some instances by speaking about their own experiences, which are nevertheless not shared by every member of the group.

Reconceptualizing Representation for Marginalized Groups

The literature on representation for marginalized groups has tended to focus on the question of whether women should represent women and African Americans should represent African Americans, that is, on the descriptive representation of these groups. Moreover, this literature has mostly focused on *legislative* descriptive representation. Descriptive representation in the legislature is an important aspect of representation for marginalized groups, but it is limited as an avenue of substantive representation. Indeed, in this chapter, I suggest that the idea that *individuals* can substantively represent groups merely through their persons or behavior is based on a problematic understanding of the relationship between individual experience and group perspective. I propose that group perspective is a *collective* product of social groups, developed through intragroup interaction.

Conceptualizing group perspective this way suggests that other avenues of representation (e.g., women's policy machineries and social movements) may provide substantive representation for marginalized groups. I illustrate this argument using an analysis of policy development in Canada, one of the most responsive governments in the world when it comes to violence against women. I then apply this argument in an examination of the impact of women's representation on policies to address violence against women in 36 democratic countries in 1994. Using OLS regression analysis, I find that women's policy agencies (e.g., women's commissions or women's bureaus) and women's movements provide more effective avenues of expression for women than the presence of women in the legislatures: in combination, they give women a stronger voice in the policy-making process. Thus, studies of representation for marginalized groups would do well to consider institutional changes and increased political mobilization as potential sources of political representation.[1] The point is not that individual bodies provide *no* representation but that bodies are limited as an avenue of *substantive* representation, and that multiple sources of representation should be considered and compared. The contributions of and interactions between modes of representation can then be more effectively evaluated (Schwindt-Bayer and Mishler 2005).

Political scientists have developed an impressive body of work arguing that in order for historically marginalized groups to be effectively represented in democratic institutions, members of those groups must be present in deliberative bodies. In this chapter, I focus mainly on these arguments as they apply to women as a historically marginalized group.[2] However, I think that many of the issues I raise here are also relevant for other such groups, such as historically disadvantaged racial minorities and gays and lesbians.

There is an extensive literature examining the consequences and determinants of better representation for women and minorities in bureaucracies and legislatures.[3] The majority of these studies conceptualize and operationalize representation as the presence or behavior of individual women or minorities in the bodies in question, although there is an emerging movement to question this equation.[4] Many studies employ Pitkin's (1967) distinction between descriptive representation and substantive representation (or passive/symbolic and active representation).[5] These studies tend to define both forms of representation in terms of the behavior or characteristics of individual legislators. Descriptive representation is defined as individual legislators "standing for" their groups.[6] Substantive representation is defined as individual legislators having opinions or behavior favorable to the minority community or to women (Tremblay 1998, 439; Cameron, Epstein, and O'Halloran 1996).[7] This focus on whether individuals are present or how they vote stems from the idea that individual members of marginalized groups can stand and/or speak for the group as a whole. As I explain shortly, this assumption is problematic, and it obscures more effective means for the articulation of the group's perspective.

The Limits of Individuals as Spokespersons for Marginalized Groups

Political theorists argue that historically marginalized groups have a distinctive voice or perspective that is unlikely or unable to be articulated effectively in deliberative contexts from which members of those groups are absent. This distinctive perspective often differs from or conflicts with the perspectives of the dominant group. The group perspective, or set of shared concerns, derives from shared experiences and/or social position and is manifest in narratives or histories that members develop collectively (Mansbridge 1999, 2005; Phillips 1995; Williams 1998, especially 138–41; Young 1997).

Ideally, on this view, representation for marginalized groups should reflect the diversity of the group's membership and should not assume a false homogeneity of interest or identity (Phillips 1995; Mansbridge 1999, 2005; Dovi 2002). Substantive political representation requires political processes through which marginalized groups authorize and hold accountable those who speak for them (Phillips 1995; Young 1990, 2000). Finally, substantive representation requires the representation of the group perspective in such a way that the group's voice is articulated and heard in policy processes.

These works offer helpful accounts of when and why descriptive representation matters. But these arguments bring to the forefront a theoretical problem, a seeming tension or contradiction, that arises from two conflicting but powerful intuitions. On the one hand, women can, at least in some circumstances, represent women more broadly when they speak from their own experiences; on the other hand, women (like men) are a diverse group, riven by other social axes like race and class, and they sometimes have conflicting interests as women, so that there is a sense in which there is no singular "women's experience." Indeed, theorists of descriptive representation emphasize that they are not claiming that women or African Americans share a set of similar experiences or identities (Mansbridge 1999; Williams 1998). But if women do not share a set of similar experiences, in what sense do women in office represent women?

Despite their acknowledgment of intragroup diversity, theorists of descriptive representation sometimes seem to argue that individual legislators can speak for the group by drawing only on their personal experiences. For example, Williams (1998, 141) suggests that when a legislator from a disadvantaged group speaks, "the needs she articulates are not hers alone, but the needs shared by members of the group she represents . . . In articulating the group's perspective on behalf of her constituents, the representative does not need to take up the standpoint of an other; the perspective is hers *immediately,* although it is not the full expression of her individuality"(emphasis in original). Similarly, Mansbridge (1999, 645) argues that descriptive characteristics often act as a proxy for identifying shared experiences and that reflecting on these shared experiences provides a limited basis for representing the group. This method results in substantive representation when the person in question is in fact most similar to their constituents. When representatives do, in fact, share the experiences of their constituents, argues Mansbridge, "representatives engaged in introspective representation will reflect the policies their constituents would choose if they had greater knowledge and time for reflection" (646; see also Whitby 1997, 6). This is an important qualification, but as scholars increasingly emphasize differences among women (e.g., Crenshaw 1993; Collins 1998; McCall 2004), the extent to which women's diverse experiences are shared by such descriptive representatives seems quite limited (Dovi 2002).[8]

If a group perspective resides complete in any individual from the group, including individual members of the group is sufficient to represent the group perspective. Epistemologically, any individual has the knowledge to articulate a group's distinctive voice. This conclusion conflicts with the recognition of within-group diversity that these theorists explicitly recognize and affirm (Mansbridge 1999, 637–39; Williams 1998, 293). Even if a woman is typical in a statistical sense, as Mansbridge suggests, she cannot "speak for" women. If she is a white, straight, middle-class mother, she cannot speak for African American, poor, or lesbian women *on the basis of her own experience,* any more than men can speak for women merely on the basis of theirs (or at least, she can only do so in a very limited way). Moreover, marginalized group perspectives are not transparent to *individual* members of the group. As noted, these theorists see group perspective as a *collective* phenomenon, developed by the group. How can individuals come to have access to these collective phenomena on the basis of their own, relatively limited experience? The link between individual experience and knowledge of the group perspective appears to be a complex one that requires more elaboration.

Individual Experience, Group Perspective, and Representation

I propose an account of the link between group perspective and individual experience that seeks to reconcile these seeming contradictions. Group perspective is related to group members' individual experiences, but not in a direct, transparent way. A social perspective is a type of knowledge that groups have. It reflects the vantage point of the social position in which a group finds itself (Young 1994, 1997, 2000). Members of the group have the experience of being marked out by society as members of a particular class (Williams 1998). As members of the group, they confront obstacles and issues that others need not confront.

But individuals can rarely provide a complete account or analysis of the obstacles confronting the group without interacting with others from the group. The distinctive voice of marginalized groups flows from group organization and mobilization; it is a product of the interaction among members of a social group. Only a small part of this group perspective is reflected in the experience of any particular individual. The group perspective is created when individual members of the group interact with other members of the group to define their priorities.

Group perspective can be thought of as a puzzle of which each member of the group has a piece. The more pieces of the puzzle we have, the better picture we have. When additional pieces are very similar to existing pieces (the same color or texture), we learn little about other areas or features of the puzzle. The greater the diversity in our pieces is, the better idea we have about the different areas and parts of the puzzle. Moreover, when members of the group come together, they can compare their puzzle pieces, and after seeing the puzzle pieces of others, each person gains a greater understanding of the larger puzzle to which she or he holds a piece. Thus, the process of putting together the puzzle pieces is interactive rather than simply aggregative. One's puzzle piece likely gives one more information after interaction with others than before, but there is a point of diminishing returns: the last pieces are not as valuable as the first few.

It may seem as if this analogy suggests that interaction among women will produce agreement on the meaning or implications of the picture. But merely identifying similar obstacles or issues does not suggest that women will experience or interpret these phenomena in the same way. Like interpreting an abstract painting, viewers could have very different reactions to or experiences of the painting, although they could agree about the physical characteristics of the work. Sharing a perspective on women's social position does not suggest agreement on the meaning of or political dynamics that produce that position.

Having said this, even when women have conflicting interests, the issues that divide them are strikingly similar. For example, middle-class and working-class women have conflicting interests in relation to the issue of wages for child care. The former would benefit from lower wages for child care, while the latter would benefit from higher wages for child care. But in both cases, it is *women* who have responsibility for child care, and it is *women* for whom the issue has the most serious consequences. The important thing is to note that all of these women confront the issue of the relationship between motherhood and work. What they share is not a list of policy proposals but more like a list of "women's issues."

Group perspective resides most fully in collective products, such as the agendas of coalitions of organizations, or in the issues identified in the body of newspapers, magazines, and other cultural productions where the group discusses its own issues and concerns. A group perspective is not as specific as a policy position or recommendation: it is more like an agenda of topics for discussion or a list of problem areas (Weldon 2002). Because social perspectives are developed through interaction among the members of a social group, no individual member *on her or his own* has a full understanding of the conditions that confront the group. Participating in group activities provides deeper knowledge of the issues and concerns that members share with others of their group. Individual members of the group cannot legitimately claim to speak for the group without having participated in such interaction, because they lack the epistemological bases (as well as the normative bases) for doing so.

Of course, interaction among women often involves conflict, and subordinated subsets of women often have difficulty getting their issues recognized as issues of importance by women who are more privileged. But debate among women makes these divisions themselves the topic of discussion, particularly when marginalized subsets of women can organize as such. For example, when women's organizations and activists from all over the world gathered in Beijing in 1995 for the Fourth United Nations Conference on Women, they pushed governments to attend to the way race, ethnicity, disability, sexual orientation, and other factors create additional barriers for women of marginalized subgroups.

Although this view of group perspective is consistent with theoretical arguments for the self-representation of marginalized groups, it undermines much of the empirical work on representation previously outlined. It suggests that there is no reason to assume that the greater bodily inclusion of members of marginalized groups, in itself, should significantly increase their substantive representation. Small improvements can be expected, but significantly improving substantive representation for groups requires that representatives be able to articulate the group perspective. The individual alone cannot effectively articulate this perspective.[9]

Marginalized groups are poorly represented in most contemporary democratic policy processes because their perspectives are not equally reflected or considered in the policy process. Better substantive representation for these groups would provide mechanisms for the effective articulation of their distinctive perspective as a regular part of policy processes and would seek to eliminate barriers to the equal treatment of the marginalized group perspective in policy deliberations. Mechanisms for the articulation of these perspectives must attend to both the interactive nature of group perspective and the requirements of accountability and authorization.[10]

Women's Movements as Sources of Political Representation

I have already argued that the focus on representation by individual legislators has distracted scholars from examining other, more important avenues of substantive representation for marginalized groups. Women's movements provide an important but generally unexplored avenue of representation for women, another important mechanism for the articulation of women's perspectives (Dobrowolsky 1998; see also Vickers et al. 1993 on the representation of women's interests). This is not to suggest that women's movements are a perfect incarnation of "women's voice." Women's movement articulations can only ever be partial articulations of women's perspectives, because some subgroups of women are always dominated or excluded. But this is true of every grouping of women in relation to all women (Young 1994). More important, because women's movement activities provide an arena where women interact as women to define their priorities, women's movements are likely to come closer to articulating women's perspectives than is a disparate, unorganized group of women in the legislature.

Some scholars argue that it is not just the existence but also the autonomy of women's groups that is important for their success in influencing policy (Elman 1996; Busch 1992). An autonomous women's movement is a form of women's mobilization that is devoted to promoting women's status and well-being independently of political parties and other associations that do not make the status of women their main concern. For example, if the only women's organizations are women's wings or caucuses within the existing political parties, the women's movement is not autonomous (Molyneux 1998). Autonomous organizations must be self-governing, must recognize no superior authority, and must not be subject to the governance of other political agencies.

Autonomous women's organizing improves women's ability to articulate their perspective. Organizations that are not mainly focused on women's concerns are more likely to adopt as priorities those "women's issues" that fit easily into the existing organizational agenda. When women's groups are only subsidiaries or wings of larger organizations, it can be difficult for them to make the case that considerable amounts of organizational resources should be spent on a "women's issue." Violence against women is an issue that is of concern mainly to women. As such, political parties, trade unions, and other political organizations may find it more difficult to adopt such an issue as a priority than to adopt other women's issues that can be subsumed under a universal category, such as old-age pensions, minimum wage, or family and medical leave. Thus, women's wings or suborganizations of larger organizations will have a harder time using organizational resources to articulate women's perspectives than will independent women's organizations that can directly translate women's issues into organizational priorities (Weldon 2002).

In addition, autonomous women's movements can improve the accountability of government bureaucrats in ways that nonautonomous movements may not. If the women's movement is entirely contained in the state, the ability to criticize government policy may be curtailed. Autonomous groups can challenge the existing order of priorities by drawing attention to issues that are not on the agenda. Thus, autonomous women's movements can improve the representation of women in the policy process.

Institutions as Sources of Representation

Another mechanism that has received little consideration as an avenue for representation is the creation of public agencies whose responsibility it is to provide an intragovernmental voice for particular marginalized groups. Many governments now have such offices. Most national governments, for example, now have a women's policy machinery, that is, a government body responsible for promoting the status of women (Mazur 2002; Staudt 1998; Stetson and Mazur 1995; Weldon 2002).

Perhaps one reason why these offices have not been more widely considered as avenues of representation is the concern on the part of some scholars that states are male-biased: they cannot be mechanisms for advancing women's rights, because "the master's tools will never dismantle the master's house" (Lorde 1984; MacKinnon 1989). But feminist scholars have discovered that the relationship between public policy and women's status is far more complex than this view would suggest, not least because the degree to which governments promote women's rights varies over time and across nations (Mazur 2002; Htun and Weldon 2007; Banaczak et al. 2005).

Understanding why women's policy agencies can provide a mechanism for representation requires an understanding of the limitations that political institutions place on the individuals who fill particular positions within them. Policy outcomes, as noted, are not just a product of the legislators that enact them. They are shaped and implemented by the institutional structure in which they are formed. This institutional structure does not affect all policy ideas in the same way. As Bachrach and Baratz (1962) noted, every organized undertaking involves the mobilization of bias: the very creation of categories makes some issues and concepts salient and renders others irrelevant. The very organization of the administrative structure facilitates some policies and obscures or obstructs others. The organization of government, for example, tends to reflect the priorities of the dominant groups who defined the basic administrative categories, creating a sort of institutional bias in the structure of public administration, in favor of the issues important to historically dominant groups. In this way, institutional structures can also formalize and entrench the understandings of policies ("policy images") preferred by dominant groups (Baumgartner and Jones 1993). As a result, organizational priorities sometimes conflict with or obscure the interests of marginalized groups, making it difficult to propose or enact policies that further their interests. Without reform, the current structure of public administration tends to provide an unrecognized form of substantive representation for historically dominant groups, while blocking or stifling the articulation of the perspective of marginalized groups.

Such an institutional bias might affect women as a marginalized group in democratic policy processes. The current construction of administrative categories in most of the political institutions in question makes it difficult to address issues of concern to women. Policies addressing violence against women, the protection of reproductive freedom, and economic inequality between men and women usually require coordination among a number of major government departments. Government response to violence against women, for example, requires action in areas of policy as diverse as criminal justice, education, and income assistance. But these areas are usually the responsibility of a variety of different agencies, posing considerable coordination problems (Weldon 2002).

Because administrative structures tend to reflect the particular problems (and the understandings of those problems) that prevail at the time of their creation, most public administrative systems are designed to address problems other than women's issues. Moreover, traditional understandings of these problems tend to reflect the context of sexual inequality in which these bureaus were created (Staudt 1997). For example, in the United States, the official definition of unemployment excludes women who are looking for paid employment but cannot obtain work because they cannot find child care. The current mobilization of bias present in political institutions disadvantages women and their concerns, creating a sort of gender bias in the fundamental structure of political institutions.

Women's policy agencies are one way of creating state institutions that at least partially reflect women's perspectives. A women's policy machinery can focus on issues of concern to women in their entirety: one need not segment problems confronting women (e.g., violence) into their health aspects, criminal justice aspects, and so on in order to address them. Stetson and Mazur (1995, 288) argue that those agencies that have centralized, cross-sectoral approaches to promoting gender equality are the most effective. These agencies must be set up to coordinate women's policies in an authoritative manner, having the power to direct policy-making across a number of departments. This suggests that a subdepartmental desk in a low-ranking ministry is unlikely to be an effective mechanism for representing women in policy deliberations. Similarly, an agency with few resources will be unable to carry out the monitoring and analysis required. This suggests that to be effective in representing women, a women's policy machinery must have a degree of independence, some of its own resources, and positional authority.

The representativeness of the perspective articulated by women's policy agencies can be improved if the represented have the opportunity to comment on and critique the agency's proposals. Women's bureau consultations with women's movement organizations and activists can improve agency proposals. Examples of such consultations are advisory committees set up in both Canada and Australia whereby women's organizations had regular access to government officials. In addition, in Australia (and in Canada for a while), there were regular meetings between political officials and women's movement activists to discuss a "women's agenda."

Where access is based on informal channels, it usually depends on good relations between women's movement activists and the individual bureaucrats. If consultation with women's groups is a formal part of the policy agency, access is likely to be more uniform across policy areas and over time. When formal, regularized channels for consultation exist and are part of the normal operation of government, it may be more difficult for new administrations (who may be hostile to women's groups) to shut women's organizations out of the policy-making process.

However, improving institutional capacity is not the same as providing the political will to address a problem. As Kathlene (1995) notes, gender mitigates "position power," that is, influence derived from one's position in the bureaucratic hierarchy: women obtain less benefit from powerful institutional positions than do men. Thus, as a prominent former bureaucrat in a women's policy agency in Canada explains, "Without external pressure, these structures have little hope of doing more than holding the fort or maintaining the status quo" (Geller Schwartz 1995, 57). In addition, providing mechanisms by which women's movements can be consulted will not be of much use if there is no one with whom to consult. This suggests that political support from external social movements is necessary to provide women's bureaus both the political pressure and input that is necessary to capitalize on improved institutional capacity. Thus, when women's policy machineries have positional authority and adequate resources, they can improve substantive representation for women by providing a mechanism by which women's distinctive perspective can be articulated and by providing some mechanism of authorization or accountability for women (through consultations with women's organizations). But this impact depends on the presence of a women's movement, and we should expect little in the way of direct effects.

Interactions between Sources of Representation

Distinguishing multiple sources of representation makes it possible to conceptualize interactions between these different sources and to theorize their combined impact on democratic political processes. Women's policy agencies provide an important avenue of representation for women, but this is only likely to have an effect on the policy process in the context of an autonomous women's movement. Strong, autonomous women's movements improve the institutional capabilities of government in addressing women's issues. This magnifies women's voice inside government. When the women's movement is strong, the women's policy machinery has more influence with other government departments. Bureaucrats inside the women's policy machinery seeking to articulate women's concerns can point to public pressure from the women's movement. Thus, a strong, autonomous women's movement improves the representative function performed by a women's policy agency.

Conversely, women's policy agencies can strengthen women's movements. By providing financial support for organizing and independent research, women's policy machineries provide additional resources to women's organizations. In addition, by providing research support and opportunities for input on policy development, women's policy machineries can assist women's movement activists in publicly articulating women's perspectives. Thus, strong, autonomous women's movements and effective women's policy agencies reinforce one another in improving women's representation. This effect is interactive: each factor magnifies the effect of the other.

Women's Representation and Policies on Violence against Women

Although descriptive representation may have positive effects on the political process (e.g., improving the legitimacy of representative bodies or improving symbolic inclusion of marginalized groups), the argument that it significantly improves substantive representation has important weaknesses. Moreover, descriptive representation is rarely empirically compared with other modes of substantive representation, such as articulation of group perspective through social movements or through institutional reforms. Such a comparison reveals that descriptive representation in the legislature is a relatively ineffective way to ensure that policy outcomes reflect the perspectives of marginalized groups (although it may accomplish other important goals).

In this section, I examine the impact of different sources of political representation for women on policies to address violence against women. Violence against women is central to women's subordinate status: violence hinders women's efforts to achieve parity with men in the areas of employment, education, the family, and public life. Violence against women is consistently identified as an important issue in women's collective endeavors to advance their status: activists and governments from more than 180 countries have identified violence against women as an issue of literally vital importance.[11] This agreement reinforced the growing body of evidence that violence against women in the form of sexual assault and wife battering is a serious problem nearly everywhere in the world (Heise 1994; Weldon 2002). Still, there is great variation among democratic governments in terms of their responsiveness to violence against women. Some governments undertake broad, multifaceted initiatives to address violence against women, while other governments do not even recognize the problem.[12]

Until very recently, despite the importance of this issue, there have been only a few systematic cross-national analyses of policy outcomes (Avdeyeva 2007; Busch 1992; Elman 1996; Johnson 2007; Weldon 2002). None of these studies investigated the question of the impact of women's representation on policies on violence against women.[13] Thus, this policy issue provides an important but unexamined test case for examining the impact of women's representation on national policies of importance to women.

The institutional forms and policy outcomes affecting women vary most clearly across national contexts. The strength and other characteristics of women's movements also vary most clearly across countries. This suggests that a cross-national study of the impact of the representation of women on democratic policy-making may provide insights into the effectiveness of different modes of political representation for women that are difficult to discern when only a single national context is considered. In the remainder of this chapter, I provide, first, an illustrative comparative discussion of how policies on violence against women developed in Canada and other established democracies and, then, a statistical analysis of policy outcomes.

GOVERNMENT RESPONSIVENESS TO VIOLENCE AGAINST WOMEN

Violence against women takes a number of forms. This study focuses on two categories: sexual assault of women by men and battering of intimate female partners by males. Action on violence is an important indicator that women's perspectives are influencing policy-making, since it suggests that government is responding to the articulation of an issue of importance to women. Despite the many differences among the countries considered, similar features of the problem and the existing policy structure make it possible to identify a common set of needed actions to address violence against women. A cross-national data set developed in Weldon 2002 includes data on seven different aspects of government response to violence against women:[14]

1. Has there been any legal reform dealing with domestic violence?
2. Has there been any legal reform dealing with sexual assault?

3. Is there any national government funding for shelters for victims of domestic violence?
4. Is there any national government funding for rape crisis centers?
5. Are there any government-sponsored training programs for service providers?
6. Are there any government-sponsored public education initiatives?
7. Is there a central agency for coordinating national policies on violence?

Asking how many of these types of policy action a government undertakes provides a good measure of government responsiveness: a government that addresses more areas is enacting a broader, more multifaceted response. Although these seven types of policy action are important for different reasons, all seven policy areas are important for addressing violence against women.[15] The seven policy areas are weighted equally: the indicator simply sums the scores (1 for each area in which policy action occurs, 0 for a lack of action) across the seven areas. This variable therefore measures the scope of government response, that is, the amount or breadth of government activity, rather than the particular substantive focus or quality of the individual initiatives (Powell 1982; Putnam 1993).[16] This indicator does not measure which governments enact the policies that result in the greatest reduction of violence. Indeed, some of the policy measures considered here are aimed at raising awareness or serving victims, rather than at directly reducing the overall incidence of violence.[17]

The data set includes these seven aspects of national government response to violence against women for all stable democracies. The focus is on national government response because, in general, action by the central government, even if it is only providing funding to local areas, is a key symbolic indicator that the political community is seriously addressing a problem. Thus, even in federal systems such as those of the United States, Canada, and Australia, action by the national government vastly increases the importance given to the issue and the consistency with which it is addressed. In Australia, where some relevant areas of law are state responsibilities, the federal government has developed model laws and pushed for state adoption. Freedom House data are used to select stable, democratic countries for comparison.[18] The data used are for 1994. See the appendix for a ranking of countries by number of areas addressed.

These data on government response are based on a variety of primary and secondary sources, including academic, government, and activist publications; materials from the proceedings of the Committee on the Elimination of All

Forms of Discrimination against Women (CEDAW); U.S. Department of State human rights reports; Human Rights Watch reports; and communications (emails, faxes, and letters) with activists and government representatives in the countries concerned. There are multiple sources for every country, and the sources for each country include at least one government source and one source independent of the national government.

Using this measure, the most responsive democratic governments are in Canada, Australia, and the United States, and the least responsive are in Botswana, Italy, Nauru, Papua New Guinea, and Venezuela. In 1994, the Nordic countries, where women have such an impressive presence in the legislature (between 25 and 40 percent), lag behind the governments of Canada, Australia, and the United States, where women are fairly poorly represented in descriptive terms (with women comprising about 10 to 20 percent of the legislature).

Looking at the process by which individual measures were adopted in Canada reinforces the sense that although the efforts of individual women can be important, it is not necessarily the number of women in the legislature that matters for the substantive representation of women in this area. After more than a decade of activism and lobbying by women's organizations, a series of important amendments (including a rape shield law) were adopted rather expeditiously in 1983. (Rape shield laws protect complainants of rape from a "second violation" as prosecutors probe their backgrounds and suggest—explicitly or implicitly—that sexually active women likely consent to all sexual activity.) Women's organizations were quite influential in getting attention to this issue, and a proposal from the National Association of Women and Law (NAWL), endorsed by the National Action Committee on the Status of Women (NAC), formed the basis for the amendments. Indeed, women's organizations had impressed many with their political strength during the constitutional reform process that led to the Charter of Rights and Freedoms adopted in 1982, and scholars agree that elected representatives perceived the women's movement as having considerable clout (Los 1994; Bashevkin 1998). Observers have noted that the minister overseeing the drafting, passage, and implementation of the measures (Jean Chrétien, a man) undertook a number of measures to ensure the success of the legal reform—investing resources in public education, special units in police stations across the nation, and similar measures. Reportedly, women's organizations and the minister worked closely throughout this process (Roberts and Gebotys 1992; Tang 1998). Indeed, in the years leading up to the passage of the amendments, the Secretary of State

Women's Program funded groundbreaking research on wife abuse that provided critical background and support for the 1983 measures (Weldon 2002).

The rape shield law was struck down in a 1991 Supreme Court decision. The minister of justice at the time (a woman and a conservative) quickly worked with women's groups to draft a new law. The resultant amendment is known as the "no means no" sexual assault law (Bill C-46). The process was undertaken by Canada's first female minister of justice, Kim Campbell, a member of the Progressive Conservative Party (a center-right party). Campbell held a broad set of hearings with women's groups on the subject of the bill, hearings that raised awareness and understanding of the issues surrounding sexual assault and built support for the feminist amendment that followed. Among other measures, the sexual assault law puts the onus for determining consent on the initiator of sexual activity. Previously, the burden was often on the woman victim of sexual assault to show she did not consent to sexual activity (Weldon 2002; Tang 1998; Roberts and Gebotys 1992).

In this process and in the development of policies on violence against women in Canada more generally, it is not the number of women in the legislature that figures prominently. The 1988 election did bring 12 additional women (including Kim Campbell) into office, increasing the proportion of women in the Canadian parliament from 13 to 18 percent. But the process of reform began much earlier and under the auspices of a male minister. In both instances, despite the varying sex and party of the ministers, the minister of justice appeared very supportive of and responsive to demands of the women's movement to act on violence against women (Roberts and Gebotys 1992; Vickers et al. 1993; Los 1994).

More generally, major expansions of policies on violence occurred when there was a relatively small proportion of women in government. Amendments to criminal law began in 1983; special initiatives funding shelters, training police, disseminating information, and aiming to prevent family violence were launched in 1986, 1988, and 1991 (Weldon 2002). The trend toward greater responsiveness toward violence against women appears to have preceded the increase in numbers of women and, indeed, to have begun in the early 1980s, when there were comparatively few women in public office even for Canada. (Women were less than 10 percent of the parliament, and fewer than 30 women were present [table 1].)

In Sweden during the same time period, in the 1980s, women's movement efforts to raise the issue of violence against women were suppressed and char-

TABLE 1. Women's Descriptive Representation in the Canadian Parliament and Developments in Violence against Women Policy, 1980–2001

Year and Party in Power	Number of Women MPs	% Women MPs	Developments in Violence against Women Policy
1980 Liberals (Center Left)	14	5.0	Canadian Advisory Council on the Status of Women publishes report on wife battering (1980) Status of Women Canada funds women's groups working on violence (1981, 1982) Amendents to criminal code (including rape shield law) (1983)
1984 Progressive Conservative (Center Right)	27	9.6	1986 first family violence initiative (FVI) launched
1988 Progressive Conservative (Center Right)	39	13.3	"No means no" sexual assault law adopted (1992) Canadian Panel on Violence against Women (1993, before election) Cuts to Secretary of State Women's Program begin 1986, continue through 2001
1993 Liberals (Center Left)	53	18	FVI is shut down (1994) Funding for shelters slows, is shifted to provinces (1995) Training for police officers in First Nations communities is undertaken (1994–98)
1997 Liberals (Center Left)	62	20.6	FVI reinstated Laws against female genital mutilation, trafficking, and sexual exploitation of children (including by Canadians abroad) take effect
2000 Liberals (Center Left)	62	20.6	Funding for shelters slows further Some increase in funding to Secretary of State women's program for preventive measures on violence against women (2001)

Source: Cool 2008; Weldon 2002a, 2004b.

acterized as divisive (Elman 1996). At that time, there were about three times as many women in parliament in Sweden as there were in Canada (96 women in the Swedish parliament in 1982 and 133 by 1988), constituting between 26 and 38 percent of total seats (IPU 2009). Indeed, legal reforms such as protective orders were adopted at least a decade later in Sweden (1988) than in the United States and the United Kingdom, where they were in initial use in the late 1970s (and where there are many fewer women in the legislature) (Elman 1998).

These brief stories suggest that whether or not public policy addresses women's substantive interests in addressing violence against women depends on more than just having the issue raised by the women's movement (as it was in both Canada and Sweden), although that seems to have been the catalyst for government response in the stable, democratic countries (Weldon 2002). It also depends on more than number or proportion of women in government: the larger number of women in government in Sweden (even under a labor government) did not make that government more responsive to women's movement demands regarding violence (Elman 1996). In addition, measures to address violence against women were adopted under both left and right governments in Canada. Similarly, in the United States, the Violence Against Women Act of 1994 (VAWA) was adopted unanimously by the House of Representatives: no member of either party voted against it.

Indeed, in Canada, where governments adopted the most expansive policies on violence most quickly, these policies seem to be the product of an unusual relationship between the state and the women's movement. The state strengthened, supported, and responded to a women's movement that nevertheless remained autonomous. This strong and autonomous women's movement benefited from the resources and political support of a powerful set of agencies dedicated to raising women's status. This state-movement relationship provided a powerful mechanism for the articulation and substantive representation of women's perspectives on violence. In what follows, I define and operationalize these terms and specify exactly how I see this influence obtaining (Weldon 2002).

WOMEN'S MOVEMENTS AND POLITICAL REPRESENTATION

I argued earlier that autonomous women's movements provide an important avenue of representation for women. A women's movement is a kind of social movement (Tarrow 1998; Beckwith 2000). A social movement is a form of political organization in which membership and action is based on a shared sense of purpose and/or identity, aimed at changing social practices or prevailing power relations (McBride and Mazur 2008; Meyer et al. 2005; Tarrow 1998). Women's movements are those social movements in which women make up the membership and leadership of the organization. In this chapter, I examine only those women's movements aimed at furthering women's status or undermining patriarchy, that is, feminist women's movements (Beckwith 2000; Mazur and Stetson 2008).

The vast majority of nations in this study had active feminist movements by 1994 (Weldon 2002).[19] As noted, scholars of feminist movements and public policy have argued that the autonomy of such movements is key to determining policy influence. Feminist movements can be coded as autonomous if they have an organizational base outside political parties, unions, and other political institutions. They must also be independent of organizations that do not make the condition of women their primary concern. Autonomous women's organizations are not subsidiaries, auxiliaries, or wings of larger, mixed-sex organizations. Data on organizations was taken from published historical accounts of these women's movements and encyclopedias of women's organizations (Weldon 2002).

In addition to gauging the autonomy of women's movements, we need some sense of whether they are strong or weak. Movements might be independent but have little impact on the attitudes or awareness of the broader public. Strong women's movements can command public support and attention, while weaker movements have trouble convincing others that their positions and opinions are important. Such strength is indicated by the size and number of protest activities, the degree of support expressed for feminists in opinion polls, the degree of support for women's organizations, the diversity and membership of women's organizations, the proliferation and diversity of women's cultural institutions (e.g., women's festivals, newspapers, concerts, etc.), and so on. Given what we know about democratic policy-making, it seems likely that strong women's movements will influence policy outcomes more than weak ones, but strong movements do not *always* influence policy outcomes.[20]

Although it is notoriously difficult to construct accurate measures of women's movement activities across national contexts (Beckwith 2000), there is considerable convergence among experts' assessments of the relative strength of women's movements (i.e., the Swedish women's movement is considered to be relatively weak, while the U.S. women's movement is considered relatively strong) (Elman 1996; Gelb 1989; Kaplan 1992; Bergqvist 1999; Randall 1987; Nelson and Carver 1995; Stetson 1997; Stetson and Mazur 1995; Norris 1987). Movements are coded as strong if they are described by expert observers as strong, influential, or powerful; as mobilizing widespread public support; and so on. Comparative and country-specific accounts of women's movements explicitly assess the strength of women's movements over time and/or relative to other countries, relying on multiple data sources, including size and frequency of demonstrations; public support for the women's movement, as expressed in public opinion surveys; the proportion of women belonging to women's organizations; the proliferation of feminist organizations, bookstores, magazines, and the like; and the frequency with which women's movement activists are consulted in the media and in other public deliberations.[21] Where the women's movement is both strong and autonomous according to these criteria, the country is coded 1, and where either strength or autonomy is absent, the country is coded 0 (see table A1 in the appendix).[22]

WOMEN'S BUREAUS AS A FORM OF POLITICAL REPRESENTATION FOR WOMEN

I have already argued that women's bureaus can provide a form of political representation for women, especially in combination with an active, independent women's movement. Women's bureaus likely play an important role in the area of policies on violence against women. We would expect women's policy machineries to improve the political representation of women when they have (1) formalized channels of access for women's organizations and (2) the independence and resources needed to formulate and implement aspects of a women's agenda. If the women's policy agencies in the 36 stable democracies in this study are categorized according to these criteria, only 8 of the 34 agencies actually meet them (the agencies in Australia, Canada, Costa Rica, Netherlands, Belgium, Venezuela, Portugal, and Germany). Countries are coded 1 on this variable if they meet both conditions, 0 if they do not.[23]

THE INTERACTION BETWEEN WOMEN'S MOVEMENTS AND POLITICAL INSTITUTIONS

As I have argued, a women's policy machinery does not, on its own, guarantee any government response to violence against women. Rather, the interaction of the apparatus with a strong, autonomous women's movement results in better representation for women in democratic policy processes. Where such women's movements interact with effective policy machineries, we should see greater responsiveness to violence against women. This interactive effect can be captured by using a multiplicative term (*strong and autonomous women's movement × effective women's policy machinery*) in the regression analysis.

REPRESENTATION BY WOMEN LEGISLATORS

I have argued that alternative modes of representation were more important than descriptive representation in the legislature in improving policy outcomes for women. What measure of women's legislative presence should be used in making this case? Some accounts claiming a substantive impact of descriptive representation have argued that women legislators should only be expected to speak or act for women after the proportion of women passes a threshold or tipping point, usually thought to be between 15 and 30 percent (Grey 2006; Bystydzienski 1992; Thomas 1994). As the proportion of women reaches 10 or 15 percent, women legislators feel freer to express their distinctive concerns. However, they may still not be sufficiently numerous or powerful to be able to diffuse their concerns throughout the legislature. This is more likely to occur when women regularly comprise a greater proportion of the legislature, say 35–40 percent (Thomas 1994, 154). As Thomas (1994) observes, it is possible that the proportion of women constituting a critical mass varies over time and location; Grey (2006) argues further that the proportion must vary across contexts and over time. Nevertheless, Thomas argues, "the concept that greater percentages of women legislators will lead to a diffusion of their perspectives throughout the governing body is sound. And the issues of special concern to female representatives . . . will permeate legislative bodies as women's representation is closer to parity" (154). This implies, I think, that we would expect a greater proportion of women legislators, especially a proportion of 35 or 40 percent, to be associated with greater policy responsiveness to violence against women.[24] In contrast, I have argued that, in itself, a greater number or proportion of women (even the presence of a critical mass) in the legislature would not have a consistently large effect on government responsiveness to violence against women.

THE PROPOSED MODEL

In general, then, the interaction between strong and autonomous women's movements and institutional structure produces better representation in the policy process, which is here measured by responsiveness to violence against women. We might also expect strong and autonomous women's movements to have an impact independent of this interaction, since such agencies are not necessary for women's movement influence. We would not necessarily expect such an independent effect from women's policy agencies. In addition, the number of women in the legislature does not determine responsiveness to violence against women. Level of development and culture are thought to be fundamental factors influencing politics and policy.[25] I control for these factors using dummy variables to measure level of development, region, and dominant religion (the latter two as proxies for culture).

Analysis

I employ OLS regression to examine the association between different sources of political representation for women and responsiveness to violence against women. Multivariate regression analysis can be used to examine whether (and how strongly) each of these modes of representation is associated with more government action on violence against women (table 2). Scope of government response is coded from 0 to 7, depending on the number of areas of policy action that a national government undertakes. If a mode of representation produced better policy outcomes for women, we would expect the mode to be associated with governments addressing an increased number of additional areas.

REPRESENTATION BY WOMEN LEGISLATORS

As expected, there is no linear relationship between proportion of women legislators and government responsiveness to violence against women (table 2, model 1). More generally, a critical mass effect is not visible in this policy area. Of those governments where women comprise more than 30 percent of the legislature, none have addressed more than four policy areas (see table A1 in the appendix). Moreover, among those governments that have been the most responsive to violence against women (i.e., that have adopted five or more policies), the percentage of women in the legislature varies from 6.4 to 21.2 percent.[26] It may be that individual feminist women are important in getting policies passed as policy entrepreneurs. Indeed, it may be that the presence of at least one woman is a necessary condition for policy development. But there is no linear relationship between the overall proportion of women in the legislature or in cabinet and government responsiveness to violence against women. This finding is robust using various specifications of the proportion of women, or the number of women. It also holds up when the analysis uses robust standard errors (not shown).

WOMEN'S MOVEMENT

The presence of a strong, autonomous women's movement is more strongly positively associated with scope than is the proportion of women, with standardized betas of .50 and .00, respectively (table 2, model 1). Controlling for level of development, the presence of a strong and autonomous women's movement is associated with about one or two additional areas of policy action on violence against women ($B = 1.90 \pm 0.55$). This supports the argument that the existence of strong, independent women's movements improves women's representation in the policy process more effectively than does increasing women's presence in the legislature.

TABLE 2. Regression Coefficients; Dependent Variable = Scope of Government Response to Violence against Women, 36 Stable Democratic Countries, 1994

Model	Independent Variables	*B*	S.E.	Beta	*T*	Sig.	R^2
1	Level of development	1.20	0.64	0.30	1.87	0.07	0.37
	Strong and autonomous women's movement	1.90	0.55	0.50	3.44	0.00	
	Percentage of women in legislature	0.00	0.02	0.00	–0.02	0.98	
	Effective women's policy machinery	0.45	0.66	0.10	0.68	0.49	
2	Level of development	1.09	0.54	0.27	2.03	0.50	0.43
	Strong and autonomous women's movement	1.39	0.59	0.36	2.33	0.02	
	Effective women's policy machinery	–0.86	0.96	–0.19	–0.90	0.37	
	Effective women's policy machinery × strong and autonomous women's movement	2.33	1.27	0.42	1.82	0.07	
3	Level of development	–0.28	1.43	–0.07	–0.20	0.85	0.61
	Strong and autonomous women's movement	0.80	0.67	0.21	1.21	0.24	
	Effective women's policy machinery × strong and autonomous women's movement	2.30	1.34	0.43	1.71	0.10	
	Logged number of reps	0.01	0.42	0.04	0.17	0.87	
	Region—Africa	–1.12	1.84	–0.14	–0.60	0.55	
	Region—Asia	2.31	1.48	0.34	1.56	0.13	
	Region—Latin America	–0.88	1.68	–0.18	–0.53	0.61	
	Region—North America	2.44	1.23	0.3	1.99	0.06	
	Region—Oceania	1.22	1.25	0.18	0.98	0.34	
	Dominant religion—Protestant	0.00	0.65	–0.01	–0.06	0.94	
	Dominant religion—Other	–2.30	1.30	–0.47	–1.70	0.08	

Note: I report statistical significance as a matter of interest, but I consider this set of countries to be a complete set of stable democracies (i.e., a population), and I am not employing sampling techniques.

S.E. = standard error; Sig. = significance.

WOMEN'S POLICY AGENCY

The presence of an effective women's policy machinery is not associated with government responsiveness to violence against women (table 2, model 1). This may seem to contradict the hypothesis that these institutions have an effect on government responsiveness to this issue. But I argued earlier that the policy impact of these institutions depended on the presence of a strong and autonomous women's movement and that we should not expect to see an independent effect. If this argument holds, a term capturing the interaction between effective women's policy agencies and strong and autonomous women's movements should be strongly associated with government response to violence against women and should explain more than either term alone.

INTERACTION EFFECTS

An indicator representing the interaction of a strong, autonomous women's movement and the presence of a women's policy machinery (one that provides access and resources) is a very strong predictor of government responsiveness to violence against women (table 2, models 2 and 3), being associated with more areas of government action than either of the two parts alone (model 2). The interaction of a strong, autonomous women's movement and an effective women's policy agency is associated with about two additional areas of policy action ($B = 2.33 \pm 1.27$) (model 2). This association seems to hold even controlling for level of development, region, and religion (model 3). In sum, then, strong, independent women's movements and effective women's bureaus interact to provide an effective mode of substantive representation for women. Indeed, in the area of policies on violence against women, cross-national data suggest that women's bureaus and women's movements together are more effective at securing policy action than are large numbers of women in the legislature.

Conclusion

The literature on representation for marginalized groups is currently focused on whether individuals in the legislature can represent diverse social groups. I argue that although individuals can provide a partial or limited articulation of group perspective, group perspectives are best articulated in those forums where members of marginalized groups interact to formulate their distinctive concerns. This suggests that legislatures, as currently organized, may not be the only (or best) place to examine whether representation of marginalized groups is occurring. Group perspectives can be articulated by social movements or even by government agencies. Political institutions, I have argued, tend to reflect the social perspectives of the historically dominant groups that created them, thereby embedding a bias toward these groups in the very structure of public administration and providing a type of substantive representation for these groups. Institutional reforms to remove or mitigate these biases can improve representation for marginalized groups.

Discussions of substantive democratic representation, then, should consider multiple sources of political representation. Considering a number of modes of representation makes it possible to compare different modes of representation and explore interactions between them. In this study, the interaction between modes of representation appears to be critical. The interaction between women's movements and institutional structures is more important for understanding policy responsiveness to violence against women than is the proportion of women in the legislature.

I am not arguing that individual members of marginalized groups in legislatures provide no representation. Indeed, the presence of such representatives can have important symbolic and substantive effects on policy processes. The question is whether it is the only or best avenue for such representation, because the literature on representation for marginalized groups often seems to treat it as such by focusing on it to the exclusion of other avenues. But descriptive representation in legislatures is limited as an avenue for providing substantive representation. Although it may be true that "descriptive representation by gender improves substantive outcomes for women in every polity for which we have a measure" (Mansbridge 2005, 622), it does not follow that the presence of more women (or a larger proportion of women) in the legislature always means better representation. For example, in France, the proportion of women in the legislature decreased during the key period of policy innovation on violence against women (Weldon 2002, table 4-1); the same was true in Indonesia and South Africa (Htun and Weldon 2010b); in Israel, an increasing number of women in the Knesset has not led to greater policy action for women, in the view of leading feminist activists (perhaps because there are more women in conservative parties now and because the most feminist members of the Knesset were voted out) (interviews with Israeli feminists, 2007); and an analysis of women's representation in Belgium similarly shows that increasing the number of women in the legislature did not result in greater substantive representation for women (Celis 2008). So even if an increased women's presence in the legislature improves representation for women under some circumstances, this does not mean that it is the best avenue for substantive representation or that the presence of more women in the legislature will always improve substantive representation for women.

Of course, as noted, social movements and women's policy agencies are also limited in terms of substantive representation: some women feel excluded or dominated in women's movements, and lines of accountability are unclear. Women's policy agencies are characterized by similar exclusions and weaknesses. Nevertheless, examining multiple sources of representation provides a more complete picture of the possibilities for—and limits on—influence in democratic policy processes.

This analysis, then, adds to the growing body of research pointing to the importance of thinking more broadly and in more nuanced ways about possible mechanisms of representation for women. It is becoming increasingly clear that an overemphasis on descriptive representation in the legislature has obscured other important, unexamined avenues for representation, ignored the way different avenues of representation interact, and resulted in a tendency to overlook the institutional context (Weldon 2002; Childs 2006; Mansbridge 2003; Poggione 2004; Wolbrecht and Hero 2005). Exploring the relationship between these multiple avenues of representation and public policy suggests many new avenues for research (Schwindt-Bayer and Mishler 2005). For example, it may be that individual women legislators are more likely to promote women's perspective when they participate in women's movements or at least belong to women's organizations (Carroll 2003; Sawer 2004; see also Costain 1998). Swers (2002) has argued that political party and political context determine whether women in the legislature represent women (see also Poggione 2004). This analysis did not examine the influence of political party, although studies of violence against women have suggested that political party is a poor predictor of support for measures on violence. In the United States, for example, VAWA has enjoyed bipartisan support for years. In Canada, as noted, significant reforms of rape law were undertaken under both left and right governments. Still, party might be more important for other issues of importance to women. Last, scholars of gender and politics are increasingly emphasizing the complexity of the relationship between gender and other, crosscutting axes, such as race, class, and sexuality (McCall 2005; Hancock 2006, 2007; Smooth 2007; Beckwith 2005a; Weldon 2006, 2008). I try to explore some of these issues further in later chapters.

More generally, this analysis shows the value of examining the structural conditions in which policy is made (Ashford 1978; Bobrow and Dryzek 1987; Duncan 1995; Giddens 1982; Walby 1990). Examining the social order, the patterns of political inclusion and exclusion established by institutions and norms, is important for understanding democratic policy-making (March and Olsen 1989). Understanding the impact of such patterns, I have shown, is key to understanding whether and how social groups are represented in democratic policy processes. Thus, the study of women and politics and of democratic policy-making more generally should focus as much on political structures such as institutions, social movements, and other macrolevel phenomena as it does on individual-level variables and characteristics.

CHAPTER 2

Social Movements, Representation, and Family Policy

In the last chapter, we saw that women's movements were important for explaining policy outcomes on violence against women and that numbers or proportion of women in government did not seem to explain the very different degree of government responsiveness to this important issue across countries. I used this finding to buttress the theoretical argument that social movements, even more than political parties or legislators, provide critical avenues of substantive representation for marginalized groups such as women, ethnic and racial minorities, and working-class people. Although violence against women is an important issue, it is not the only issue of importance to women or the only area of law and policy in which we might hope to see women's perspectives, interests, and concerns reflected. Indeed, scholars of gender and public policy are increasingly emphasizing that the politics of women's rights vary by issue (Sanbonmatsu 2003; Htun 2003; Mazur 2002).

Another important area of public policy, leave policies related to bearing and caring for children, shows quite a different cross-national pattern. Indeed, some of the most exciting and progressive policies for such leave, policies that seem to greatly facilitate women's work, have been adopted in precisely those countries in which women have a sizable presence in government (e.g., Norway, Denmark, and Sweden). Moreover, scholars of the politics behind these policies report little influence on the part of organized feminist movements in determining these policy outcomes. They argue instead that the critical determinants of policy outcomes are the general configuration of social policies, struggles over secularism, or the presence of women in government (Mazur 2002; Morgan 2006; Kittilson 2008). If this finding is true, how can we reconcile it with the idea that social movements are better representatives for women than are women in government?

There has been little systematic cross-national analysis of the politics of policy in this area[1] and no quantitative cross-national analysis that takes into account women's organization in civil society. In this chapter, I use an analysis of maternity and parental leaves and antidiscrimination policy to argue that women's interests as women are best represented by women's movements but that women's class interests may be better articulated by labor movements. Social movements, or third-sector representatives such as unions, are still the most effective avenue of policy change—more effective than left parties, for example. Women's movements are still critical for advancing policies that challenge *gender* hierarchies, while labor mobilization is more critical for challenging *class* divisions. I find that the number of women in government does seem to produce more generous policies on maternity and parental leave but does not make policies challenging gender hierarchies more likely. These findings, I contend, support the general argument that extralegislative avenues of representation (e.g., social movements) are more effective avenues of representation than those intralegislative avenues traditionally considered to be the primary avenues of democratic representation for movements seeking to advance transformative agendas, agendas of social change.

Leave Policies

Examining leave policies advances the discussion of social movements and representation for at least two reasons. First, leave policies are important for advancing women's interests. Second, the extant scholarship on leave policies suggests that women in government influence policy development in this area (Kittilson 2008; Schwindt-Bayer and Mishler 2005) and that women's movements have little impact (Mazur 2002; Morgan 2006). So, as already noted, this area presents a "hard case" for the theory that movements best represent women.

Although rates of labor force participation by women vary cross-nationally (from 40 to 91 women active for every 100 men), a majority of women in most countries work in the paid labor force at some point in their lives, and a majority become mothers. Worldwide, more than 1.1 billion women work in the paid labor force. Although rates of labor force participation vary across countries, differences between women and men in active labor force participation have been decreasing, with 80 women active for every 100 men in most regions (ILO 2004). Thus, most women work, most women become mothers, and opportunities to combine work and family roles are significantly affected by measures such as leave policies. Perhaps this is why all stable democratic countries have adopted some sort of leave policy to accommodate workers' childbearing and child care responsibilities (Mazur 2002; ILO 2004).

There has been much analysis of the impact of leave policies on women and men, and scholars have devoted a great deal of attention to categorizing leave policies and social policies more generally in various countries. Perhaps the best-known typology of social policies as they relate to gender roles is Lewis's (1993) categorization of welfare states according to how strongly they reinforce a "male breadwinner" model of the labor market (see also O'Connor et al. 1999; Gauthier 1996).[2] But few scholars have examined the comparative politics of reconciliation policies, that is, the determinants of better or worse work-family policies for women cross-nationally (Mazur 2002, 109). Even fewer analyses actually focus specifically on leave policies (Kittilson 2008) or the needed antidiscrimination policies that too seldom accompany them (Zippel 2007). Thus, such policies constitute an important and widespread but understudied type of policy.

DIMENSIONS OF A MODEL LEAVE POLICY

While leave policies are clearly critical for women's equality, even some of the more generous leave policies reinforce sexual inequality in some important ways. Indeed, although generous family policies do seem to narrow wage inequality to some degree, probably by facilitating women's access to work, they also widen inequality between women and men indirectly, by increasing occupational segregation (Mandel and Semyonov 2005; Gornick and Meyers 2007). This increased gender segregation of the labor market likely occurs because 95 percent of family leaves are taken by women and because women miss out on promotions and lose seniority when they are absent from the workplace for long periods (Lewis 1993; Mandel and Semyonov 2005; Gornick and Meyers 2007). When social norms are such that women are expected to take long leaves (but men are not), employers are less likely to invest in women, and women are less likely to pursue occupations that involve competition with men (Gornick and Meyers 2007). In addition, many generous leave policies do not distinguish between medical leave needed for pregnancy and the two to three years of leave or part-time work that is often needed for care of young children (parental leave). Sometimes, such leave is explicitly restricted to biological or adoptive mothers, reinforcing the norm that women have primary responsibility for child care, especially of young children, even when they are already working. Leave provided to fathers of newborn or adopted babies and young children, if it is provided at all, is often unpaid, only a few days, and/or contingent on the mother being dead or incapacitated. Such leave policies reinforce the norm that women must take responsibility for child care (and not just childbearing). Are such policies feminist? From a feminist perspective, because such leaves provide women with some benefits but reinforce regressive gender stereotypes and roles, they are at best a mixed bag (Gornick and Meyers 2007; Zippel 2007).

Even leave policies that are facially gender neutral (e.g., the leave policy in the United States) tend to reinforce the traditional sexual division of labor in the family because of social norms and the structure of incentives created by gender inequality in the paid labor market. Because men tend to have higher salaries, it is often more economically rational in the short run for the woman to take leave. In addition, social norms create strong social pressures for women to take leave and simultaneously reinforce expectations that the father stays on the job or even increases his efforts at work (to be sure to solidify the economic well-being of the family). Even where policies are gender neutral, women take the vast majority of leaves. Taking lengthy maternity and parental leaves seriously weakens women's position in the labor market, often undermining their access to seniority, promotions, pensions, or even employment itself (Gornick and Meyers 2007; Mandel and Semyonov 2005).

Some governments have adopted policies that specifically seek to challenge this gender division of labor in child care. For example, Norway was the first country in the world to introduce "daddy leave," a parental leave allocation (in this case, four weeks) that is specifically targeted to fathers and cannot be transferred to mothers if it is not used. This leave policy has increased the number of men taking parental leave (ILO 1994, 40; Bergman 2004). There are also provisions prohibiting discrimination on the basis of sex or pregnancy or because an employee avails himself or herself of any kind of family leave. In addition to being very generous, then, Norwegian reconciliation policy involves measures to challenge established gender roles in caring for young children. This is in stark contrast to leave provisions in Switzerland, which include only maternity leave and are available only to women workers. Although Swiss law mandates paid maternity leave, it is paid by the employer, creating a financial disincentive to hire women. Making matters worse, there is no protection against sex or pregnancy discrimination in hiring (although there is some provision to eliminate firing for reasons of pregnancy). Turning to a different configuration of these policies, federal policy in the United States offers quite strong protections against pregnancy discrimination and offers a gender-neutral, family leave policy that is very limited in terms of the time allowed away from work (12 weeks, or about three months, under the Family and Medical Leave Act [FMLA]). Since the leave is unpaid, this policy has been criticized for mainly benefiting middle-class women, who can best afford to avail themselves of leave without state support (ILO 1994; Gelb and Palley 1996; Gelb 2003). In fact, the unpaid nature of the leave means that even middle-class women have strong incentives to return to work right away, and few families can afford to make use of the unpaid leaves guaranteed by the FMLA. Although the leave is gender neutral, it does nothing to alter the status quo, where women take primary responsibility for child care. Unlike the daddy leaves offered in Norway and Sweden, there are few incentives to encourage fathers to take on care of babies and young children.

There are at least two distinct aspects of leave policies, then, that are relevant for thinking about whether such policies further sexual equality. First, we can ask whether these policies seek to change gender roles with respect to paid work and child care (or at least to support those who seek to change such roles) (Gelb and Palley 1987). To answer this question, we will want to know about the provisions for maternity leave, paternity (or supporting parent) leave, and parental leave. Are these issues addressed separately, or are they all assumed to be subsumed under maternity leave? In addition, we want to know whether any paternity leave is provided for, whether it is paid leave, and whether this leave can be transferred to the mother or is specifically reserved for the second parent (if there is one). Last, we want to know whether workers who become pregnant, have parental responsibilities, and take leaves to accommodate these conditions are protected from discrimination. If workers can be fired for taking maternity leave or for being pregnant, the generosity of the policy on the books does not count for much. These aspects of parental leaves are critical for gender equality (Zippel 2007).[3]

A second aspect of these leaves focuses more on the class basis for these leaves. Public responsibility for paying for these leaves is especially relevant from the perspective of working-class women and families. Families that have higher incomes are better able to take advantage of unpaid leaves (although this can still be a struggle, especially for single mothers). Moreover, publicly paid leaves are more easily adopted where the principle of government support for the indigent is already well established, and this can be as much a matter of class politics as of gender politics. Thus, we would expect that class politics and the structure of the welfare state would play a much greater role in the area of the generosity and public funding of leaves than in determining whether or not they challenge gender roles. We would expect that women's movements matter more for the latter. So the finding that women's movements play a relatively small role in the development of leave policies and that these policies are often cast as pro-labor or pro-family policies likely stems from a focus on the generosity of these leaves and the public funding of these leaves. If these policies are importantly based in class, as I have argued, then one would expect the structure of class politics, including the degree of the mobilization of labor, to play a role in determining some aspects (the most class-relevant ones) of these policies. If we are looking at whether social movements influence public policy, then, we may need to consider labor movements as well as women's movements in order to understand the dynamics of policies in these sorts of hybrid policy issues.

Maternity, Paternity, and Work in the United States and Norway

A brief examination of the dynamics of policy developments in the United States and Norway suggests the plausibility of the approach I have recommended. I start with this comparison because Norway has been an important innovator in the area of feminist leave policy, while the United States has been a notorious laggard using traditional measures focused on generosity, providing a clear contrast on the dependent variable (family leave policy) that should help to illuminate differences in the national contexts that produced these outcomes.[4] In both the qualitative and quantitative analysis in this section, I focus on national-level policies.[5] I show that examining different aspects of leave policy reveals that there are different political dynamics for leaves of different types. For aspects of leave related to gender discrimination and challenging patriarchy, women's movement mobilization is key. For policies aimed at changing state-market relations, class-related mobilization is pivotal.

THE UNITED STATES

In the United States, the Pregnancy Discrimination Act (1978) is often thought of as a model of feminist policy influence (Gelb and Palley 1987; Stetson 1997; Mazur 2002). In the early 1970s, the Supreme Court issued somewhat contradictory decisions on the legal status of pregnant workers,[6] prompting feminist groups' efforts to clarify matters by proposing a statute to protect workers from pregnancy discrimination. Working in a coalition of more than 300 groups, including unions and civil rights groups and even pro-life antiabortion groups, feminist organizations formed the Campaign to End Discrimination Against Pregnant Workers (Stetson 1997; Gelb and Palley 1987). The proposal became law in less than two years, resulting in the Pregnancy Discrimination Act (PDA). Business interests were not unified against the proposal, perhaps because some large and influential companies already offered benefits to pregnant workers. Those corporate interests who had testified against protections for pregnant workers in the Supreme Court were unwilling to do so in the more public venue of Congress. The main threat to the bill was opposition from pro-life activists concerned that the bill would mandate payment for abortions. However, a compromise bill passed both chambers with wide margins of support (Gelb and Palley 1987; see also Stetson 1997).[7]

The PDA is the first national policy for pregnant workers in the United States. It amends Title VII of the Civil Rights Act to add language prohibiting discrimination against pregnant women in all aspects of employment (hiring, firing, job security, seniority, and fringe benefits). The PDA also explicitly requires that employers with programs for disability or health benefits include pregnancy in these plans. At the time the PDA was adopted, women comprised about 4 percent of Congress (IPU 1995).

A very different process produced the Family and Medical Leave Act in the United States, a process characterized by delay, opposition from business, and little participation by organized feminism. Feminists working on the issue of maternity leave in the United States initially tried to craft a gender-neutral solution to it by framing the problem as medically needed leave or family leave. The proposal was quickly taken up by labor unions and conservative groups who saw it as either a pro-labor or pro-family idea. The FMLA was first introduced by representatives Patricia Schroeder (D-CO) and William Clay (D-MO) in 1985 but finally passed both houses only in spring of 1990. By this time, the feminist content of the proposal was watered down (Gelb 2003; Stetson 1997). Indeed, the bill that ultimately became the Family and Medical Leave Act of 1993 was seen mainly as a labor- or "family"-related bill (Stetson 1997, 270–71). Opponents also saw it (or were happy to have it seen) as labor legislation. Business interests and states rights groups effectively and publicly opposed the legislation. Apart from helping to propose the original idea, then, it seems that women's organizations did not play a major role in the development or passage of the FMLA (Mazur 2002, 114).

As with many labor issues, the FMLA was supported by Democrats and opposed by Republicans. Some Republican legislators broke ranks and sponsored the act, arguing it was a family measure that would help workers, especially women, to cope with demands of work and family. But President George H. W. Bush vetoed the bill anyway in 1990. This happened again in 1991–92: both houses passed the FMLA, and the president vetoed it again. The Senate overrode the veto (but the House did not), and the FMLA became an election issue. In the election campaign, Bill Clinton pledged to sign the law. The Congress once more passed the bill, and it was signed into law in 1993 by President Clinton (Stetson 1997).

Although the original act was strongly supported by a woman legislator, there were not many women in the legislature over this period. From 1985 to 1987, the number of women in Congress increased from 22 to 29, from about 5 to almost 7 percent. The number of women in Congress increased even more in 1992 (the year the bill was passed), to 48 (11 percent of Congress).

The FMLA applies to private employers with more than 50 employees and to public agencies, requiring that they provide up to 12 weeks of leave (which can be unpaid) in a 12-month period for medical leave or for purposes of childbirth or adoption, caring for a sick parent, and the like. The act likely covers about 60 percent of all workers and probably even fewer women workers. Only 4 percent of those eligible actually take leave (Mazur 2002, 115).

NORWAY

In Norway, we also see different processes producing antidiscrimination laws and generous maternity leaves, with women's movements more important to policies advancing the status of women (but not challenging state-market relations) and with labor movements more important for policies expanding the role of the state vis-à-vis the market. As background, it is worth noting that Norway is distinctive among the Nordic welfare states for its strong emphasis on gender difference. There, feminists and the political culture more generally strongly emphasize a sort of maternalist difference in matters relating to gender (Skeije 1991; Sainsbury 2001).

The 1978 Equal Status Act was passed in the context of a series of important feminist policy and political successes achieved in the 1970s in Norway, including the legalization of abortion on demand and the election of large numbers of women to political office (Leira 2005). These issues came to the forefront at that time because of the "interaction of women's groups and movements outside the formal political power bases and women in the political parties" (Leira 2005, 68). The Labor Party formed a committee on the equal status issue and invited feminist groups to formulate a proposal. The feminist proposal was watered down by the union representatives (from the Norwegian Confederation of Trade Unions) on the committee who were concerned about the feminist proposals for comparable worth legislation. These measures were stripped from the final version of the bill. Since the labor government was in a minority, even this bill was subjected to more compromises in order to ensure the support of the Socialist Left, Labor, and Conservative parties, all of whom ultimately voted for the bill. Nevertheless, the final bill did include protections against discrimination for women workers and ensured a measure of implementation, creating an ombuds as an enforcement agency. Women's organizations were very active in ensuring the enforcement and implementation of the act (Mazur 2002).

In Norway as in the United States, the political struggle for maternity leave took quite a different form from that characterizing antidiscrimination policy. In Norway, maternity leave developed much earlier, in the late nineteenth century, in the context of the class struggle over social reform and the nationalist struggle to be free of Swedish domination (Leira 1993; Sainsbury 2001). In 1885, a commission was appointed to make proposals for social reforms to prevent social unrest and to reduce class conflict. At the same time, feminist activists were contesting traditional gender hierarchies or roles as they mobilized in pursuit of suffrage. As part of the social policies that emerged from this process, which constituted the beginnings of the Norwegian welfare state, a maternity leave policy was adopted as part of a more general health insurance act (Sainsbury 2001). Thus, Norwegian working women have had access to paid maternity leave since 1909, well before women won the right to vote and stand for parliamentary elections in 1913 (Leira 1993).[8]

Feminists tried to expand maternity leave in the late 1970s, in the aftermath of both the 1971 "women's coup" that brought many more women into government and the successful subsequent campaigns in 1977 and 1979.[9] The women elected as a result of these feminist campaigns report immediately getting to work changing policies on child care and equal pay and setting up shelters for battered women (Leira 1993). By 1978, there were 37 women in the Storting (national parliament), constituting about 24 percent of the seats. This was the biggest change in women's representation across the Nordic world at that time (Raaum 2005). Nevertheless, efforts to pass expansions of maternity leave were unsuccessful. It is worth noting, though, that Norwegian men and women first obtained the right to shared maternity and paternity leave for childbirth in that process, a significant change in the role-changing dimension of Norwegian leave policy.

In the 1980s, the discussion of expanded maternity leave again rose to the forefront, and a series of expansions making maternity leave more generous was adopted in the late 1980s.[10] In 1986, a government commission was struck to examine the male gender role and aspects of maleness and masculinity, including fatherhood. This commission was chaired by a dynamic young Social

Democratic man (who later became prime minister). In 1989, the committee recommended extending parental leave to 12 months, with three months reserved for the father. In this discussion, the division of unpaid care was framed as an issue of gender equality.

In Norway, family values and the father-child relationship were widely discussed, although this discussion focused on child well-being and family values rather than on advancing employment equality for women. The commission's proposal was scaled back in the process leading to enactment. The three months reserved for the father was cut to four weeks, and the father's right to care was made conditional on the mother's employment. The Labour government introduced the *fedrekvote* (daddy quota) that came into effect in 1993 (Leira 2002, 95). Norway was the first country in the world to introduce this kind of a leave.

There was little opposition to the final version of the measure, probably because it was seen as a modest expansion of existing leave provisions and did not take any time from the mother. It is also likely that general discussion about the importance of a father's involvement for a child's well-being paved the way for the measure. Fathers were granted an independent right to parental leave in June 2000. The measure has proven very popular, with 70 to 80 percent of eligible fathers taking it up.

Comparative Conclusions

Examining the previously described cases in terms of the number and proportion of women in government, the political strength of labor, and the strength and involvement of the women's movement allows us to draw some conclusions about what makes policy processes more substantively reflective of women's interests and concerns in relation to child-related leaves and antidiscrimination policy (table 3).

CLASS POLITICS

The political power and support of labor seems to be very important for success in expanding maternity leave policy but not especially important for successfully passing initiatives that solely address women's status. In Norway in the 1970s, the women's movement was ascendant and was able to pressure the government to pass some measures fairly narrowly tailored to focus on gender status, such as the Equal Status Act and abortion rights bill. Neither measure took aim at state-market relations, so the relative power of labor and business did not matter. Those elements opposed by organized labor (e.g., comparable worth measures) were removed, and all parties voted for the Equal Status Act. Efforts to significantly expand maternity leave, however, failed. The minority labor government was too weak to force it through, even with a supportive women's movement and with women comprising 24 percent of government. In the 1980s, labor was strong enough to push through the changes to maternity leave. None of the expansions of maternity or parental leave took place under a Conservative-led government. In contrast, the Conservatives did support the Equal Status Act.

Similarly, the FMLA passed both houses of the U.S. Congress three times between 1990 and 1992 but failed the first two times because of a veto by a Republican president. The act was picked up and supported by the unions, but labor is politically weak in the United States. The women's movement in the United States was strong and autonomous (though largely extraneous to this particular debate) all through the period. The main change between the failed and successful passage was the change in party, from Republican to Democratic. While the Democratic Party is not a European-style left or labor party, it is certainly more pro-labor and has closer relations to unions. Thus, partisan changes along the left-right continuum seem critical for explaining the passage of maternity leave policies. Antidiscrimination measures, however, which challenge gender roles but leave state-market relations basically unchanged, sometimes do draw conservative support and can sometimes be passed when labor is weak. Such measures pertain more to gender status in general than to class status.

Over the longer term, one can see a broad pattern in which cross-gender coalitions based on class support those programs requiring more direct spending on social services and programs, while gender-specific cross-party (and cross-class) coalitions support measures focused on gender status. In Norway, unions opposed some measures to promote gender equality that they viewed as being inimical to the interests of "labor," such as comparable worth. But unions strongly supported family leaves as measures reducing inequality between families, and Conservatives have more strongly supported measures providing cash for stay-at-home parents (mostly mothers). Both measures maintain gender roles to some degree.

WOMEN IN GOVERNMENT

It is indisputable that women within the political parties in Norway have advanced proposals to improve policies on child care, flexible hours, part-time work, and the like for women (Bystydzienski 1995; interviews with Norwegian politicans, 1995). Indeed, in the cases considered here, both women in the leg-

TABLE 3. **Comparison of Outcomes of Policy Debates on Family Leave and Sex Discrimination Policies, United States and Norway, 1978–93**

Measure Passed/Type (country, year)	Women in Government (%/role)	Women's Movement Mobilization	Policy Party in Power	Outcome
PDA: Gender role change, state-market relations unchanged (United States, 1978)	4%	Strong, supportive	Democratic president (Carter)	Passage
FMLA: Gender role maintaining, state-market relations slightly changed; framed as pro-family, pro-labor measure (United States, 1990, 1991–92)	5–6%/Measure is initially proposed by a woman (Schroeder).	Women's movement is strong and initially supportive; some opposition.	Congress passes measure with Democratic support and some Republican votes. Republican president vetoes measure twice.	Failure
FMLA: Gender role maintaining; state-market relations slightly changed (United States, 1993)	10%	Women's movement is strong but divided and marginalized on this issue.	Democrats control all three branches of government (center-left).	Passage
Equal Status Act: Gender role change; state-market relations unchanged (Norway, 1978)	24%/Women in political parties supported measure. Norway passes 20% threshold for first time in 1977.	Strong, autonomous women's movement support	Minority Labor government; all three parties (Socialist Left, Labor, and Conservative) support final measure. Unions oppose comparable worth elements. They are stripped from final bill.	Passage
Maternity leave expansions: Gender role maintenance, expanded role of state in market (Norway, 1970s)	24%/Norway passes 20% threshold for first time in 1977.	Strong women's movement support	Labor minority supportive but weak. Conservatives oppose expansion of spending. Conservatives grow stronger and win in 1981 election.	Failure to expand maternity leave generosity. Men and women share access to leave for first time (gender role (change).

TABLE 3.—*Continued*

Measure Passed/Type (country, year)	Women in Government (%/role)	Women's Movement Mobilization	Policy Party in Power	Outcome
Maternity leave expansions: Gender role maintenance, expanded role of state in market (Norway, 1986–88)	34%/Norway passes 30% threshold for first time in 1985.	Women's movement support	Labor minority takes power in 1986. Labor supports the policy.	Passage (except that gender role change policy [daddy leave] is omitted from final package)
Daddy leave: Gender role change, slightly expanded role of state in market (Norway, 1993)	39%	Strong women's movement support	Labor minority elected in 1990 and 1993. Labor supports daddy leave measure.	Passage

Source: Brandth and Kvande 2009; Bystydzienski 1992; Gelb 1989, 2003; Gelb and Palley 1996; Leira 1993, 2002; Mazur 2002; Morgan 2006; Raaum 2005; Sainsbury 2001; Skjeie and Teigen 2005; Stetson 1997.

islature and autonomous social movements of women supported expanded maternity leave and role-changing policies like the daddy leave. In the United States, similarly, a feminist woman legislator from the Democratic party (Patricia Schroeder) was an initiator and one of the cosponsors of the first version of the FMLA in 1985. But in neither case did increased numbers of women in the legislature determine the passage of these policies or even make it more likely that they were proposed. In Norway, whether the Storting was comprised of 11 percent or more than 30 percent women, support from a strong labor party and from the unions was the deciding factor. Women's mobilization and increasing numbers of women in government (which appear to be closely related in Norway, particularly in the 1970s and 1980s) were likely catalysts for starting the discussion of maternity leave, but these discussions fizzled, and efforts to pass measures were unsuccessful when political support from labor was lacking or when labor itself was in a weaker political position (table 3). Similarly, in the United States, the additional political influence acquired when an opponent (President George H. W. Bush) was replaced by a more supportive ally (Democrat President Clinton) made the difference. The FMLA passed both houses in 1990, when the proportion of women in Congress was less than 6 percent. Despite the fact that this proportion has more than tripled over the past two decades (the proportion of women in Congress now stands at 17 percent), no further improvements to maternity leave have been made at the federal level (Center for American Women and Politics 2009).[11]

These cases support the idea that while having some women in government (rather than none) enhances women's effective substantive representation, it is not the number or proportion or even the attainment of a critical mass that matters. Maternity leave provisions in Norway were adopted before women even had suffrage. One Norwegian feminist activist argues that although there were fewer women in the Storting in the 1970s, they were more vocal advocates for women than the large numbers of women elected later through national party lists (Torild Skard in Bystydzienski 1995, 45–67). Moreover, women legislators themselves report that the requirement to vote along party lines often trumps their own predilection to vote for or against a particular policy. Only about a third of the women in government are actually vocal, active supporters of feminist policy proposals (Bystydzienski 1995).

WOMEN'S MOVEMENTS

In both cases discussed in this chapter, supportive, autonomous women's movements were critical for the passage of antidiscrimination measures and for role-changing elements of family leaves (e.g., shared access to leave for men and women or the introduction of daddy leave), but they proved less important for expanding such leave to make it more generous (table 3). Feminist activists were successful at creating broad political coalitions in favor of antidiscrimination measures and pushed hard for role-changing elements of maternity policies. Where labor is weak, even strong women's movements and large numbers of women in government were unable to overcome business opposition, and sometimes unions opposed measures more squarely focused on sex equality. In Norway, this opposition effectively killed some comparable worth measures.

SOCIAL CHANGE AND WOMEN'S STATUS

For the working-class women for whom they are most important, paid maternity leaves enable women to continue to take primary responsibility for child care and domestic work while maintaining their attachment to the labor market. They do not challenge the traditional association of women with "care" work. In some ways, they reaffirm the idea that women's roles as mothers are more important than their roles as workers (which is why some U.S. feminists have opposed such policies). Indeed, this debate about whether government policies should challenge the burden of women as they bear the bulk of domestic labor or should ease that burden (thereby maintaining the gender division of labor by making it easier) has been an important debate among Nordic feminists as well (Bergman 2004; Gornick and Meyers 2007).

Policies like the Pregnancy Discrimination Act or equal opportunities acts challenge the primacy of the male worker in the labor market, requiring that women's biology be accommodated within the workplace. Such policies have encountered the objections that pregnant women do not belong in the workplace. Before the PDA, pregnant women were traditionally confined to the private sphere and even fired from their jobs as teachers lest their pregnant forms suggest inappropriate ideas to their students (Gelb and Palley 1987). Thus, demanding that pregnant workers be permitted to continue in the workplace and that they be entitled to the benefits that male workers enjoy directly challenges gender hierarchy in the workplace and traditional attitudes about gender roles. So these antidiscrimination policies are role-changing policies. Similarly, policies allocating to men parental leave that cannot be transferred to women is a direct attempt to involve more men in child rearing, a direct attempt to change gender roles. One might expect to see autonomous women's organizations play a greater role in determining these types of policies.

The Politics of Leave Policies: A Cross-national Analysis

The preceding discussion suggests that labor movements are more important for class-based dimensions of policy and that women's movements are more important for dimensions that challenge gender roles. I expect the role of women in government to be less important relative to these civil society phenomena. In addition, overall generosity of social policy here will be mostly determined by class politics. For the role-changing dimension of these policies, however, I would expect that women's movements are the most important actors. If such an approach is vindicated, this analysis suggests new ways to interpret extant research on how women in government affect policy outcomes in the area of maternity leave (Kittilson 2008; Schwindt-Bayer and Mishler 2005; Swers 2002), as well as new questions to investigate in this area.

MEASURES AND DATA SOURCES

In the next sections, I explore this argument by examining policies toward pregnant workers and parents in 34 stable, democratic countries—specifically leave policies for pregnancy and parenthood and antidiscrimination policies.

I examine a number of dimensions for each of these policy areas. For leave policies, I ask whether policies distinguish between or explicitly provide for maternity, paternity (or second parent), and parental leave. I also examine the generosity of these leaves, asking both how much time is available for each type of leave (as well as how much total time is permitted) and how much paid leave is available. I also ask about the source of pay (public or private). For antidiscrimination policies, I ask whether there are policies that prohibit discrimination on the basis of pregnancy or parenthood (especially taking family leaves) and whether these policies apply to both hiring and dismissal or to just one of these areas. I take data on these leave policies from the 1994 *Conditions of Work Digest* of the International Labour Organization (ILO) (see table A2 in the appendix for a list of countries and a summary of these provisions cross-nationally). As in chapter 1, I use OLS regression analysis to examine the relationships between these dependent variables (policies) and various independent variables representing different modes of representation: women's movements, labor mobilization, women in government, women's policy machineries, and relevant control variables (I explain the operationalization of each variable in the text that follows). Summary tables showing values for the dependent variables and key independent variables are provided in the appendix.

DEPENDENT VARIABLES: POLICY OUTCOMES

The Generosity of Leave Policy. The generosity of leave policy is measured as the total time, in months, available for three types of leaves (maternity leave, paternity leave, and parental leave), plus a measure of the generosity of any income support provided (leave time multiplied by a measure of how many paid leaves there are and by the rate of wage replacement for maternity leave, ranging from 0 to 1). In other words, it is *time* + (*time* × *number of leaves* × *percent wages covered*). The family leave index ranges from 12 to 184 and has a median of 37.

Paid Leaves. Focusing just on the dimension of leaves that is most salient for class politics, I examined the determinants of publicly paid leaves. The focus on public provision is important because mandating private provision of paid leaves (leaves provided by employers) can make it more expensive to hire women or those who take family leave. This can result in difficult-to-prove discrimination against women. Public provision of funding, moreover, reflects a commitment to collective, as opposed to individual, responsibility for paying for reproduction. Feminist analysts have emphasized the importance of these aspects of paid leaves. This index ranges from 0 to 3 and is constructed by adding one point for each type of leave that is publicly paid: one for paid maternity leave, one for paid paternity leave, and one for paid parental leave. Denmark and Norway score the highest on this measure, while the United States and Australia score the lowest.

Changing Gender Roles. I constructed an indicator of the degree to which the policy challenged gender roles, looking at two key aspects of the policy, each weighted to account for half the indicator (1 point out of 2 total points). First, I asked whether the policy took into account that the primary caregiver for the child might not be the biological mother. In other words, if the policy challenged the assumption that being a biological female made one the logical caregiver for the child, that counted for something. If the policy recognized that the parent who is not the biological parent might also have some interest in the birth or parenting of the child, this also counted as challenging gender roles. For example, if a government only recognized one sort of need (usually just maternity leave), the policies would receive only one of the three points possible for this aspect of policy. A government that recognized these distinct areas of need would get a full score for this aspect of role-changing policies (3/3 = 1). I also examined antidiscrimination policies. If a government protected pregnant women and parents from discrimination in hiring and firing, the government received full points on this score. If the government protected workers in only one aspect of employment, it received only half marks. Each type of role-challenging policy counted for a whole point, so that the highest possible score was 2 and the lowest possible score was 0.

INDEPENDENT VARIABLES: EXTRALEGISLATIVE REPRESENTATION

Labor Movements. I have argued that labor movements should be critical for determining the generosity and public character of leave policies and that women's movements should be most important for predicting the role-changing aspects of policies. Defining and measuring the strength of labor movements is a notoriously tricky business. Some have measured the political mobilization of labor by examining the proportion of legislative seats held by labor parties (e.g., Esping-Andersen 1990). Since I want to separate intralegislative representation from extralegislative representation conceptually, however, that will not do here. I do examine the importance of left (and right) parties by way of comparison, but I measure the strength of the labor movement here by using as an indicator the proportion of paid workers belonging to unions. This data is taken from the ILO's *World Labor Report.* Not all countries are covered by this data set. For those few (four) that are missing, I used data from the *CIA World Factbook.* Data from the *Factbook* and the ILO was very highly correlated (.85), but the use of a different source likely introduces some error. In some places and under some conditions, labor unions are more or less militant, elite-dominated, or co-opted. For this reason, I also include a measure of labor movement strength that focuses more on protest and conflict in industrial relations. I sum the number of strikes and lockouts over five years (1990–94). This data is taken from the ILO's *World Labor Report.*

Women's Movements. As in chapter 1, movements are coded as strong if they are described by expert observers as strong, influential, or powerful; as mobilizing widespread public support; and so on. Where the women's movement is both strong and autonomous according to these criteria, the country is coded 1, and where either strength or autonomy is absent, the country is coded 0 (see chapter 1 for more details).

INDEPENDENT VARIABLES: INTRALEGISLATIVE REPRESENTATION

Left Parties. Some have measured labor movement strength by examining labor's presence inside the legislature in the form of political parties. But I have argued that extralegislative activity can be as important, if not more important, than such intralegislative avenues of representation. In order to compare the extralegislative strength of labor to intralegislative strength, we need to measure both and compare their importance in determining policy outcomes. For a measure of intralegislative strength of labor, I use Swank's measure of left party strength (Swank 2006). Few data sets on left parties offer data on all 36 countries examined here, and Swank is no exception. Still, Swank offers data on the largest number of countries in the data set, so I used this indicator. The incomplete nature of the measure means, however, that analyses of left party importance can only use 21 countries, not all 34 countries in the complete data set. Thus, I evaluate most models with and without the variable of left parties, to make the best use of the available data.

Representation by Women Legislators. I have argued that extralegislative avenues of representation are more important than descriptive representation in improving policy outcomes for women. What measure of descriptive representation should be used in making this case? As discussed in the previous chapter, the literature suggests that we would expect a greater proportion of women legislators, especially a proportion of 35 or 40 percent, to be associated with better pregnancy/family leave and antidiscrimination policies. In contrast, I have argued that, in itself, a greater number or proportion of women (even the presence of a critical mass) in the legislature should not matter for the role-changing aspects of leave policies as much as the presence of a strong, autonomous women's movement.

Others have argued that women's identity as women is more salient when there are fewer of them, and so we would expect that individual women might be more effective as spokespersons and that women might have more symbolic power when there are fewer of them. Perhaps this accounts for the seemingly counterintuitive finding that more women are sometimes less effective, "less feminist," than fewer numbers of women, as some accounts of policy change in Norway suggest (Skard in Bystydzienski 1995). In addition, descriptive representatives are more important in the absence of a strong social movement that articulates and promotes women's perspectives, that is, when women's issues are relatively "uncrystallized" (Mansbridge 1999). Last, the impact of women representatives also depends on whether they are members of a governing or opposition party, their ideology, and other contextual variables (Swers 2002). So any impact of women representatives is likely contingent on a series of contextual factors.

Focusing specifically on maternity leave, Kittilson (2008) finds that the percentage of women in the legislature is associated with longer leaves and more paid leave. This operationalization suggests that, controlling for other factors, as the proportion of women increases, more generous policies will result. Schwindt Bayer and Mishler (2005) try a number of measures and conclude that the square of the percentage of women in the legislature best captures the relationship between women in office and policy outcomes. This operationalization suggests that there is effectively a ceiling on the proportion of women in the legislature, above which increases have little effect on policy outcomes. Even after the number of women reaches some ceiling and levels off, we would expect to see continuous improvements in laws on women's status. In addition, it also suggests that rather than increasing with proportion of women in a smooth, linear fashion, policy responsiveness increases quite dramatically and exponentially as the proportion of women grows larger. It also suggests that where there are no women in the legislature, there will be no policy responsiveness. I employ both measures in my models but report only the last measure. The reader should note that employing different measures of women's representation did not change the main findings reported in this chapter.

Bureaucratic Representation. In the previous chapter, I argued that women's bureaus can provide a form of political representation for women. As in chapter 1, we would expect women's policy machineries to improve the political representation of women when they have (1) formalized channels of access for women's organizations and (2) the independence and resources needed to formulate and implement aspects of a women's agenda. If the women's policy agencies in the 33 stable democracies in this study are categorized according to these criteria, only eight of the agencies actually meet these criteria (the agencies in Australia, Canada, Costa Rica, Netherlands, Belgium, Venezuela, Portugal, and Germany). Countries are coded 1 on this variable if they meet both conditions, 0 if they do not.

SOCIAL MOVEMENTS AND REPRESENTATION: HYPOTHESES

In general, then, I would expect that labor movements would be most important in determining the generosity of and especially the public provision for paid leaves, since this aspect of leave policy is most clearly reflective of class interests. Labor unions should be more important than left parties or women in government in determining these policies. Women's movements should be more important in determining the adoption of policies aimed at changing gender roles. Labor movements should be less important here, and left parties and women in government should be of even less importance.

Level of development and culture are thought to be fundamental factors influencing politics and policy. I control for these factors using dummy variables for region and dominant religion (as proxies for culture) and GNP per capita as a measure of level of development. Only level of development is employed in the models that follow, since the dummy variables did not seem to improve the models or change the main findings.

Results

The results of the analysis, discussed in the text that follows, are summarized in table 4.

OVERALL GENEROSITY OF FAMILY LEAVE

Using OLS regression to examine the predictors of the generosity of family leave (DV = family leave index), we see that, as expected, labor protest is the most significant determinant of family leave policies—more important than women's movements, which is not significant (table 4, model 1). In model 1,

TABLE 4. **Regression Analysis of Work-Family Policy Outcomes**

Model/Dependent Variable	Independent Variables	*B*	S.E.	Beta
Dependent variable = **family leave index**				
Model 1	Women's policy machinery	13.92	15.87	0.10
($n = 32$; $R^2 = 0.66$)	Women in legislature (% squared)**	0.04	0.02	0.44
	Union strength	0.58	0.42	0.27
	Strong and autonomous women's movement	–9.67	13.13	–0.01
	Strikes and lockouts***	0.01	0.00	0.41
	GNP per capita	0.00	0.02	0.17
. . . controlling for left party strength				
Model 2	Women's policy machinery	10.35	21.25	0.08
($n = 21$; $R^2 = 0.71$)	Women in legislature (% squared)	0.03	0.02	0.31
	Union strength*	1.04	0.58	0.48
	Strong and autonomous women's movement	–12.62	19.46	–0.11
	Strikes and lockouts***	0.01	0.00	0.47
	Left parties (government seats)	0.39	0.45	0.14
	GNP per capita	0.00	0.00	0.18
Dependent variable = **paid leaves**				
Model 3	Women's policy machinery	0.27	0.25	0.12
($n = 32$; $R^2 = 0.71$)	Women in legislature (% squared)	0.00	0.00	0.29
	Union strength***	0.02	0.01	0.56
	Strong and autonomous women's movement	–0.23	0.21	–0.14
	Strikes and lockouts	0.00	0.00	0.13
	GNP per capita	0.00	0.00	0.04
. . . controlling for left party strength				
Model 4	Women's policy machinery	0.37	0.38	0.16
($n = 21$; $R^2 = 0.73$)	Women in legislature (% squared)	0.00	0.00	0.27
	Union strength**	0.02	0.01	0.58
	Strong and autonomous women's movement	–0.32	0.35	–0.16
	Strikes and lockouts	0.00	0.00	0.14
	Left parties (government seats)	0.00	0.01	0.01
	GNP per capita	0.00	0.00	0.15
Dependent variable = **gender role change policy**				
Model 5	Women's policy machinery	0.06	0.20	0.05
($n = 32$; $R^2 = 0.47$)	Women in government (% squared)	0.00	0.00	0.34
	Union strength	0.00	0.01	–0.01
	Strong and autonomous women's movement**	0.36	0.17	0.35
	Strikes and lockouts	0.00	0.00	0.34
	GNP per capita**	0.00	0.00	0.42

TABLE 4.—*Continued*

Model/Dependent Variable	Independent Variables	*B*	S.E.	Beta
... *controlling for left party strength*				
Model 6	Women's policy machinery	–0.07	0.26	–0.06
($n = 21$; $R^2 = 0.40$)	Women in government (% squared)	0.00	0.00	0.29
	Union strength	0.00	0.01	0.19
	Strong and autonomous women's movement**	0.53	0.24	0.57
	Strikes and lockouts	0.00	0.00	0.31
	Left parties (government seats)	–0.01	0.01	–0.31
	GNP per capita	0.00	0.00	0.17

Note: *significant at the .1 level; **significant at the .05 level; ***significant at the .01 level; ****significant at the .001 level; S.E. = standard error.

however, the number of women in government appears to be at least as important as labor protest: the squared number of representatives has the largest (by a hair) standardized coefficient (beta) of any of the independent variables and, with labor militancy (strikes and lockouts), is one of two most significant variables (although labor militancy appears to be a stronger predictor). Controlling for the impact of left parties seems to mitigate the impact of women in government, however. When the strength of left parties is included in the model, union strength and labor militancy (strikes and lockouts) become more important than women in government, with larger standardized betas, and become the only significant predictors of leave generosity (model 2). This suggests that social movements, or extralegislative representation, are very important for policy change—more important than some intralegislative avenues (in this case, political parties and women in government).

The number of women in government may make a difference to overall leave generosity, or the number of women may partly reflect the impact of left parties. Recall that I argued that leave policies are generally perceived as importantly (or even primarily) class issues; they are not always perceived as feminist issues. Extant research suggests that left parties are more likely to promote women as candidates. It is possible that some of the seeming impact of women in office is actually an indirect effect of left parties. Indeed, controlling for the impact of left parties appears to diminish the direct effects of women in government on policy outcomes. Moreover, to the extent that there are such direct effects of women in government, it appears that extralegislative avenues of representation for working-class people (unions, labor protest) are more important in prompting generous family leaves than are women in government. The point is not that women in government do not affect policies of importance to women. Rather, the point is that extralegislative avenues of representation appear to be more effective in this case.

PAID LEAVES

The class politics model performs even better for this aspect of leave policy than for the overall generosity measure (table 4, models 3 and 4). For paid leaves, the strength of unions is by far the single most important determinant of government action, providing income support for maternity, paternity, and parental leave. Unions are more important than left parties, women in government, and the strength and autonomy of women's movements.

CHANGING GENDER ROLES

The examination of policies that challenge gender roles supports the theory advanced here. The most important thing to notice is that the model that explains overall generosity of family leave policies and that is especially good at accounting for the adoption of paid leave policies performs relatively poorly at capturing the dynamics behind role-changing policies (table 4, models 5 and 6). The most important determinant of these policies appears to be the presence of a strong, autonomous women's movement. This variable is more important than labor movements, left parties, or women in government. For the full data set (not including left parties), the presence of strong and autonomous women's movements is the only significant variable (albeit only significant at the .1 level) (table 4, model 4). Their presence makes the adoption of role-changing policies more likely, being associated with an increase in the role-changing score of about .27 (nearly a third). This could mean that where such movements are present, governments are more likely to recognize a distinction between maternity and parental leave, to recognize the specific need of fathers for leave for childbirth, or to adopt nondiscrimination policies in an additional area (hiring or firing).

The dynamics of policies related to role changes, then, are very different from those related to social spending and public provision of support for families. The class-based models and analyses of welfare states do a much better job of predicting the generosity and public provision of leaves than they do in predicting the adoption of antidiscrimination laws for women workers or in predicting whether policies will support feminist or traditional family forms. Although better models of this dimension of policy are needed, it seems, from the explanations considered here, that strong, autonomous women's movements are most important for facilitating the adoption of role-changing policies and that the numbers of women in government are not central to the policy dynamics behind such policies (although individual women officeholders often play an important role).

Conclusion

The extant literature suggests, then, that women in government are important determinants of women-friendly policies, such as family policies, and that women's movements (and feminist activists) do not seem to play a central role in policy adoption. But this analysis suggests that different aspects of social policies affecting the reconciliation of work and family may have different catalysts. Policies that aim to expand public provision for families tend to follow the pattern of class politics, more than do issues where gender is more obviously salient (e.g., violence against women or antidiscrimination legislation). The strength of labor unions is more important than women's movements in determining this aspect of public policy. Unions are also more important than left parties, supporting my general argument about the importance of extralegislative mobilization in social movements as an avenue of policy influence. For policies that aim to change gender roles, women's movements are the most important catalysts, more important than numbers of women in government, labor unions, or left parties.

Even if women in government matter less than these extralegislative avenues of representation for both types of policy issue, it does seem that women in government have more of an impact on family policies than on violence against women. Why would numbers of women in government matter for aspects of the policy that are more labor related and not for aspects of policy that are exclusively gender related? This finding is puzzling. One possibility is that since we know that left parties tend to elect more women, the effect of women in government is primarily an indirect effect of left parties. Indeed, in Norway, the election of larger numbers of women coincides with the period in which the Labor Party dominated. Thus, perhaps counterintuitively, the number of women in government may be a better indicator of the strength of left parties than it is of political mobilization along lines of gender. Another possibility is that women in government might be more willing to take on vocal leadership roles and thus might be more effective advocates when the women's interests at issue do not challenge gender roles. Indeed, many women politicians in Norway, even in the 1990s, worried about appearing to be too feminist (Bystydzienski 1995), but they did not need to worry about appearing pro-labor if they were in the Labor Party. For policies that do challenge gender roles, women's independent organizing is critically necessary to provide an independent source of support for officeholders who aim to challenge party hierarchies and entrenched gender roles. I develop this argument—that social movements are most important for policies advancing social transformation—in later chapters.

Again, this argument is not about whether women in the legislature provide descriptive representation. Nor do I contest that there is a link between descriptive and substantive representation. Indeed, women's movements are a place where women interactively articulate their unique perspective, making women's movements an alternate site for examining the link between presence and social group perspective. At issue are the mechanisms by which descriptive representation becomes substantive representation and how best to achieve substantive representation. Extralegislative avenues are critical for effective substantive representation of women because they provide the best opportunity for women to organize as women, to develop an oppositional consciousness that identifies the problems that public policy must address to advance the social transformation required to bring about equality.

CHAPTER 3

Intersectionality, Labor, and Representation in the 50 U.S. States

WITH PATRICK JESSEE

Are labor movements good representatives of working women? The analyses presented in the last chapter suggest that they are, but labor movements have often been criticized as being poor representatives of women's interests. Recall that union opposition was critical to defeating policy proposals in Norway that were aimed at comparable worth, even as the same unions eventually supported provisions for paid family leave. In the United States, unions historically discriminated against people of color (both women and men) and white women (Stepan-Norris and Zeitlin 2003; Frymer 2008; Trotter and Smith 1997). Unions in the United States have made strides in improving diversity in leadership and membership, but women and people of color are still underrepresented in descriptive terms; unions are still subject to criticism that they represent the privileged better than the marginalized (Caiazza 2007; Roby 1995; AFL-CIO 2005). Can women really count on labor movements to represent their interests as working-class women? What about as women *workers*? Do such movements produce more worker-friendly policies?

These questions are particularly pressing in the United States. Income inequality in the United States is greater than in any other advanced industrialized state, and it is growing (Smeeding 2003; Danziger and Gottschalk 1995). Yet the last decade has seen deep cuts in programs that help low-income people, especially low-income women.[1] It is hard not to see a connection between the deteriorating position of low-income people and their lack of political power. Lower-income citizens are less likely to vote, to be represented in civil society organizations, and to be elected to public office than their middle- and upper-income counterparts (Schlozman et al. 1999; Skocpol 1999). Many have noted the lack of a strong labor movement and a strong labor party in the United States, attributing the lack of a strong U.S. welfare state to the absence of one or the other (e.g., Esping-Andersen 1993; Brady 2003; Alesina et al.

2001). Left parties and unions may be important for representing women's interests as workers more generally and, in some instances, their gender-specific interests as working women.

The literature on political representation for disadvantaged groups gives little attention to the problems of representing the interests of poor and working-class people (Dovi 2002). It may be that the problem of the political representation of those disadvantaged by economic class is not amenable to the same "fixes" available for addressing gender and race inequality, such as descriptive representation. Perhaps left parties or protest are better courses of action for working-class people (Piven and Cloward 1993; Dovi 2002).

In this chapter, I evaluate various avenues for substantive representation of class across the 50 states. I show how disaggregating the analysis by social group (asking which women and which men are well represented) can provide insights not offered by an undifferentiated analysis. This intersectional approach to analysis helps to illuminate the complex relationship between gender, race, class, and the democratic state (Crenshaw 1992; Strolovitch 2007; Hancock 2007; Weldon 2008).

This chapter explores a variety of avenues for the representation of working-class interests in the United States, comparing representation by unions, other civil society organizations, and political parties. The analysis compares the impact of these different types of groups on various labor policies in the 50 U.S. states, in order to evaluate the effectiveness of these different avenues of representation. I use some qualitative research (interviews, document study) to supplement these analyses and to demonstrate their plausibility. Through a series of OLS regression analyses, this chapter shows that vibrant civil society organizations—not just unions, but also women's organizations—are most strongly associated with pro-labor policies, while political party appears to have a weaker, more contingent effect. This is especially true for women workers. This suggests that civil society representation is the most important avenue of political influence for labor interests in the United States and that those seeking to strengthen labor movements should not only work to strengthen unions but also look beyond unions to other civil society groups. It may also suggest the need for a political party that is a more effective partner for these civil society groups.

More generally, I argue, important aspects of processes of representation remain hidden when we fail to disaggregate our questions about representation and to consider the distinctive perspectives of specific social groups. Social movements are more important avenues of substantive representation when policies in question challenge existing patterns of social organization. Those marginalized groups not explicitly recognized in established institutional mechanisms of representation tend to fall through the cracks of existing categories of political organization. For such groups, social movements are especially important avenues of substantive representation in democratic politics. For more advantaged groups, however, more traditional electoral mechanisms may provide adequate means of representing their interests.

Representation and Working-Class Interests

THE STATE AND SOCIAL INEQUALITY

Even asking how we can improve political representation and policy influence for working-class people presupposes that such improvements are possible. Some theorists would deny that truly emancipatory policies are possible, because the state plays the functional role of defending ruling-class interests or, at best, aims to co-opt the oppressed classes in order to preserve the capitalist system from its own excesses (Poulantzas 1973; Engels [1884] 1978). Many have argued that a more nuanced view of the relation between social structures of inequality and state power is needed, pointing out that ruling-class interests are never homogeneous and that state policies can produce real improvements in the lives of working-class people (Block 1987; Piven 1990).[2] Indeed, if we think that it is better to have a higher minimum wage, more generous work supports, and antitrafficking legislation and if we think it is better not to have laws that weaken union organizing, we still want to know why some states have such policies while others do not and how to promote these policies where they are absent.

CLASS AND DESCRIPTIVE REPRESENTATION

Political theorists have long recognized the importance of self-representation as a mechanism for the protection of individual and group interests (Mill [1861] 1926). More recently, the theoretical literature focusing specifically on political representation for disadvantaged groups has emphasized the physical presence of group members (descriptive representation) as a critical mechanism for improving group representation (Mansbridge 1999, 2003; Williams 1998; Phillips 1995; Young 2000). But this literature focuses mainly on women and ethnic and racial minorities, discussing class chiefly to explain why descriptive representation will not work as a solution to the underrepresentation of disadvantaged economic classes (Dovi 2002): if people do not subjectively identify as members of particular classes, advocating quotas or special representation on the basis of class would smack of vanguardism (Williams 1998); classes are too complex and difficult to delineate, and class is different than race and gender anyway and so requires different solutions (Phillips 1995).

Yet the problem of class cannot be dismissed so easily. At least in the United States, poll data show that people *do* identify themselves in class terms (Perrucci and Wysong 1999, 6). Successful politicians play up working-class credentials in order to emphasize the experiences they share with voters. John Edwards and Orrin Hatch, for example, repeatedly emphasize in their publicity materials and speeches that they are the children of industrial workers. Many state legislators in the United States point to their work experience or economic background when explaining their policy positions and qualifications for public office. For example, one Indiana state legislator that has been a prominent advocate of pro-labor policies points to his background as a third-generation plumber on his Web page (Niezgodski 2009). Moreover, even if class divisions are complex in modern societies, class cleavages can be identified. For example, if we think of the division between professionals and nonprofessionals as a critical class division in modern society (Young 1990; Wright 1997), it does seems that in the United States, the former group (including lawyers, businesspeople, professors, and doctors) dominates politics more than the latter (including clerical workers and industrial workers).[3] As one U.S. legislator (David Obey) commented on criticisms of the World Trade Organization, "The trouble with the WTO is that guys in suits are making rules for guys in overalls" (cited in McGrory 1999). The distinction between the class (and gender) position of "guys in suits" versus "guys in overalls" (or women in overalls) is one that is easily spotted in contemporary society.

Despite the salience of class in the United States, the conceptual definition and delineation of classes is controversial. Rather than enter here into a debate about how to define class, for which there is not space, I will rely on Perrucci and Wysong's (1999) approach, since it seems to me to combine the strengths of traditional class analysis, which is still useful, with a more nuanced account of social structure in contemporary U.S. society (cf. Wright 1997). Perrucci and Wysong (1999) propose a scheme that defines classes according to four distinct forms of capital, which they call "consumption capital" (income), "investment capital" (wealth), "skill capital" (operationalized as formal education), and "social capital" (organizational resources and power). Variations in access to these forms of capital stem from links people have to corporate, government, and cultural structures. Based on this scheme, the major class division is between a privileged class (consisting of owners, managers, and elite professionals) and a working class. The working class is itself broken down into a comfort class (including teachers, nurses, high-paid tradespeople, and social workers) at the upper end; a contingent segment comprising the large middle of the working class, made up of wage earners; and, at the bottom of the hierarchy within the working class, those who are largely excluded from good jobs and who work in a variety of unskilled, temporary jobs.

Adopting this schema means that becoming an elected representative alters one's class position. On Perrucci and Wysong's accounting, the organizational power (social capital) one gains from being a member of legislature definitely catapults one into another class. The ability to change one's class status more than one's race or gender could make descriptive representation less effective for disadvantaged economic classes. It is unlikely that one's background and life experiences are irrelevant: class might have some residual impact due to the occupational or family background one had before entering politics or due to persistent family or personal ties. But there is a chance that this effect would be muted by a changing class position as the legislator becomes increasingly professionalized.

Following the argument advanced in this book so far, testing whether descriptive representation within the legislature resulted in substantive representation would best be done by examining whether the proportion of legislators of, say, working-class background resulted in more pro-labor policies. It would be best to compare the effects of descriptive representation within the legislature to extralegislative descriptive representation. Comparable state-level data on the occupational composition of the legislature, however, is not available for all or even many states.

There is some relevant data at the individual level (see chapter 1 for a discussion of the limitations of such individual-level analysis): a 1995 study of state legislators included data about occupation and family income and also asked which groups the legislators perceived as their strong supporters (and which they perceived as not supporters) (Carey et al. 2000). This study covered about 7,000 state legislators, and the response rate for the mail survey was 47 percent. Among the 40 percent or so of the legislators who did not currently work, it seemed that occupational background had little influence on perceived support from business or labor. Among the majority who worked, however ($N = 1{,}997$), overall many more legislators saw themselves as supported by business and not supported by labor unions or women's groups. Most of these legislators were lawyers, farmers, or businesspeople. Farmers tended to perceive more support from farmers, and businesspeople tended to perceive much more support from business:[4] neither group thought unions were supporters. Teachers saw unions as supportive. This suggests that current occupational ties have a stronger impact on representative relationships than those that are further in the background. Indeed, in some states, legislators hold union positions or are actively running businesses while also acting as state legislators.[5] Family income can be a rough proxy for class, and it certainly taps access to what Perrucci and Wysong (1999) call "consumption capital." It seems that higher family incomes are significantly associated with a perception of greater support on the part of business and are negatively related to labor union support.

Legislators likely have stronger, more sympathetic relationships with those groups they perceive as stronger supporters, making them better representatives of that group. The class position of state legislators (as defined by occupation and wealth) influences their relationships with constituents and may well influence their policy positions. It is hard to know whether these individual differences translate into differences at an aggregate level or how they compare to self-representation by working people through extralegislative means. Still, it suggests that descriptive representation in the legislature cannot be dismissed out of hand as irrelevant or too difficult to define and that class may well be an important dimension of representative relationships.

The greatest difficulty in exploring descriptive representation by class has to do with the way that becoming an elected representative transforms one's class position. State legislators likely have weaker ties to their occupational categories even when they continue to work in their preelectoral occupations to some degree, and some do not continue to work at all. Indeed, since most states pay legislators some salary and expenses for their public service, serving as a legislator itself affects the family income and occupational category of the legislator.[6] It certainly affects a legislator's access to powerful organizations, a key dimension of class in contemporary American society (Perrucci and Wysong 1999). Looking for descriptive representation for groups defined by class thus involves some complications that are less salient when considering descriptive representation for women or African Americans.

CIVIL SOCIETY AND THIRD-SECTOR REPRESENTATION

Extralegislative representation may be most effective for the poor and working-class people (Dovi 2002; Piven and Cloward 1971). Civil society organizations provide benefits and fulfill needs that neither the state nor the markets have the ability to fulfill (Goodin 2003). Compared to individual legislators, unions and other civil society organizations have the distinct advantage of forming a collective perspective that renders them better equipped to represent marginalized groups. This collective representation flows from interaction between members of the group. The group perspective offered by civil society organizations can be more representative than an individual legislator drawing on his or her own experience, which may be more or less representative of the group. This section explores the various ways to think of the importance of civil society representation, explicating the specific implications for representation of labor as a class group.

Pluralism. Recall that pluralist theories of political representation focus on competition between organized interest groups (Truman 1951). On the pluralist view, those groups inadequately represented through electoral processes (e.g., minorities) can recover some of this influence in the arena of interest group competition, where it is the intensity of interest, rather than the sheer number of complainants, that matters. The problem with this theory, in the case of class, is that disadvantages in electoral processes (lack of electoral influence) are reinforced by inequalities present in civil society. Far from compensating or countering their lack of influence in the arena of formal politics, inequality in civil society reinforces the lack of influence of the poor and working classes. Lower-income people are less likely to participate in civil society organizations (Schlozman et al. 1999; Skocpol 1999). The systemic nature of this disadvantage across political, social, and economic arenas, combined with the seeming inability to exercise influence through established political channels, grounds arguments that we need special measures to ensure the representation of poor and working-class people (Williams 1998).

Social Capital. Recent theories of social capital argue that the key to eliciting government responsiveness is to develop a thick network of civil society organizations, not just the large bureaucratic interest groups envisioned by pluralist theory, but also informal networks and ostensibly apolitical groups such as religious organizations and social gatherings. This thick network of organizations is thought of as social capital. Where social capital is greater, we can expect greater government responsiveness to all groups of citizens, including disadvantaged groups such as women (Putnam 1993, 2000; Caiazza and Putnam 2002).

Social capital can be thought of as a feature of a polity that can benefit the society as a whole, even those individuals who do not belong to any organizations, as a public good (Putnam 1993, 2000). But social capital can also be thought of as an excludable good, a primarily private good. For example, all social capital may not be equally valuable: belonging to networks of elite people and institutions brings significantly more power and advantage than belonging to networks of poor or working-class people and institutions (Perrucci and Wysong 1999; Hero 2007). Hero (2007) argues that many of the benefits attributed to social capital are really benefits to white Americans, of racial homogeneity and racial inequality. Even when citizens belong to the same organizations, the benefits of social capital are distributed unequally: for example, women churchgoers get fewer benefits in terms of access to leadership positions and the like than their male counterparts (Djupe et al. 2007). Some citizens have fewer such connections to begin with: for example, African Americans have less access to social networks than do their white counterparts (Dawson and Cohen 1994). Some scholars characterize social capital as having both individual and collective effects and see these effects as potentially both positive or negative (Bourdieu 1986; Coleman 1988). Even if the benefits of social capital are distributed unequally and if some organizations are better avenues to influence than others, it is still possible that a thicker network of organizations provides some benefits (albeit less than to members of advantaged groups) to members of marginalized groups.

One long-time activist in a conservative state with a weak Democratic party said that personal relationships with legislators were critical to eliciting government responsiveness on her issues (interview with a U.S. activist, 2009). Activists work to train, inform, and build relations of trust with government officials. Unfortunately, the personal (as opposed to institutionalized) nature of these links means that elections, retirements, and other reasons for turnover in personnel in both organizations and government necessitate rebuilding these links. So personal connections to people in government and probably to people in other positions of influence likely facilitate marginalized group efforts to influence policy. Such connections may, however, be more difficult for members of marginalized groups to form.

Social Movements. Others have argued that it is social movements that create social capital for marginalized groups (Fuentes and Gunder Frank 1989) and that a generalized measure of social capital will not capture whether there are civil society organizations capable of advocating for women, racial and ethnic minorities, the poor, and so on (Young 2002; Weldon 2006, 2002). Civil society groups are likely to be more effective advocates for the poor and other groups when they are representing themselves, telling their own stories (Schlozman et al. 1999; Williams 1998; Mill [1867] 1926). In addition, sometimes social movement action can overwhelm even partisan loyalties. When unions in Indiana organized a massive protest at the statehouse that brought in 73 buses of union members from all over the state, it influenced even conservative Republicans, who had to worry about union members in their district (interview with a U.S. state legislator, 2009). Similarly, a Republican politician in New York explained that although he (and others like him) had doubts about legislation on violence against women, they would never express any such thoughts publicly: "Nobody wants to be caught voting against this one . . . It'll come back to haunt you that you opposed a law protecting women from crime" (Bernstein 2000).

The argument is not that social movement organizations compensate for inequalities in formal electoral processes, nor is the focus on the resources and organizational ability of established, bureaucratic lobby groups. Rather, the idea is that civil society offers the possibility of forming counterpublics—each of which may consist of one organization or many—where marginalized groups may withdraw and regroup. In this arena, marginalized groups may identify problems and develop arguments they later press in the broader public. These counterpublics provide a base for agitational activity directed both at the state and at society at large. The less formal nature of many social movement organizations means that the entry costs are lower, and this avenue is thus more accessible for marginalized group members than traditional electoral avenues or professional interest group politics (Fraser 1992, 1995; Young 2000). In addition, the group-focused nature of many of these organizations means that they can focus on generating group-specific concerns and issues, something that more broadly focused, encompassing or "bridging" organizations cannot do.

Social movements create alternative avenues to power for working-class people, creating an organizational basis for challenging the large organizations that define modern class society. They create networks of working people that are more accessible than the networks of university-educated owners, managers, and lawyers that comprise the privileged class. Nevertheless, these more accessible networks can have considerable influence on public policy, promoting legislative measures that empower working people. For example, policy can provide working people greater autonomy vis-à-vis particular employers—what Esping-Andersen (1990) calls "decommodification"—through measures such as unemployment insurance. Policy can set floors for working people through measures such as minimum wage laws and can improve the autonomy of women vis-à-vis men by improving women's ability to escape domestic violence, by ensuring they have economic independence when violence threatens their livelihood.

Long-standing, more established social movements generally include both large bureaucratic organizations (like unions) and less formal groups, and there are often multiple links between these different sorts of organizations. In the United States, the labor movement includes both unions and community groups, women's organizations, and other groups that focus on improving conditions for workers (e.g., Women for Racial and Economic Equality [WREE] or the Indiana Coalition for Worker's Rights). If these groups are effective advocates for labor, we should expect better policies for labor where these groups are more numerous. Such labor-specific groups should be more important than social capital more generally.

For example, in 1998, 10 unions formed a coalition to press the state of New York to expand its funding of child care. The coalition included the United Federation of Teachers; the Union of Needletrades, Industrial and Textile Employees; District Council 37 (which represents 120,000 municipal workers); the Communications Workers of America; and 1199 (the Service Employees International Union). The initiative, known as the "Child Care That Works" Campaign, was also supported by dozens of other groups, including the League of Women Voters, the Federation of Protestant Welfare Agencies, and the United Jewish Appeal. Union officials spoke out strongly in favor of increased funding, with the teachers union (headed by a woman, Randi Weingarten) apparently taking a particularly prominent role. National labor movement spokespeople such as the then president of the AFL-CIO (John Sweeney) were also prominent in publicly advocating for child care and paid parental leave. When the Republican governor (Pataki) failed to increase funding for child care as much as union representatives and Democrats thought he should, he was roundly criticized in the media, even as he promised to increase funding beyond his original pledge. National and local union officials joined with local Democratic politicians in public events at day cares, where toddlers tumbled behind them. They portrayed the governor as out-of-touch with the struggles of working families and as "turning his back" on children (Swarns 1998; Greenhouse 1998).

Political Parties. It seems unlikely that policy outcomes can be explained entirely with reference to extrainstitutional factors. Indeed, many studies of women's movements and public policy emphasize that women's movement activists partnered with insiders to create the alliances necessary to get legislation (e.g., Gelb 1989; Mazur 2002). These internal allies are important for translating political pressure into real, rather than merely symbolic, policy change. What would make legislators particularly disposed toward partnering with pro-labor groups?

Labor parties have been critical for the development of welfare states in Europe (Esping-Andersen 1990; Korpi and Palme 2003). Such parties have also been allies for women's movements advocating for more generous leaves or for income support for lone mothers (Stetson and Mazur 1995; Norris 1987; Bergqvist 1999; Berkman and O'Connor 1993). A larger number of left legislators should make pro-labor policies more likely. Although there is no party in the United States that identifies itself as a "labor party" as such, the Democratic Party is often seen as an ally of labor. In states where the Democratic Party is stronger, one should see more pro-labor policies.

If we look at the politics of an antiunion measure such as right-to-work laws across the 50 states, it seems clear that political parties are important avenues for expression of political conflict about these issues. Democrats and Republicans seem to fall fairly consistently on opposite sides of the issue, as do their traditional allies: unions tend to oppose right-to-work laws, while chambers of commerce tend to support them. In the 2005 Virginia gubernatorial race, for example, the Democratic candidate for lieutenant governor argued that right-to-work laws allow "moochers" to free ride on those who sacrifice their money and time to support unions and raise prevailing wages. Her Republican opponent said that right-to-work laws make states attractive to business and so are good for economic development and job creation (Odell 2005). In the 2001 gubernatorial race in Oklahoma, the Republican incumbent argued that a right-to-work law would send the message that the state was open for business, while his Democratic counterpart in Iowa characterized it as putting a "cheap wage" sign on the state (Jenkins 2001). In Nevada in 2005, Democrats strongly supported a measure to get around the right-to-work law, while Republicans denounced any perceived effort to weaken the 60-year-old laws (Associated Press 2005). Which political party is strongest seems like an important element in determining whether these measures get enacted (see also Associated Press 2002).

In U.S. politics, the party system works differently in the North than in the South, because of the way the party system in the South is entwined with struggles over slavery and white dominance (Rae 1994).[7] At one time, the Republican Party was the party of racial equality, and the Democratic Party defended slavery. When the Democratic Party dramatically shifted positions on this issue, positioning itself as the party of affirmative action and civil rights, the Southern Democratic Party split. Today, Southern Democrats tend to be more conservative than their Northern cousins (a prominent example is Zell Miller, a Southern Democrat who often supported Republican policies and complained about the liberal bent of the national Democratic Party). So one might not expect better labor policies in Southern states where Democrats are strong. Indeed, cross-national studies of left political parties code the Democratic Party differently in the North than in the South (e.g., Swank 2006). This may be why most right-to-work laws are in the South, where the Democratic Party is more conservative or relatively weak.

The Democratic Party has also been important at both the federal and state level in advocating for paid family leave, while Republicans have opposed such leave. President Clinton introduced a scheme that allowed states to augment their unemployment insurance programs to provide paid leave to new parents. Several states were also developing or had developed their own paid leave schemes at that time. Democratic state legislators, women's groups, and unions all pushed for such measures. In Massachusetts, a change to state unemployment benefits to permit women to use unemployment insurance for pregnancy and maternity leave (Baby UI) was championed by a coalition of union groups, women's groups, and Catholic groups. President Bush repealed the measure early in his first term (2002), with the support of state and federal chambers of commerce and over the opposition of unions and women's groups, eliminating paid maternity leave where it had briefly existed with federal support. Five states—California, Hawaii, New Jersey, New York, and Rhode Island—still provide an average of 10 to 12 weeks of paid maternity leave through temporary state disability insurance. Similar political dynamics are at play here. In New Jersey, for example, a Democratic governor and mostly Democratic legislators strongly supported the measure, with support from the unions and women's organizations, while business interests strongly opposed it, and Republicans were split on the issue (Raghunathan 2001; Parmley 2001). In supporting these measures, Democrats have framed them as "family issues," "children's issues," or "family values" policies, not as women's rights or labor policies.

INTERSECTIONALITY AND POLITICAL REPRESENTATION

The claim that marginalized groups share any interests or perspectives has been criticized as essentialist, in that all marginalized groups are riven by internal cleavages and inequalities (Lugones 1994; Butler 1993). The experiences of dispossessed subgroups can be qualitatively different (not captured by speaking merely in terms of more or less—e.g., "more violence" or "less wealth") than the experiences of more privileged segments of the marginalized group (Crenshaw 1994; Brewer 1999; Collins 1998; Harris 1990; Hancock 2007). When such privileged segments (e.g., professional women) claim to speak for the whole marginal group (women), their voices can crowd out or drown out the interests or voices of marginalized subgroups and can falsely seem to present a united or homogeneous front. Indeed, Dara Strolovitch's important work on U.S. interest groups shows that marginalized subgroups tend to "fall through the cracks" in a system constituted by groups focused on economic justice, women's issues, and racial equality (Strolovitch 2006, 2007). We would not expect, then, that all avenues of representation work equally well for all workers. It could be that social movements are the best avenue of representation for marginalized subgroups because movements are more accessible and fluid. This means that poorly resourced populations would find it easier to penetrate such informal, fluid forms of political organization than to penetrate more formal institutions such as political parties.

Intersectional dimensions of political representation would be manifest in distinct political dynamics for policies affecting different groups of people. In particular, we might expect the policies affecting the most advantaged women or the most advantaged segment of the working class to result from different political dynamics from those affecting the least advantaged segment of the working class. Similarly, we would expect the determinants of policies primarily affecting working-class women to be different from those primarily affecting working-class men.

Although disaggregating the analysis by social group provides insight, this does not mean we can say nothing about the broader social group. There may well be some cases where we can speak of representing women as women or workers as workers. But never going beyond these broader categories means we miss some important dimensions of the process of representation that would otherwise become apparent (Weldon 2008). I advance this argument here by looking at the intersection of gender, class, and race/region in the United States.

Labor Policies across the 50 States

DEPENDENT VARIABLE

Let us examine the relative importance of various avenues of representation in terms of their likely impact on policies that affect low-income workers. As noted, comparable, cross-state data are not available to examine the impact of the occupational composition of the state legislature, but it is possible to compare the impact of the Democratic Party, unions, other civil society groups (e.g., women's movements and living wage campaigns), and social capital more generally on labor policies, controlling for relevant background conditions (e.g., cost of living, ideology). In order to analyze the relationship between these types of representation and labor-favorable policy across the 50 U.S. states, we examined a range of policies affecting workers with lower incomes and/or levels of formal education. Policies examined include policies traditionally associated with labor rights, such as right-to-work laws. However, given the trend away from full-time, full-year, industrial-sector "good jobs," especially for the most disadvantaged workers, the analysis also covers minimum wage laws, public spending on work supports, and whether the state offers income support for lower-income workers in the form of a state earned income tax credit. We also looked at whether unemployment insurance (UI) is available to part-time workers. Finally, the most disadvantaged workers (e.g., garment workers or sex workers) are often working in a realm of shady legality, where undocumented workers and traffic in people comprise part of the workforce. Measures to redress trafficking therefore aid not only the workers who are trafficked themselves but also those who work in the same occupations as trafficked workers. For this reason, we also examine antitrafficking provisions across the states.

Women comprise nearly one-half of all workers in the United States, so labor policies affecting women may affect more workers than policies affecting union members (12.1 percent of wage and salary workers) or minimum wage workers (2.5 percent of all hourly paid workers) (Bureau of Labor Statistics 2005a, 2005b). A large majority of women have children, and a majority of women with children (even very young children) continue to work after childbirth in the United States. Maternity leave makes it possible for more women to retain their attachment to the labor market and resume work after childbirth, so rules that permit women to use unemployment insurance for pregnancy (sometimes called "Baby UI") are important for working women. In addition, since poor women are about seven times more likely to be victims of domestic violence than middle-class women, we also examined whether problems stemming from domestic violence were seen as a valid reason for claiming UI.

In all, then, we examined policies including the following:

1. right-to-work laws
2. minimum wage laws
3. social spending on work supports
4. whether there is a state earned income tax credit
5. whether unemployment insurance is available to part-time workers
6. whether unemployment insurance is available to pregnant workers as a sort of paid maternity leave
7. whether unemployment insurance is available to workers who lose their jobs due to domestic violence
8. whether there is antitrafficking legislation

Each of these policies was examined for the 50 states (see table A4 in the appendix). First, we coded these policies to create an index of labor-favorable policy. If a state had a minimum wage policy higher than that required by the national minimum wage law, we coded it 1 (17 states scored 1). If a state had an earned income tax credit (15 did), we coded it 1. If a state did not have a right-to-work policy, it received one point (29 states did not; note reverse coding here). If the state UI program had rules that permitted pregnant workers to use UI for leave (8 states did as of 2005) or permitted workers suffering job loss as a result of domestic violence to claim UI (24 states did as of July 2003), then a state received one point for each policy. The state policy on part-time workers was given a score between 0 and 1 based on the evaluation of the National Employment Law Project as of May 2005. If a state had an antitrafficking policy, it received a score of 1; if an antitrafficking measure had been introduced but not passed, the state was scored 0.5; otherwise a state was coded 0. Three states had such measures, while an additional 6 had introduced (but not passed) policies by 2004.[8]

We also included a measure of spending on work support programs in 2005 as a proportion of the national average, which ranged from 0.5 (Utah) to 2.0 (Maine). Data were drawn from an Urban Institute analysis of Current Population Survey data. This means that this spending variable is weighted more than the other measures included here, but if a state spends twice as much as the national average on work supports for workers, it probably should be weighted more than the other policy measures included. The results of this labor-favorable policy index are reported in table A4 in the appendix.

The most labor-favorable policy regimes (scoring 9) are found in California, Maine, Minnesota, New York, and Vermont. The least favorable states (scoring 1) are Alabama, Georgia, Idaho, Nevada, North Dakota, South Carolina, Tennessee, Utah, and Virginia. An average score was about 5 (the score for Arkansas, Illinois, Iowa, Oregon, and Wisconsin).

AVENUES OF REPRESENTATION: INDEPENDENT VARIABLES

We use regression analysis to examine the relationship between independent variables tapping different avenues of representation for working people as well as control variables. We expect to find strong positive relationships between the civil society variables and the adoption of these policies. We expect union involvement to be especially important, since it is a labor-specific organization, although these formal organizations may be less important for policies aimed at less-privileged workers, such as antitrafficking legislation and perhaps minimum and living wage laws.

Union Strength. Our measure of union strength is the percentage of employed individuals within the state who are represented by unions. The variable is an interval-level scale from 0 to 100, with a mean of 12.7. This data is for 2004 and was collected from the Bureau of Labor Statistics (2005b).

Number of State Living Wage Campaigns. Other than unions, there are many civil society groups focused on economic justice (e.g., Jobs with Justice in Minnesota). Cohen and Rogers (1992) emphasize the importance of organizations other than unions in representing workers. We wanted some way of getting at this less formal avenue of civil society representation. One rough measure of activism on economic justice issues might be the presence of a state living wage campaign. The nonprofit community group ACORN tracks living wage campaigns across the country. These data are for 2004 (ACORN 2005).

Social Capital. We utilize a measure of social capital created by Putnam that combines his earlier data from *Bowling Alone* (2000) and five other measures of public and private social capital (Caiazza and Putnam 2002). This method of operationalizing social capital treats it as a public, rather than private, good. The result is an interval-level scale that ranges from –1.39 to 1.76, with a mean of –.0325.

Women's Movement Strength. As noted, we aim to include multiple sources of civil society representation of labor, and many of the measures included here are policies of particular interest to working women as women. For example, many women's organizations argue that the minimum wage is a "women's issue" because women comprise the majority of minimum wage workers. As noted earlier, women's groups in California, New York, New Jersey, and other states joined with unions in pressing for expanded parental leave and child care. For these reasons, the analysis here includes women's movements as a possible source of political representation for labor.

We have included a measure for the strength of women's movements within each state. We use the same definition here as that used in previous chapters: women's movements are social movements organized by and for women or some subgroup of women (Tarrow 1998; Beckwith 2000). In this chapter, though, we make use of the available comparable, cross-state data on women's organizations (such data is not available cross-nationally). The number of women's organizations for a given population tells us the rate at which women are mobilizing as women. It is important to note that these groups are not limited to interest or lobby groups—they include women's cultural institutions (e.g., women's festivals, writers workshops, bookstores, newspapers, and so on), women's centers, groups oriented toward consciousness raising and protest, and the like.[9] The number of organizations standardized for population indicates the intensity of women's movement activity (Weldon 2004, 2006). This measure ranges from 0 to 1, with a mean of .30.

Democratic Party Strength. We use two separate measures of Democratic Party strength within each state. First, we calculate the percentage of Democrats in the state legislature. This variable has a mean of 50. We also ask whether the state had a Democratic governor (scored 1 if the state has a Democratic governor, 0 if it does not). This data is from State Net (2005b).

Women in Legislature. Especially for those policies of particular interest to working women, women in the legislature could affect the likelihood of policy adoption. Of course, the impact of women should depend not only on the number of women in office but also on how numerous they are compared to the size of the legislature as whole (see chapter 1). We include the proportion of women in the legislature as an independent variable. Data are from the Center for American Women and Politics.

Women in the legislature may matter in ways that are hard to detect at an aggregate level. One activist said she thought women and men were equally responsive as state legislators to women's concerns but that they understood them in different ways because of their differing experiences (interview with a U.S. antiviolence activist, 2009). This suggests that there could be qualitative differences in influence on state response that are not picked up by a macrolevel analysis. In addition, it is likely that women in the legislature have to "toe the line" and be careful about criticizing their fellow party members. One woman state legislator told me that the state legislature was still an "old boys' club": "One has to get along and go along a bit to get things done. Don't challenge the men. Don't frighten or threaten them. You need to be nice—but then be firm in making one's demands at some point. There have to be some things you really demand" (interview with a U.S. state legislator, 2009). This could be the reason why, at the federal level, as Katha Pollitt of *The Nation* magazine observed, not one single Democratic congresswoman defied Bill Clinton's 2006 welfare reform initiative (PRWORA), despite the likely negative impact of this law on low-income working women. Still, to the extent that the raw number or proportion of women in the legislature makes a difference to state policy responsiveness, this analysis should reveal that phenomenon.

CONTROL VARIABLES

Political Culture/Liberalism. We wanted to control for a general openness to progressive ideas and policies that might be associated with a more liberal political culture. We used the liberalism scale devised by Wright, Erickson, and McIver, created from an aggregation of data drawn from the *CBS News/New York Times* national polls from 1977–99. The scale is an interval-level scale ranging from −1 (conservative) to 1 (liberal), with a mean of −.13.

Cost of Living. We expected that a higher-than-average cost of living would make it more likely that a state would adopt living wage laws and minimum wage laws.

Population Diversity. There is a burgeoning body of literature suggesting that greater racial diversity is associated with a weaker commitment to welfare spending (Schram et al. 2003; Hero 2007). We initially controlled for racial and ethnic diversity by including a measure of the population that is white and non-Hispanic. This measure proved to be a source of multicollinearity, undermining our confidence somewhat in the assessment of the significance of some key theoretical factors, and its inclusion did not change the significance or relative strength of the other variables, so we ended up leaving it out of the analyses reported here.

AN INTERSECTIONAL ANALYSIS OF LABOR REPRESENTATION: RESULTS

Overall Indicator of Labor-Favorable Policy. In bivariate terms, the variables most strongly associated with labor-favorable policy were union density and women's movement strength, but multivariate analysis showed somewhat different results: women's movements and social capital appeared to be the most important determinants of pro-labor policy, with the largest standardized betas and strongest predictive relationship. The proportion of Democrats in the legislature was also strongly, positively associated with labor-favorable policy, although it appears that women's movements and social capital are slightly more important. Contrary to our expectations, unions and less formal economic justice associations appeared to have a weak positive relationship or no relationship to labor-favorable policy in the states (table 5).

The results of this analysis are consistent with the idea that civil society organizations (women's movements and social capital) are the most important influences on pro-labor policies. Democratic Party strength was also expected to be supportive of labor-favorable policies. But the idea that women's movements and social capital are so much more important than both unions and Democratic Party strength seems counterintuitive. Although we certainly

TABLE 5. Association of Various Avenues of Representation with Labor-Favorable Policy (Robust Standard Errors)

Independent Variables	*B*	S.E.	Beta	Sig.
Model 1 ($R^2 = 0.59$)				
Union density	0.06	0.04	0.17	0.185
Social capital	0.86	0.26	0.37	0.003
Women's movement	13.52	3.83	0.39	0.001
State living wage campaigns	0.25	0.37	0.07	0.512
Democrats in legislature	0.04	0.01	0.31	0.003
Model 2 ($R^2 = 0.69$)				
Union density	0.02	0.04	0.06	0.644
Social capital	0.71	0.25	0.32	0.009
Women's movement	11.32	3.89	0.34	0.006
State living wage campaigns	0.28	0.35	0.08	0.426
Democrats in legislature	0.02	0.01	0.19	0.067
Cost of living	0.01	0.01	0.11	0.321
Liberalism	3.47	1.94	0.21	0.083

Note: S.E. = standard error; Sig. = significance.

thought that women's movements might be important for labor-favorable policy, especially since we included so many policies of importance to working women, we did not expect women's movements to be overwhelmingly important and for unions to be unimportant. We wondered if these surprising results would hold up if we disaggregate the policy indicators into those more focused on women and those policies more traditionally thought of as pro-labor policies.

Gendering Labor Policy Analysis. Right-to-work policies, minimum wage policies, and social spending on work supports (e.g., food stamps, medical care, tax credits, etc.) have traditionally been thought of as the sort of workers' rights policies that unions would address. Although women comprise a significant minority of union members (44 percent), women are still not well represented in union leadership (Caiazza 2007). It is possible that unions are more effective political actors with respect to those policies seen as squarely within their purview (policies that are important to workers *as workers* unmodified) and that policies affecting women workers tend to receive less attention. Indeed, as noted, Strolovitch's 2006 study of interest groups in the United States, which included economic justice groups, found that issues that affected less advantaged subgroups (e.g., women workers) were often perceived as too specialized to be part of the mandate of the organization. If this were true in this case, unions would do better at representing advantaged subgroups (like union members) and policies that appeared more universally applicable to all workers (e.g., minimum wage policies, the earned income tax credit [EITC], and work support policies).

Examining just those policies previously described (right-to-work, minimum wage, work supports, and EITC), we created a measure of labor-favorable policy that focuses on these traditional labor policies (see the appendix for specific scores). Based on these traditional measures, Washington, DC, Maine, New York, and Vermont had the most labor-favorable policy (scoring 5), while 19 states received a score of 1. Controlling for ideology and cost of living, unions were the most important influences on these policies, followed by social capital and the strength of the Democratic Party. Women's movements did not appear to significantly determine these policies, nor did less formal economic justice organizations seem to have much impact (table 6, model 1).

These findings support the argument that civil society organizations are the best avenue of influence for working people, although the Democratic Party does also appear to be an important influence. Social capital more generally, though, also seems to have a role in improving government responsiveness to labor.

Women's organizations and feminists often argue that if they do not pay attention to women's issues, no one will. Our findings from examining the remaining labor issues support this contention. Let us turn to an examination of the labor policies that women's movements tend to define as women's issues: spending on child care (as a percent of maximum), UI provisions for paid maternity leave, access to UI for part-time workers, regulations recognizing domestic violence as a legitimate reason to claim UI, minimum wage laws higher than the national average, and laws against trafficking. If we evaluate state labor regimes based on how they address this combination of policies of importance to working women, we see different patterns of policy and political response. California stands out as the state with the policy regime most favorable to women's labor, and 13 states (e.g., Alabama) do nothing in any of these areas (see table A4 in the appendix). Table 6 (model 2) shows the OLS regression analysis of the association of each of the avenues of representation with a more favorable policy response to women's labor. The most important influence for policies affecting women's labor is the strength of women's movements, and the second most important is social capital. Neither unions nor Democratic

TABLE 6. Association of Various Avenues of Representation with Traditional and Women-Friendly Labor Policies

Independent Variables	*B*	S.E.	Beta	Sig.
Dependent variable = Traditional labor policies				
Model 1 ($R^2 = 0.75$)				
Union density	0.07	0.03	0.29	0.01
Social capital	0.39	0.15	0.24	0.02
Women's movement strength	3.44	2.8	0.14	0.23
State living wage campaigns	0.19	0.24	0.07	0.43
Democratic Party strength	0.02	0.01	0.21	0.09
Cost of living	0.00	0.01	–0.04	0.74
Liberalism	4.64	1.62	0.39	0.01
Dependent variable = Labor policies primarily impacting working women				
Model 2 ($R^2 = 0.47$)				
Union density	–0.04	0.04	–0.15	0.35
Social capital	0.50	0.22	0.31	0.03
Women's movement strength	9.63	4.05	0.41	0.02
State living wage campaigns	0.21	0.35	0.08	0.55
Democratic Party strength	0.01	0.01	0.13	0.46
Cost of living	0.02	0.02	0.24	0.18
Liberalism	0.61	2.33	0.05	0.80

Note: S.E. = standard error; Sig. = significance.

strength in the legislature appear to make these policies more likely. Unsurprisingly, a generally favorable political climate, such as a liberal political culture, also appeared to influence the likelihood that pro-labor policies would be adopted.

Two key findings emerge from these analyses. First, the perceived beneficiaries of the policy (or framing) likely affects the dynamics of political support. Those policies perceived as women's labor issues seem to have derived greater support from women's organizations than from either unions or more liberal political parties. Those policies less clearly perceived as women's issues are more likely to receive support from unions and from more liberal or left political parties (in this case, the Democratic Party).

Intersectional Analysis of Class, Gender, and Race/Region. Some might argue that the impact of party will be more evident if the impact of Southern Democrats is taken into account. As noted, in the South, the Democrats are more conservative, and one might not expect them to be particularly strong as labor allies. To examine this claim, we present further analyses for two distinct groups of states: those of the South (defined as the states of the former Confederacy) and those outside the South so defined. (For convenience, I have used the term *North* for the latter group of states, though some of the states included here are not really "Northern.")

Disaggregating the analysis this way provided some intriguing results, complicating the picture we have developed so far. For Northern workers working in traditional jobs (full-time, union jobs), predominantly male workers, the Democratic Party does become the most important source of policy influence in a multivariate analysis, although not statistically significant. (It is significantly and strongly positively correlated in bivariate terms, however. The lack of statistical significance in the multivariate analysis here most likely reflects the small number of cases compared to independent variables.) Social capital, women's movements, and unions also seem to have a positive relationship with this traditional (male) workers' policy regime, although not statistically significant (table 7, model 1). Women's movement strength and unions are significantly and strongly positively related to these regimes in bivariate analysis, but social capital is not (not shown).

For Northern *women* workers, however, women's movements remain more important sources of influence than political party, and unions seem to offer little additional influence. Women's movements are the only avenue of representation that is significant in bivariate analysis and are the strongest predictors of a

TABLE 7. **Analysis of Labor Policies by Region and Gender**

Independent Variables	*B*	S.E.	Beta	Sig.
Northern workers, Model 1:				
Dependent variable = traditional labor policies ($R^2 = 0.65$)				
Union density	0.05	0.05	0.17	0.32
Social capital	0.40	0.26	0.21	0.13
Women's movement strength	4.23	4.27	0.18	0.33
Number of living wage campaigns	0.15	0.36	0.06	0.68
Democratic Party strength	0.02	0.02	0.27	0.13
Liberalism	4.41	1.99	0.38	0.04
Northern workers, Model 2:				
Dependent variable = women-friendly labor policies ($R^2 = 0.39$)				
Union density	–0.01	0.06	–0.05	0.84
Social capital	0.45	0.32	0.25	0.18
Women's movement strength	7.83	5.37	0.35	0.16
Number of living wage campaigns	0.02	0.46	0.01	0.96
Liberalism	2.57	2.51	0.24	0.31
Democratic Party strength	0.02	0.02	0.21	0.39
Southern workers, Model 3:				
Dependent variable = traditional labor policies ($R^2 = 0.89$)				
Union density	0.04	0.02	0.28	0.13
Social capital	0.26	0.21	0.24	0.27
Women's movement	–3.93	1.84	–0.35	0.08
Number of living wage campaigns	0.52	0.16	0.56	0.02
Democratic Party strength	–0.02	0.01	–0.59	0.02
Cost of living	–0.04	0.02	–0.44	0.06
Liberalism	2.51	1.42	0.33	0.13
Southern workers, Model 4:				
Dependent variable = women-friendly labor policies ($R^2 = 0.68$)				
Union density	–0.14	0.1	–0.37	0.21
Social capital	2.23	0.9	0.81	0.05
Women's movement	6.94	7.85	0.25	0.41
Number of living wage campaigns	1.57	0.68	0.67	0.06
Democratic Party strength	–0.02	0.03	–0.20	0.55
Cost of living	–0.17	0.07	–0.78	0.05
Liberalism	–3.33	6.05	–0.17	0.60

Note: S.E. = standard error; Sig. = significance.

labor regime favorable to women's interests in multivariate analysis. Women's movements (beta = .35) appear to be more important than general social capital (standardized beta of .25), strength of the Democratic Party (.21), unions (.05), or less formal economic justice organizations (.01) (table 7, model 2).

Shifting focus to the South, however, we see quite different regional dynamics (table 7, models 3 and 4). For both Southern women and Southern men, the most important avenue of influence is less formal economic justice organizations, such as living wage campaigns. For Southern women, women's organizing does still have a positive effect (but only significant in bivariate terms). Unions have little impact on policies favorable to women workers in the South but may have a more favorable impact on policies for traditional, mostly male workers (table 7, model 3).

This may reflect the relative weakness of unions in the South and perhaps a general hostility toward women's movements or organizations. Indeed, the strength of the Democratic Party appears to have a negative effect on policies favorable to both men and women workers in the South. This suggests that traditional avenues for left or liberal political organizing (e.g., liberal political parties) may not be available for workers in the South, making less traditional civil society avenues all that more important. In the South, general social capital is important for women and may be important for other workers as well, although there is less support for the latter claim. It seems that strong women's movements are unrelated to (or may even have a negative effect on) policies promoting traditional workers' rights in the South. The small number of cases in these multivariate analyses relative to the number of independent variables necessitates caution in drawing any firm conclusions, but makes the statistical significance of the fundings regarding social capital and other informal economic justice associations even more noteworthy.

Conclusion

Disaggregating the analysis by perceived beneficiary and region, then, provides some support and some refinement of the argument. For traditional workers in the North, political parties (in this case, the strength of Democrats in the legislature) seemed to offer an effective avenue of influence. But for women in the North and workers of both sexes in the South, civil society organizations such as women's organizations and state living wage campaigns seemed to be associated with better policy regimes for workers. Unions seemed to enhance political representation mostly for Northern men but also for men in the

South to some degree. Women's movements, far more than unions, seemed to enhance the representation of women workers' rights. For both women and men in the South, less formal civil society organizations aimed at social justice may be the best avenue of political representation, although even in these hostile contexts, women's movements and unions seem to improve representation somewhat for these constituencies.

Descriptive representation for women did not seem to improve policies for workers, even when focusing on policies targeted to women workers. Disaggregating the analysis by policy, we found that the presence of women in the legislature seemed to matter only for policies focused on pregnancy leave, mirroring cross-national findings in this policy area (not shown). Interestingly, though, women in office did not seem to have a positive effect in areas that would seem to be closely related, such as spending on child care for working families or access to unemployment insurance for domestic violence victims or part-time workers. Disaggregating the analysis did suggest that political party mattered more for spending issues (e.g., work supports in general and even child care in particular) than for the other issues, but women's movements and unions appeared more important in analyses disaggregated by issue. Again, women in government appeared to have little impact on policy regimes affecting women workers (not shown).

We were unable to compare these avenues with descriptive representation by class, although survey data suggests that occupational background has some influence on state legislators representative relationships with constituencies such as business, labor, and women's groups. It seems that those with a business background favor business, those with farming backgrounds favor farmers, and so on. The only group that seemed to favor labor was teachers, perhaps because of their experience with teachers' unions. Overall, the most common occupational backgrounds for state legislators were lawyers, businesspeople, salespeople, and other professionals. Legislators from these groups, who mostly report seeing business but not labor as strong supporters, comprise a majority of those legislators reporting any occupation (with the remainder working in teaching, politics or government, media occupations, farming, or office administration). This suggests that most legislators are not drawn from the working class and that the largest and most disadvantaged sections of the working class (the contingent and excluded classes, as defined by Perrucci and Wysong) are underrepresented in descriptive terms. Improving descriptive representation by class background in the legislature would likely improve substantive representation for working people (Dovi 2002).

However, we also see that even in the context of descriptive underrepresentation by class, unions, women's movements, and other civil society organizations offer relatively accessible and influential routes to substantive representation. Political parties offer an avenue of influence for the most advantaged workers—those working in traditionally male forms of work and occupations (full-time, unionized jobs). But for workers that have not been well represented by unions and political parties (part-time workers, women), women's organizations and other civil society organizations seem to offer a more effective alternative route to policy influence. Especially in the absence of a strong left or labor party (as in the South), such organizations offer a way to effect policy change for workers.

Many studies of the influence of descriptive representation and political parties on policy issues have focused on abortion rights or maternity leave policies (Kittilson 2008; Hansen 1993; Berkman and O'Connor 1993). Other studies have explicitly excluded from analysis some of the issues that are of concern to working women, such as welfare reforms affecting child care spending (e.g., Swers 2002). This analysis suggests that women's organizations are the most effective route to influence for working women—more than parties or unions. This could change if parties and unions were to become more inclusive, as some are striving to do. But for now, these more traditional routes to representation for workers appear to be less effective for women workers.

Wolbrecht (2000) has argued that gender issues such as abortion have been fundamental to a process of party realignment in which the Democrats have become the party representing women's rights while Republicans have become the party of backlash. Contesting this view, Sanbonmatsu (2002) has argued that the influence of political parties on policies affecting women is more complex, varying across issues. When it comes to conflicts about gender roles, about women's place, Sanbonmatsu argues, the Democratic and Republican party platforms both reflect ambivalence. This analysis suggests that even if Democrats are staunch defenders of women's rights on abortion at a national level, they have not been reliable advocates for working women's rights at the state level. Democrats were influential in advancing traditional workers' rights in the North, but for policies more obviously associated with women, Democratic strength in the legislature was not associated with better policies for working women. In the South, neither party seemed a reliable ally for workers of any kind, leaving workers to rely on other civil society organizations to advance their interests. Even disaggregating the analysis by issue, Democrats mainly seemed to influence policies related to social spending. For Southern workers, for women, and for the great mass of workers who do not fit the profile of the full-time, union worker, civil society groups provide better substantive representation than political parties.

An unexpected but strong and interesting finding is the role of social capital in enhancing policies on workers' rights in all regions and for all groups, especially for Southern women. Where strong, focused movement organizations or unions exist, general social capital is less important (though it seems to have a positive effect even there). But in the absence of strong movements and strong party allies, general social capital seems important for working men and women.

As noted, theorists of intersectionality argue that disaggregating the analysis of political phenomena by examining social groups created by the intersection of social structures (e.g., gender and class) provides insights that are obscured in the aggregate analysis. This seems true here: although the overall analysis did suggest that civil society groups provide a critical avenue of representation for workers, disaggregating the analysis revealed a differential role for political parties based on the gender of the workers. Further disaggregating the analysis by region suggests the importance of different sorts of civil society groups for different groups of workers in different locations. So an intersectional analysis of labor policies across the 50 states helped to explicate the political dynamics behind particular policies.

In terms of political implications for advocates of workers and women's rights, this analysis supports the focus by women's movements on the rights of *women* workers. It is true that the other advocates of labor rights have not been effective advocates for women. This analysis also suggests that the charge that women's organizations (as standard-bearers for critics of "identity politics") are undermining the Left and distracting activists' attention away from issues of material well-being and toward "cultural" issues is unfounded: women's movements are important advocates for economic justice for women. I return to this issue in a later chapter.

This chapter began by asking how we can improve representation for workers. The answer, this analysis shows, partially depends on *which* workers we consider, since different groups are effective in representing different groups of workers. Nevertheless, it seems clear that the more marginalized and disadvantaged the worker is, the more important civil society avenues for self-representation appear to be, and the less it appears that intralegislative representation (parties, descriptive representation in legislatures) offers a feasible and effective avenue of change.

CHAPTER 4

Inclusion, Identity, and Women's Movements: State Policies on Violence against Women of Color

Are group-specific movements necessary to the representation of particular marginalized groups? So far, the answer seems to be yes: labor movements are not as effective as advocates of women's labor interests (at least when they require challenging gender hierarchies) as are women's movements. It seems that more generally focused organizations tend to overlook or downplay the interests of intersectionally marginalized groups and to overemphasize the interests of intersectionally privileged groups, as previous research suggests (Strolovitch 2006; Crenshaw 1993).

Some scholars are concerned about what they perceive as the increasing fragmentation and specialization of social movements. Are "identity politics" weakening contemporary social movements? Some social movement scholars and political theorists have argued that identity politics divides movements and reduces their political effectiveness (Gitlin 1995; Tarrow 1998; Taylor and Whittier 1999; Echols 1989; Harvey 1996). In particular, the impulse toward *separate organization* around specific social positions (e.g., women's caucuses or groups centered around African Americans) is seen as particularly balkanizing. Others have argued for a more nuanced view of identity politics, arguing that separate organization can be critical for empowering and engaging marginalized groups in democratic political life (Young 2002; Gutmann 2003; Weldon 2006). Drawing on this work, I suggest that separate organizing around social position can create more inclusive social movements and lay the groundwork for cooperation across social cleavages.

I engage this debate by investigating the relationship between the organizational efforts of women's movements to recognize racial divisions and policy responsiveness to violence against women across the 50 states. Policy responsiveness is examined both as it pertains to women in general and as it relates specifically to women of color.[1] I find that states where women of color organize separately are likely to have stronger women's movements and, consequently, greater government responsiveness both to violence against women of color in particular and to violence against women in general. This suggests that the most vulnerable segments of society and social movements more generally benefit from organizational mechanisms that recognize diversity.

Are Identity Politics Divisive and Distracting?

Do identity politics advance or undermine social movements?[2] The answer to this question depends partly on what is meant by "identity politics" (Young 2000). Todd Gitlin (1995, 141), one of the best-known critics of identity politics, defines identity politics as an impulse toward separate organization (e.g., the formation of caucuses) with an aim to imbue formerly denigrated group identities with more positive meaning or to develop a group culture. Such organization requires drawing strict boundaries around group members based on ascriptive characteristics (gender, race, etc.).

Critics of identity politics worry that organizing around separate identities weakens social movements. Gitlin, for example, argues that identity politics have fractured and weakened the Left in the United States. Tarrow (1998, 119) notes, "In fact, identity politics often produces insular, sectarian, and divisive movements incapable of expanding membership, broadening appeals, and negotiating with prospective allies." Similarly, Taylor and Whittier (1999, 174) note that they "agree with the dominant view that disputes over sexuality, class and race contributed to the decline of the radical feminist branch of the movement" (see also Echols 1989).[3] Critics of identity politics argue that separate organization undermines movement identity, distracts activists from important political issues, and prevents the construction of a common political agenda. Let us turn to a critical assessment of these claims.

Much organizing according to social position is misrepresented by the term *identity politics.* Indeed, separate organizing is often focused on developing analyses of social relations and policy agendas. Sometimes groups aim to develop positive self-characterizations to counter the negative images that dominate social life, but this is usually part of a broader effort to address group inequality, rather than an effort to develop a group culture for its own sake (Young 2000). Some refer to all women's organizing as a sort of identity politics. Politically, such language is sometimes used to diminish the claims of marginalized groups, falsely portraying them as primarily focused on symbolic characteristics and as having selfish goals (Gutmann 2003).

Some forms of separate organizing are radically separatist, while others are more cooperatively oriented. The balkanizing effect of the more extreme forms of separatism seems obvious. But radical separatism does not characterize all or even most organizing around social position. Many organizations are favorably disposed to coalition and cooperation (Mueller 1995; Whittier 1995; Davis 1998; Gutmann 2003). Moreover, it is not merely extreme separatism that raises the scholarly concerns previously cited. Indeed, social movement scholars specifically note that separate organizing of constituents contributed to the decline of organizations that successfully pursued coalitional strategies (Snow and McAdam 2000).

Finally, it seems unlikely that creating movement organizations that affirm specific social identities undermines activists' feelings of affiliation with the broader movement. Since many activists participate through specific organizations, the act of belonging to a specific organization in and of itself cannot undermine the feeling of solidarity that unites social movements. Nor does cooperating in a movement require the deep level of identity that would conflict with separate organizing around social position. Indeed, the collective identities created by social movements are contingent identities, forged for political purposes, rather than primordial or essential ones (Rupp and Taylor 1999; Snow and McAdam 2000). Such a thin identity need not conflict with thicker, more specific categories of identity, such as "Hispanic women."

Social movements emphasizing a group identity that precludes the organization of marginalized subgroups risk alienating the most disadvantaged sectors of their constituency by delegitimizing efforts to draw attention to unjust social relations within that constituency. Efforts to gloss over deeply divisive conflicts by emphasizing similarities likely make matters worse and weaken social movements (Davis 1998; hooks 2000).

Separate Organizing as Enabling Inclusion and Cooperation

There are reasons to be skeptical of the argument that identity politics undermines social movements, and there are also reasons to think that separate organizing strengthens movements. Such organizing facilitates the development of more inclusive movement identities and agendas, thereby strengthening movements. If inequality among adherents, rather than separate organizing, is the challenge for movements, efforts to address inequality can strengthen cooperation (Beckwith 2000; Mueller 1995; Snow and McAdam 2000). For example, women of color have argued that it is racial inequality itself, not the efforts to procure recognition of such inequality, that weakened the women's movement (Davis 1998; hooks 2000).

Organizing on the basis of social position activates or enhances group consciousness, thereby engaging new participants or intensifying the commitment of existing participants. Indeed, some social movement scholars argue that *solidary identities* (identities derived from social positions such as gender, race, or class) are critical for mobilization (Rupp and Taylor 1999; Gamson 1991). Organizing around social position can provide a forum in which to develop group perspectives. A group perspective is grounded in the experiences of members, but it is not reducible to any particular set of experiences. It is a set of issues that are salient for members of solidary groups and that emerge in intragroup discussions (Mansbridge and Flaster 2007). The articulation of a perspective helps us understand the social relations that produce the groups in question (Young 2002). This furthers our understanding of social relations of exclusion that define marginalized groups, and it helps to develop more representative policy agendas.

Separate organizing sometimes takes place within organizations—for example, in the form of caucuses (Mueller 1995). In the absence of such mechanisms, marginalized groups may feel alienated from the organization and broader movement (Gutmann 2003). Even separate organization that is wholly independent of extant movement organizations can help to strengthen a social movement. The presence of independent organizations creates the possibility of coalition building on specific issues and increases the legitimacy of efforts to establish other such dedicated organizations (Minkoff 1995), perhaps even within the broader mass organizations. This increases the ability of marginalized groups to obtain public attention for issues that are important to them. Cooperation in the form of coalitions can occur even in the context of disagreements about ideology or a lack of shared identity (Davis 1998, 318; Crenshaw 1994; Strolovitch 2004; Weldon 2006).

Mass organizations without separate organization for marginalized subgroups provide no mechanism by which these intersectionally marginalized groups can develop and articulate their distinctive perspective, their oppositional consciousness. No matter how effective they are, they are unlikely to articulate the policy priorities and distinctive concerns of marginalized groups. Even when mass organizations do include separate organizations of marginalized subgroups, such internal organizations must compete with other groups to get their issues on the organizational agenda. Perhaps this is why such organizations tend to do a better job of representing advantaged constituencies (Strolovitch 2006).

This account of identity politics suggests that separate organization strengthens movements by activating group consciousness. The improved political analysis and broader base of support that result from separate organization should make movements more effective in addressing public issues. Yet if critics of identity politics are correct, those movements that eschew separate organization, adopting a more universalistic structure, should be more politically influential than those comprised of organizations based on social location.

This debate is clearly relevant to movements that aim to speak for solidary groups. Less obvious, perhaps, is whether this argument is relevant for movements that do not appear to be based on solidary identities, such as environmental, antiglobalization, and peace movements. Interestingly, activists often organize around solidary groups within these movements: for example, people of color organize against environmental racism (Hines 2001; Gedicks 1993). Indeed, some scholars argue that all movements draw on and/or create the identities of their constituents.[4] If organizing solidary groups within these movements strengthens or conflicts with broader movement identities, these arguments may apply to these other contexts as well.

Organizing to Address Racial Inequality in the U.S. Women's Movement

In this section, I examine the previously delineated debate in the context of how women's movements across the U.S. states have addressed racial inequality. Women's movements in the United States face the challenge of maintaining solidarity despite deep inequalities among women. Women of color have responded to racism in the women's movement by organizing separate caucuses or institutions. How has such organizing affected women's movements?

Across the states, the degree to which women are organized both as women and as women of color varies. This presents the opportunity to compare the degree and consequences of such variation. Does separate organizing by women of color weaken the women's movement and undermine policy influence? Or does such organizing strengthen the women's movement and improve responsiveness to important women's issues? I argued earlier that separate organizing exerts an indirect effect on policy processes, strengthening women's movements so that they have greater influence. Critics of identity politics maintain that movements are less politically effective when they are divided into separate caucuses and thereby weakened (an indirect effect) and distracted from important policy issues by their focus on symbolic politics and "cultural issues" (a direct effect).[5]

I examine the association between the degree to which the women's movement is organized to recognize racial differences and greater government responsiveness to violence against women. By the term *responsiveness,* I refer primarily to the scope and timeliness of the policy response, rather than to its implementation, effectiveness, or impact (Weldon 2002a).[6] Violence against women is now recognized as a pressing public problem across the United States. Violence against women is an excellent policy issue for examining the impact of women's movements, since the issue is first articulated by women's movement activists (Weldon 2002b).

Although women of all races and classes are subject to violence against women, low-income women and women of some marginalized races are likely subject to a larger number of sexual and domestic assaults than are white women (Tjaden and Thoennes 1998). Recent surveys suggest that African American women, American Indian/Alaska Native women, and women of mixed race are more likely to experience violence in intimate relationships (Tjaden and Thoennes 2000; Rennison and Welchans 2000).[7] However, it is not known how much of the variance across groups can be accounted for by differences in reporting, bias in the criminal justice system, and other demographic variables (Tjaden and Thoennes 2000; Crenshaw 1994).

Racism makes women of color more vulnerable to violence at the same time as it makes it more difficult for women of color to access services after the fact. For example, racial discrimination in wages and employment (Fix and Struyk 1993) results in an overrepresentation of women of color among the poor: in 2001, 40.8 percent of single-parent families headed by African American women and 43.2 percent headed by Hispanic women were poor, compared to 33 percent for all single-parent families (U.S. Bureau of the Census 2003). Discrimination in the housing market makes it more difficult for women of color to leave violent situations and to establish independent households (Crenshaw 1994). Poverty and other barriers to independence are associated with higher rates of violence (Raphael 1996, 1997; Levinson 1989; Sanday 1981).

Compounding the problem, the limited services that now exist for women victims of violence tend to be modeled on white, Anglo women's experiences and needs. For example, women's shelters tend to be located in white neighborhoods (Matthews 1993). Women of color often require types of assistance that white women need less frequently, including assistance in securing housing (Crenshaw 1994). It would be easier for women of color to obtain services provided in their own communities and/or languages, but such services are even more limited than services provided to white, Anglo women (Matthews 1993; Crenshaw 1993; Agnew 1998). Indeed, some women's shelters make English proficiency a precondition for access, arguing that such language skills are necessary in order for women to participate in support groups and to comprehend house rules. As a result, many non-Anglo women are effectively excluded from available shelters (Crenshaw 1994). Language barriers obstruct the ability of legal advocates and service providers to help women for whom English is not a first language (Richie and Kahuna 2000).

Native American women confront seemingly higher rates of violence and distinctive obstacles in relation to the criminal justice response. Most of the violence suffered by Native American women is perpetrated by non-Indians (it is interracial). This is quite different from most of the violence suffered by white or African American women (which is mostly intraracial). Native American women living on tribal lands are twice as likely to be raped or sexually assaulted as other women, and assaults on Native women are particularly violent. But criminal justice response is hard to obtain because of the complex jurisdictional problems that stem from the overlapping legal authorities on tribal lands (Duthu 2008).

In addition, women of color confront racist attitudes from shelter workers, police, health care providers, activists, and others who assume that their victimization is a result of their membership in a "backward" or traditional cultural group (Richie and Kahuna 2000; Agnew 1998, Smith 2001). They also face sexism and resistance to acknowledging violence within their own communities (Crenshaw 1994; Richie and Kahuna 2000; Smith 2001). These conflicts have motivated women of color to establish their own organizations to address violence against women (Smith 2001). Thus, women of color confront barriers to addressing violence that white, Anglo women do not confront (Matthews 1993; Smith 2001).

Although most governments do not address the distinctive problems confronted by women of color, some governments are beginning to adopt policies that specifically seek to address the barriers that prevent women of color from accessing services. These policies include bilingual hotlines; shelters located in communities of color; trained interpreters in shelters, health care facilities, and criminal justice settings; legal advocacy regarding immigration; and public information and outreach programs.[8] Examining whether governments adopt such policies is an important part of assessing government response to violence against women.

I explore the relationship between separate organizing, movement strength, and policy impact by comparing the 50 American states. There is variation in women's movement activity and policy across the 50 states, but the degree of institutional and cultural variation across the states is somewhat less than it is cross-nationally. In addition, comparable demographic, policy, and other data on the states are readily available. For this reason, the American states offer an especially good context in which to explore these relationships.

SEPARATE ORGANIZING

In this analysis, I examine the degree to which women's movements recognize racial differences among women, by examining the degree of separate organization of women of color. I compare the amount of women's organizing overall to the amount of organizing focused on women of color, by examining the percentage of women's organizations that focus on women of color. Conceptually, the latter category should include both freestanding organizations of women of color and caucuses and other internal suborganizations of women of color. This does not include organizations that aim for racial inclusion but are not, on the whole, focused on women of color. Nor does it include organizations that pursue universalistic policies and, as a matter of course, address issues of concern to women of color. This makes sense because I seek to examine the effect of *separate* organizing of women of color. These data are taken from a database of women's organizations called the Electrapages (2000) (see note 9 and Weldon 2004). Organizations for women of color include, for example, the White Buffalo Calf Woman Society (South Dakota), Mujeres por la Raza Unida (Texas), Black Women in Sisterhood for Action (Virginia), the Asian and Pacific Women's Caucus (Washington), African American Women Veterans (Pennsylvania), the African Studies Association Women's Caucus (Georgia), Lesbianas Unidas (California), and the Conference of American Women Writers of Color (Maryland).

STRENGTH OF THE WOMEN'S MOVEMENT

Women's movements are social movements organized by and for women or some subgroup of women (see Introduction and chapter 1 for more discussion; cf. Beckwith 2000). Women's movement strength refers to the political support for and resources commanded by the women's movement. Strong women's movements are able to mobilize grassroots action. Partly because of their ability to mobilize electoral support and partly because of the broader social changes they inspire, spokespersons for strong movements are perceived as legitimate participants in public discourse (Rochon and Mazmanian 1993;

Kingdon 1984). Movements participate in policy discussions through lobbying, protest, cultural productions, and consciousness-raising activities (Katzenstein 1995; Weldon 2002a).

Some scholars seek to get at cross-state variation in women's movements by examining the number of women who are members of national women's lobby organizations such as the National Organization of Women or NARAL (e.g., Hansen 1993; Keiser 1999; Oakley and Steuernagel 2000). But a focus on mainstream organizations tends to overlook most activism by women of color (Minkoff 1997). In addition, membership in national organizations may not be the best indicator of women's movement strength at a state level, since it leaves out membership in state-level organizations. Women may be more likely to join such national organizations where state-level organizations have a lower profile. Thus, examining the membership of national organizations may somewhat understate the degree of women's movement activity in a particular state.

As in chapter 3, I use the number of women's organizations for a given population to indicate the rate at which women are mobilizing as women. The number of organizations standardized for population indicates the intensity of women's movement activity.[9] Population data are from the Bureau of the Census, and data on organizations are from the Electrapages (2000) (see Weldon 2004).[10]

MEASURES OF POLICY ON VIOLENCE AGAINST WOMEN

Chapter 1 measured responsiveness by examining the scope of government response to violence against women.[11] This study adapts this approach to measuring government responsiveness in the U.S. states and includes elements designed to tap responsiveness to women of color. Eight areas of government action were examined for each state. As in chapter 1, for each area for which the state took action, it received a score of 1 (otherwise a state was coded 0 for that area). Policy scope is simply the sum of these scores, that is, the number of areas in which the government takes action. The measure covers the following policy areas:

1. Is there a law against assault and battery between intimates?
2. Is stalking legally recognized as a felony or misdemeanor on the first offense?
3. Is there warrantless arrest for perpetrators of domestic violence?
4. Is there domestic violence training for police?

5. Is there sexual assault training for police and prosecutors?
6. Is there state funding for medical exams for victims of sexual assault?
7. Is there any state government effort focused on violence against women of color?
8. Is there state funding for shelters for victims of domestic violence?

Data for items 1–6 are taken from publications of the Institute for Law and Justice and reflect the status of state legislation as of the end of 2000. Items 7 and 8 are based on interviews conducted during fall 2000 and spring 2001 with representatives of the domestic violence coalitions in each state.[12] Policy responsiveness to violence against women of color is examined by focusing on whether state governments adopted efforts targeted specifically to addressing violence against women of color. States adopting any such policy or even multiple such policies received a score of 1; otherwise a state was coded 0.[13]

CONTROL VARIABLES

This analysis considers a number of control variables, including proportion of women (and women of color) in public office, effectiveness of the women's commission, level of economic development, diversity of the population, urbanization, variation in political culture or citizen ideology, and official rape rate.

Women in Elective Office. Theorists have argued that women in elective office are likely to be more receptive to women's issues and ideas (Mansbridge 1999; Williams 1998). Indeed, some studies find that women are more likely to advocate for and adopt policies such as police reforms to address domestic violence (Murphy 1998), abortion rights (Berkman and O'Connor 1993), and policies concerning women, children, and the family (Thomas 1994; Swers 2002). The effect of women in office on policy is expected to be greater once there is a critical mass of women, that is, when women exceed a critical proportion of the legislature. A critical mass of women, then, should be associated with greater responsiveness to violence (see chapter 1 for a fuller discussion).

However, the political and institutional context mediates the impact of women legislators (Swers 2002). Moreover, although individual women may play important roles in promoting woman-friendly policy, sheer number or proportion of women in the legislature does not have a significant impact on policy outcomes in areas such as violence against women and women's reproductive rights (Oakley and Steuernagel 2000; Weldon 2002b). This analysis controls for the proportion of women in the legislature in each state, using 1999 data from the Center for American Women and Politics. The proportion of women of color in the legislature was also taken into account but was omitted from the models shown, as it is collinear with the diversity of the population. When included, the proportion of women of color in office did not prove to be a good predictor of policies on violence in any of the analyses.

Women's Commission Effectiveness. The presence of a state government commission on women's status may strengthen women's movements and improve policy responsiveness to violence against women (Weldon 2002a). However, it is unlikely that the mere presence of a commission makes a difference. Commissions can be seriously underresourced: several are staffed by a single person (in one case, a part-time worker). Some commissions serve only as public relations offices to promote the governor and have little access or influence.

Those commissions that have better access and more resources are more likely to affect movement strength and policy responsiveness. Previous studies have found that women's policy agencies that have broad, cross-sectoral authority and that provide access for women's movements are more effective at influencing policy (Stetson and Mazur 1995; Weldon 2002a). State-level women's commissions were scored more highly if they had access to both the legislature and the executive, if they had more resources (staff and budget), and if they provided opportunities for formal or public access by women's organizations.[14] Scores range from 0 (having no resources or access) to 6 (having many resources and access) (see Weldon 2004). Data were generated by interviews with staff in the women's commissions in each state.

Other Control Variables. Several other standard control variables are included. Political culture or state ideology might influence whether a given state is predisposed to adopt policies to address violence or to organize in social movements.[15] This study controls for such an effect by using a standard indicator of citizen ideology (Berry et al. 1993).[16]

Relatedly, some might wish to control for the overall degree of civic engagement. Caiazza and Putnam (2002) find that social capital is associated with women's status in some areas (e.g., health and economic autonomy) but not in others (reproductive rights, employment equity). However, cross-national studies have found that organizing by women is critical for provoking a policy response to violence against women (Weldon 2002a). Forms of organization that are not focused on women's status, such as unions, political parties, or other civic associations, have not played an important role in galvanizing government action on violence against women (Elman 1996; Weldon 2002a). It may be that issues explicitly related to women's bodies (e.g., reproductive rights or violence against women) are less likely to be raised by organizations with other foci.[17] In addition, Norris (2002) finds that protest politics are a phenomenon distinct from traditional civic association. Bivariate and multivariate analyses showed that social capital was unrelated to policy responsiveness to violence and unrelated to movement strength. For these reasons, social capital was not included in the final models.

Previous studies have suggested that social and economic factors are important in determining government response to violence against women (Call et al. 1991; Weldon 2002a). These include measures of economic development (state gross domestic product), degree of urbanization (the proportion living in metropolitan areas), and the diversity of the population (the proportion of the population that is Hispanic or nonwhite or both) (U.S. Bureau of the Census 2000).[18] Diversity is particularly important for the analysis of government response to violence against women of color, since one might suspect that governments are more likely to respond to women of color where there are more such women present. Conversely, one might expect heightened awareness of race or greater racial conflict where racial diversity is greater. Population diversity and degree of urbanization proved to be highly collinear, so degree of urbanization was left out of the final analysis. Finally, one might expect government response to be greater where violence against women is more pervasive (Kingdon 1984). Despite the many problems with official crime statistics, particularly as they pertain to rape, I follow the common practice of using the "forcible rape"[19] rate from the FBI's Uniform Crime Reports as an indicator of the scale of the problem of violence against women (U.S. Bureau of the Census 2000).

DETERMINANTS OF WOMEN'S MOVEMENT STRENGTH

Does separate organizing weaken movements, as the critics of identity politics suggest? Or is separate organization associated with greater movement strength, as I expect? I explore this question using a least squares analysis that takes women's movement strength as the dependent variable (table 8).

Such an analysis reveals that separate organizing is indeed an important and powerful predictor of women's movement strength (sig. = .01).[20] An increase of 16 percentage points, from the minimum to the maximum value, would result in an increase of .08 in movement strength (16 × .005). Though this may seem like a small effect, the dependent variable ranges only between .22 and .42. An increase of .08, then, is 40 percent of the total range. This is a sizable effect.

Separate organizing is the most important predictor of women's movement strength (with the largest standardized coefficient, .34) of all independent variables in the equation, including citizen ideology, the racial diversity of the population, the gross state product, or the percentage of the legislators that are women. Separate organization, then, likely strengthens and revitalizes movements by creating new organizations and by preserving old ones.

Analyzing Policy Responsiveness to Violence against Women

Does the separate organization of women of color improve policy responsiveness either to women of color or to women more generally? Critics of separate organizing argue that it undermines policy influence by weakening movements and distracting activists from political issues of importance. Since violence against women is an important political issue, we can ask whether there is an association between degree of separate organization and government responsiveness. If the critics are right, an increased degree of separate organization should be both directly and indirectly associated with less government responsiveness to violence against women. Conversely, I have argued that a greater degree of separate organization should be indirectly associated with greater policy responsiveness.

Is there is an association between the degree of separate organization and responsiveness of state governments to violence against women? OLS regression analysis is a simple and straightforward way of assessing whether a linear association exists. If more separate organization decreased the effectiveness of

TABLE 8. Analysis of Women's Movement Strength

Independent Variables	*B*	S.E.	Beta	Sig.
Separate organization for women of color	0.005	0.002	0.34	0.01
Control variables				
Citizen ideology	0.001	0.001	0.15	0.27
Effective women's policy machinery	0.005	0.003	0.20	0.12
Logged gross state product	0.064	0.036	0.26	0.08
Percentage of legislators that are women	0.002	0.001	0.25	0.06
Racial diversity of population	0.000	0.000	–0.05	0.70

Note: Analysis by OLS; dependent variable = number of women's organizations standardized for population size; $R^2 = 0.39$; S.E. = standard error; Sig. = significance.

women's movements in influencing policy processes, one would expect to see a negative relationship. In fact, controlling for other relevant variables, more separate organization appears to have little relationship to responsiveness: it is not a significant predictor of the scope of government response (table 9). A greater focus on women of color, then, does not directly decrease policy responsiveness to violence against women.

At the same time, women's movement strength has a strong positive relationship with government responsiveness to violence against women. Indeed, the logged indicator is the most important predictor of government response to violence against women (with a beta of .43), followed by separate organizing (.20), citizen ideology (–.14), and effective women's policy machinery (.13). Of these variables, only movement strength is statistically significant.

Movement strength is also substantively important. To get an idea of the size of the effects, consider the difference in women's movement strength between Missouri, with the weakest women's movement at .22 (25 organizations in absolute terms), and California, with the strongest at .42 (1,403 organizations in absolute terms), a difference of .20 in the strength indicator. An increase of this size is associated with two or three additional areas of government action on violence against women.

Interestingly, the percentage of women in the legislature appears to have little predictable effect on policy responsiveness to violence against women. This finding reinforces the findings of earlier chapters and replicates other studies focusing on policies on violence against women (Elman 1996), reproductive rights (Oakley and Steuernagel 2000), and child support enforcement (Keiser 1999).[21] The percentage of women of color in the legislature (not

TABLE 9. Analysis of State Responsiveness to Violence against Women

Independent Variables	*B*	S.E.	Beta	Sig.
Separate organization for women of color	0.09	0.07	0.20	0.20
Women's movement strength	12.41	4.94	0.43	0.02
Control variables				
Citizen ideology	–0.02	0.02	–0.14	0.40
Effective women's policy machinery	0.10	0.11	0.13	0.38
Gross state product per capita (logged)	–0.35	1.18	–0.05	0.77
Percentage of legislators that are women	0.01	0.03	0.04	0.80
Racial diversity of population	0.01	0.02	0.07	0.56
Rape rate	0.01	0.02	0.07	0.66
Constant	4.64	11.35	—	0.68

Note: Analysis by OLS; dependent variable = state responsiveness to violence against women; $R^2 = 0.3$; S.E. = standard error; Sig. = significance.

shown) is not strongly associated with greater responsiveness to violence against women.

Women's commission effectiveness does not provide much explanatory leverage. Other studies have found that effective women's commissions shape policy-making on women's issues (Stetson and Mazur 1995; see chapter 1 in the present study). However, these analyses focused on women's movement access to the commissions and on whether the commission had cross-sectional authority. The measure employed in this analysis focuses on the resources and access to power of commission bureaucrats themselves. Perhaps a measure more focused on position in the administrative hierarchy and relations with women's movements would produce a different result. This would be worth investigating in future research.

Thus, stronger women's movements are strongly and significantly associated with greater responsiveness to violence against women. Separate organizing, however, does not appear to have a strong direct effect on such responsiveness. This result holds even when controlling for diversity of the population, proportion of women (and women of color) in the legislature, level of economic development, urbanization, citizen ideology, and other relevant variables.

INDIRECT EFFECTS

The indirect effects of separate organization on responsiveness to violence against women are positive and significant. Both legs of the hypothesized indirect effect are significant. We can expect an increase in responsiveness of .06 for every unit increase in separate organization ($B = .005 \times 12.41$). An increase of 16 percent in separate organization (the difference between the minimum and maximum values of the variable) would produce an increase in government responsiveness of about one additional area of policy action. One additional area can make a big difference to government responsiveness to violence against women, meaning the difference between funding shelters or not, between funding crisis centers or not, between providing outreach to women of color or not.

POLICY RESPONSIVENESS TO VIOLENCE AGAINST WOMEN OF COLOR

One might wonder whether it matters to which women the government is responding: surely, separate organization would be more critical for obtaining a government response targeted specifically to violence against women of color. After all, if separate organizing improved the *representativeness* of women's movements, as well as their strength, one might expect separate organizing to result in greater responsiveness to women of color. As previously, however, critics of separate organizing would expect that separate organizing would divide women's movements, undermining their effectiveness (an indirect effect) and distracting them from important issues.

A logistic regression analysis explores these possibilities (table 10). Overall, the model specified improves our understanding of why some state governments are more likely to respond to violence against women of color. The Nagelkerke R^2 for the model is .587, suggesting that the model explains nearly 60 percent of the variance. More important, taken together, the coefficients for the independent variables provide a significant improvement in explanatory power (correctly predicting 84 percent) over guessing the most frequent category (predicting 70 percent). Indeed, the model improves predictive accuracy by nearly half (PRE = .46).

Separate organization by women of color does not have a strong, direct relationship to the likelihood of government responsiveness to violence against women of color (sig. = .92). Women's movement strength, however, does significantly and substantively alter the likelihood of government responsiveness to violence against women of color (sig. = .00). A change in the independent variable for women's movement strength from its minimum to its maximum value increases the likelihood of government response to violence against women of color to nearly 1 (the associated change in predicted proba-

TABLE 10. The Likelihood of Government Responsiveness to Women of Color

Independent Variable	*b*	S.E.	Sig.	Change in Predicted Probability
Separate organization for women of color	0.02	0.16	0.92	0.04
Women's movement strength	50.31	17.25	0.00	0.98
Control variables				
Citizen ideology	–0.02	0.06	0.87	–0.12
Effective women's policy machinery	–0.03	0.23	0.89	–0.02
Logged gross state product	–0.54	3.21	0.87	–0.07
Percentage of legislators that are women	–0.13	0.08	0.11	0.55
Racial diversity of population	0.01	0.04	0.86	0.08
Rape rate	–0.02	0.05	0.68	–0.13
Constant	–6.82	30.72	0.82	—

Source: For raw data see Weldon 2004, table A-1, column 8.

Note: Analysis by logistic regression; dependent variable = government response to women of color (1 = Response; 0 = No response). Nagelkerke R^2 = 0.59; % correct = 84; PRE = 0.46. S.E. = standard error; Sig. = significance.

bility is .98). As previously, this result holds even when controlling for diversity of the population, proportion of women in the legislature, proportion of women of color in the legislature, level of economic development, degree of urbanization, state ideology, and other relevant variables.

INDIRECT EFFECTS ON RESPONSIVENESS TO WOMEN OF COLOR

Indirect effects of separate organization on responsiveness to women of color are expected to follow the same causal path as the indirect effects on responsiveness to women at large: separate organization strengthens the movement, which in turn elicits greater policy responsiveness. One might expect greater effects for women of color. Such women would be prime beneficiaries of a stronger movement that was more representative of their concerns.

As expected, the indirect effects of separate organization on government responsiveness to violence against women of color are substantial and positive. As noted, a 16 percent increase in separate organization should be associated with an increase of .08 in women's movement strength. An increase of .05 (one standard deviation) in women's movement strength increases the likelihood of government response to violence against women of color by 40 percent (the change in predicted probability is .40). Thus, an increasing degree of separate organization likely has an important impact on government responsiveness.

To get a sense of the scale of this impact, we can analyze policy concerning women of color by using heteroskedasticity-robust standard errors. For the variable of women's movement strength, such an analysis yields a significant coefficient of 5.96 ± 1.18 (sig. = .000). Using this coefficient to calculate the indirect effect produces a coefficient of .03 ($5.96 \times .005$). An increase in the degree of separate organization of women of color from its minimum to its maximum value (16 percentage points), then, would result in an increase of about 50 percent in policy responsiveness ($16 \times .03 = .48$). Thus, separate organization by women of color likely has positive and important indirect effects on government responsiveness to violence against women of color.

Of course, this analysis examines association and so cannot rule out the possibility that the hypothesized causal order is reversed. It may be, for example, that a more favorable policy environment encourages more organizing by women, as they expect their efforts to have a greater effect. While this is certainly possible, previous research on policies on violence against women make this interpretation unlikely. Cross-national studies of policy development on violence against women find that women's organizing is an important catalyst for policy development and that policy development never temporally precedes women's independent efforts to draw attention to violence against women (Elman 1996; Weldon 2002a). This suggests that the association most likely reflects a causal relation in the hypothesized direction.

It is also possible that women are more likely to organize and protest when policy does not reflect their interests (Costain 1998). Of course, even if this were true, women's organizing would, in the long run, still tend to be associated with better policy outcomes, as I find here. Analysis of state policy development over time could sort out which of these interpretations best accounts for the associations revealed in this cross-sectional analysis. One thing, however, is certain: separate organizing is not associated with weaker or less effective women's movements.

As noted, some scholars argue that new organizations of dedicated subgroups are more likely to occur as a movement becomes stronger and more established. In other words, strength causes diversity, rather than vice versa. This analysis does not sort out the direction of causation. This seems to me to be a minor concern: the genesis of organizations dedicated to particular subgroups is likely more complex than simply reflecting strength—reflecting also environmental changes, external support or funding, longevity of the movement, and other well-established factors (Minkoff 1995; see Romanelli 1991 for a helpful review). Moreover, there are good theoretical reasons (already outlined) for thinking that diversity reinforces (rather than undermines) strength. Last, if diversity is a sign of strength, it hardly follows that diversity undermines movement effectiveness. Scholars must be careful not to interpret the proliferation of diverse organizations as evidence of "schism" or "fracture" in itself. I have argued that it is precisely when such organizations exist and advocate for their members within the movement that they will contribute most significantly to movement strength. The question of when and why activists organize more specific organizations within a movement is an interesting one for further research, but it is not the subject of this chapter.

Conclusion

Overall, then, this analysis suggests that separate organizing by women of color is associated with greater women's movement strength. A stronger movement, in turn, is associated with greater government responsiveness both to violence against women in general and to violence against women of color in particular. Thus, as the argument previously advanced suggests, organizing that focuses on women of color is indirectly associated with greater policy responsiveness to violence against women of color and women more generally. It is not at all evident that a greater degree of separate organizing reduces the ability of the movement to influence policy on important issues, as critics allege.

When organizing strategies recognize social divisions, social movements are strengthened. This may be because such organizing increases feelings of affiliation with the movement, revitalizes social movement organizations, and prevents a fatal foundering over internal divisions. In addition, separate organizing may generate new information about how problems are shaped by social relations, contributing to a better understanding of the issues around which the movement is organized. This lays the groundwork for sounder and more representative political analysis and policy agendas. Organizing to recognize difference also creates the possibility of forging alliances on specific issues.

This study also has some practical implications for those wishing to increase state government responsiveness to violence against women. Efforts to increase such responsiveness will likely be more successful if they are supported by a strong women's movement. Activists can maintain and build a strong women's movement by supporting the self-organization of women belonging to marginalized groups, both within and outside of existing organizations.

If the experience of women's movements across the 50 states can be applied to other social movements, then, this study suggests that not only the most vulnerable segments of society but social movements in general benefit from organizational mechanisms that recognize the marginalization of specific groups. If social movements provide an avenue for the representation of marginalized groups, separate organizing within such movements may provide an amplified voice for the most marginalized of social groups. This argument is clearly important for movements that claim to speak for specific solidary constituencies. However, it may also be important for movements that do not claim to represent particular groups, such as the environmental, antiglobalization, or peace movements. Such movements could also be strengthened through the organization of marginalized constituencies whose perspectives might otherwise be overlooked or silenced and whose participation broadens their constituencies. Thus, separate organizing of marginalized constituencies, which looks divisive to some observers, may in fact provide an avenue for strengthening social movements and making democratic policymaking more inclusive.

These conclusions may seem to conflict with the findings of earlier chapters that labor movements in general are unlikely to promote policies mainly affecting women workers or that women's movements appear to be less likely to address issues that are primarily class issues. Why would women's movements be effective at advancing the interests of women of color if labor movements are not effective at advancing the interests of women? The first thing to notice is that in examining labor policies, we did not disaggregate women's organizations into those that focused on working-class women and those that were more focused on elite women or women in general. Nor did we examine whether working-class women were separately organized within labor movements or within women's movements. Doing so might help us to figure out when women's movements or labor movements are more likely to respond to the working women's issues examined.

Second, these findings could suggest an even closer, iterative relationship between movement strength and inclusiveness. The women's movement in the United States is strong, while the labor movement is relatively weak. The stronger labor movement in Norway did a better job of advocating for paid leave, even championing "daddy leaves" that challenged gender roles. Women have more mechanisms of self-organization in the labor party and unions in Norway. Weaker movements tend to be less institutionalized and produce fewer opportunities for self-organization of marginalized groups. These marginalized groups may also feel that there is less benefit to trying to work within a weak movement.

Third, these findings might appear to be less of a puzzle if the nature of the policy issue examined is taken into account. Violence against women is an issue that affects all women (a universal or at least majority issue) (Strolovitch 2006). The elements of policy concerning violence against women that are focused on women of color affect a disadvantaged subgroup but do not challenge or conflict with the interests of the majority of women in any direct way. The issue of changing gender roles in the labor market, in contrast, challenges the interests of male workers in some way and requires behavioral change on the part of men. Similarly, women and men have different interests in relation to antidiscrimination legislation. So perhaps that is why unions and left parties appear to do a worse job of representing marginalized segments of their constituency (labor) than women's movements do here. This suggests that figuring out the relation between social movements, representation, and policy outcomes depends on a theorization of issue types not only in terms of whether they challenge existing gender roles (Gelb and Palley 1996) or otherwise require fundamental social transformation but also as to whether the majorities or minorities whose interests are primarily at stake are privileged or disadvantaged (Strolovitch 2006).

CHAPTER 5

Women's Movements, Representation, and Civil Society

WITH MAURA BAHU

How well do women's organizations represent women? So far in this book, I have joined others in arguing that civil society offers an important avenue for democratic representation, especially for marginalized groups such as women (Warren 2001; Strolovitch 2006; Skocpol 2003; Goodin 2003). I have shown that for women, workers, and women of color, vibrant, strong social movements are associated with greater policy responsiveness to their distinctive perspectives and concerns. But how exactly do movements exert these effects, and how representative are they in terms of speaking for all their constituents?

Women's movements influence public agendas and policy not only through direct efforts to affect the legislative process, such as lobbying, but also through indirect methods, such as seeking to change public opinion and raise awareness. One key way that women's movements do this is by attracting media attention and intervening in public debates to advance new concepts and ways of understanding old problems, to advance women's perspective (Young 2000; Mansbridge and Flaster 2007). Some scholars are skeptical about the potential of social movement organizations for representing women. Some worry about the inclusiveness of women's organizations, noting that such organizations seem to do a better job of representing privileged women than disadvantaged women (Strolovitch 2004, 2006). Some even question whether women *as women* can be represented at all (Butler 1993). Finally, some worry that large social movement organizations, remote from their "constituencies," are replacing small participatory groups and traditional federations of groups, raising concerns about accountability (Skocpol 1999, 2003; Putnam 2000).

Most of the evidence presented so far in this book has shown associations between policy outcomes and numbers or strength of women's organizations, strength of unions, or other larger-scale measures. In this chapter, I seek to provide some evidence that women's movements do intervene in the public sphere, as I have claimed, and that they provide a particularly effective avenue of representation for marginalized women. How effective is the set of women's organizations at advancing women's perspectives in the public sphere? Are women differentially represented by this system of organizations? Many studies of women's organizations focus on individual organizations or a particular type of women's organization (e.g., pro-choice organizations), but few examine the system of all women's organizations as a set, asking what role they collectively play in democratic politics.[1] Even fewer examine these organizations at a local level, where informal, participatory organizations are more likely to be found. We need to know more about the composition of the system of women's organizations and how effective these organizations are at attracting public attention to policy issues of importance for women.[2]

This chapter examines the efforts of women's organizations to influence public discussion on policy issues at a local level, examining the set of local women's organizations in Chicago. The chapter explores the sorts of groups that comprise this set and the relationship they seem to have to the public sphere. What policy issues do they raise, and to what effect? Examining the coverage of these issues in the local press, the chapter concludes by drawing out the theoretical implications for studies of women's representation.

Women's Organizations, Civil Society, and Representation

This book argues that social movements substantively represent women better than political parties or descriptive representation in the legislature. The evidence presented so far focuses on the impact of these movements on policy. This section focuses more on the other side of the representative relationship, the relationship between the movement and the constituency. Specifically, are women's organizations more accessible to marginalized groups of women (e.g., poor women and women of color) than are traditional avenues of legislative representation? Do they advocate for these groups or mainly or primarily for privileged subgroups of women? This chapter examines whether the set of women's organizations in Chicago is indeed more accessible to marginalized women than formal avenues of participation and whether the set of organizations identifies and acts on issues of importance to disadvantaged subgroups. It also asks how effective these groups are in diffusing women's perspective in the public sphere (focusing here on print media).

It is not the argument of this chapter that all women are equally well represented by women's groups or movements. Indeed, increasingly, research is documenting the ways that multiply disadvantaged people are left out of the organizations aimed at broader groups: women, people of color, the poor (Strolovitch 2006; Cohen 1999; Crenshaw 1994). But to say that the members of marginalized groups are differentially represented is not to say that such groups are not represented at all. Indeed, all mechanisms of representation exhibit this pattern of being more accessible to privileged subgroups. Providing some political representation for women does not require that all women are served equally well by these organizations. Indeed, it is most likely that, like other civil society organizations, women's organizations do a better job of representing privileged women than disadvantaged women. But one still might expect that women's organizations, because of their greater accessibility, do a better job of representing marginalized women than electoral avenues.

EVALUATING WOMEN'S REPRESENTATION BY WOMEN'S ORGANIZATIONS

How well do women's organizations represent women? This discussion suggests there are several aspects of the representative relationship that can be explored. The first aspect is how well the set of organizations reflects the composition and views of the constituency of women. If the set of organizations represents a broad diversity of women, this would constitute good representation. If some women seem excluded or marginalized by these organizations, those women are less well represented by these organizations. One can ask: How many organizations focus on women in general? How many groups focus on particular subgroups? Which subgroups are the focus of particular organizations? Which are not? One can compare the composition of the set of organizations to the population. One can also compare this set of organizations to traditional modes of representation, such as electoral representation.

One can also ask about the substantive issues that the groups say they are working on. What do women's organizations say they are doing? Are these groups actually trying to represent women, to give them a voice? How well do they perform this goal? Are issues of concern to poor women, women of color, and other marginalized groups of women taking a backseat to issues of concern to privileged majorities? The literature suggests that this set of organizations will likely systematically overrepresent privileged women (e.g., business women and professionals), giving disproportionate attention to their concerns. It also suggests that this set of organizations should be a better mechanism for the articulation of women's shared concerns than electoral representation or traditional interest groups.

A second aspect of representation involves how effective or influential these groups are in attracting public attention to the issues that concern their constituents. Do these groups try to obtain public attention for these issues? What do they do? Does it work? Why or why not? We can start to examine this question by looking at press coverage of the activities of women's organizations. In the mainstream media, issues of importance to the broader public are examined independently of government. Sometimes these issues are taken up by government officials, absorbed into the government agenda; sometimes they are not (Kingdon 1984; Jones and Baumgartner 2005). So the mainstream press is a good approximation of a dominant public sphere. If women's groups figure prominently in the press and if the issues they raise receive extensive press coverage, we can conclude that women's organizations are very effective in bringing policy issues to public attention. If these issues receive little coverage and if women's organizations are largely ignored, we can conclude that this public sphere is relatively closed to women. How open is this public sphere to women's organizations? How are women's organizations portrayed in the media? Does the media cover the issues that are important to these groups? What is the quality and extent of this coverage? What role do women's groups play in the development of this coverage? This chapter begins to answer some of these questions.

Women's Organizations in Chicago

As noted, few studies have examined whether women are well represented by the *set* of organizations that purport to represent them. Some studies examine women's direct efforts to influence public policy through lobbying. But many scholars have argued that the most important effects of social movements may be indirect (Staggenborg 1995; Katzenstein 1995, 1998; Rochon and Mazmanian 1993). Social movements change people's minds and ideas through discursive engagement in the public sphere. Through cultural productions, protest, and the like, movements influence public discussion of issues, interpreting key events and putting women's issues on the table. These more diffuse effects are more difficult to pin down empirically. We know that membership in particular women's organizations and the number of women's organizations of a particular type seem to be associated with better policy outcomes for women. But we are less sure of the mechanism of such influence.

To examine these questions, one needs to compare discussion of women's issues in some public forum (say, the media) with the efforts of women's movements to influence that discussion. But detailed data on voluntary organizations is very difficult to get, especially if one is interested in local or social movement organizations (as opposed to registered, lobbying-oriented national groups). Lists of organizations are easy to come by, but such lists rarely provide details about the organizations apart from some contact information. By their very nature, local organizations in social movements are informal, shoestring operations and are fleeting. Finding information about which organizations are actually in existence and what they actually do is difficult.

Previous scholarship has documented the wide variety of forms that individual organizations take. Indeed, many excellent case studies focus on individual organizations or on particular types of women's organizations, documenting the structure of these organizations and how they engage with the state (e.g., Barakso 2004). But few studies examine the *set* of women's organizations as a mechanism for representing women, taking these organizations as a collectivity. But this is what is suggested by the theoretical debate about women's movements and about civil society in general. The argument is not about the potential or demise of individual organizations but, rather, about the composition and impact of these organizations as a set.

Much of the research on social capital, civil society, and women's movements, especially research that examines their impact on public policy, is at a national or state level (Caiazza and Putnam 2004; Weldon 2004; Howell and Mulligan 2005). Since voluntary associations such as women's organizations are so hard to track, this means that this larger debate has been based on data that likely overestimates the prevalence of big national organizations and underdocuments the existence of smaller local organizations. For these reasons, we chose to first try to examine the set of women's organizations in a local context, women's organizations based in and around Chicago. We chose this area for a variety of reasons. Chicago is a large metropolitan area with an active women's movement. In terms of examining efforts to influence public discourse, Chicago has more than one major local paper (with varying political ideologies) in which it would be possible to examine the coverage of women's movement activities.

What do women's movement organizations and activists in Chicago do? There is not a women's newspaper or other database documenting women's movement activity in Chicago against which to compare media coverage. To obtain information on which women's organizations exist and what they do, we tried to go directly to the organizations themselves—as opposed to relying on *New York Times* coverage or the like, which assumes that media coverage accurately reflects what movements do (Earl et al. 2004). We found several lists of women's organizations in Chicago, but many of these organizations seemed to have ceased to exist. Based on that research, we believe we have a fairly accurate and current list of active women's organizations in Chicago.[3] Based on that list, we did a survey of all the women's organizations that were active in Chicago from 2003 to 2005. Our survey asked organizations about what they thought the purpose of their organization was and how influencing public discussion of policy issues fit into those priorities. We asked if they ever sought to influence policy-making on particular issues and what those issues were. We asked them if they ever sought to obtain media coverage for the issues that were important to them and, if so, what they did to obtain it (see the appendix for the text of the questions).

Efforts to attract the attention of the media are efforts to intervene in the broader, dominant public sphere on behalf of women. How effective were these organizations at intervening in the public sphere? The responses to our survey provide a list of public policy issues that organizations claimed were important and for which they claimed to be seeking media coverage. The two major Chicago newspapers were searched for mentions of these issues, to see if women's organizations were effective in generating media coverage. The analysis examines what kind of coverage was generated and which women's organizations were sought out as sources in these stories.

NUMBER OF ORGANIZATIONS

By combining a number of different lists of women's organizations, we identified 147 distinct organizations. Of these, about 77 likely did not exist (their phone was disconnected or no longer listed). This suggests that there are about 70 active women's organizations in the Chicago area as of 2004 (table 11). All of these organizations were contacted by phone and e-mail. Of those contacted, 23 organizations completed the survey. Some of those contacted did not return calls or respond to requests. Some indicated they did not have time to complete a survey, and one or two claimed that they were not "women's organizations" (e.g., one pro-life organization rejected this characterization).

This rate of response may seem low by some standards (e.g., Babbie 2001), but recent research suggests that response rates in the 30 percent range may produce results that are not significantly different from those in the 60 percent range (Keeter et al. 2000). Survey researchers in general have become accustomed to using surveys with much lower response rates than was traditionally thought to be acceptable, as the high response rates of years gone by seem less and less attainable (even for big surveys like the American National Election Study). The key issue with lower response rates is nonresponse bias. But low response rates do not necessarily reflect a significant bias, and a theoretical argument about the specific impact of nonresponse bias on the results must be made. In this case, the concern might be that those with fewer resources have less ability to respond to the survey. Because the study started by gathering data on the population of organizations, the analysis can compare our survey group with known population characteristics. This comparison alleviates this concern to some degree: it appears that groups representing working-class women and women of minority race/ethnicity are at least as well represented in the survey respondents as they are in the population at large (table 11). Indeed, Keeter and others (2000) find that efforts to improve response rates seem to result in the overrepresentation of those most likely to respond in the first place (better-educated, well-off respondents).

ORGANIZATIONAL PURPOSE

The main purposes listed by these organizations were empowering women, advancing women's status, and representing women or giving women a voice. Providing socializing opportunities for women was least important. Most (70 percent) of these organizations aimed to represent women, and most aimed to influence public policy. Most organizations sought to obtain media coverage for their activities as a way of influencing public policy discussions of issues

TABLE 11. Women's Organization in Chicago Surveyed, Judged Active, or Listed in All Sources, by Type, 2004

Focus	% Surveyed ($n = 23$)	% Active ($n = 70$)	% Listed in All Sources ($n = 147$)
Occupational/Trade associations	35	26	21
Minority and other underrepresented women	18	18	13
Women's health	5	9	8
Reproductive rights	0	6	5
Violence against women	14	10	6
Women's poverty	9	4	3
Women's equality generally	5	12	6
Academics	5	6	11
Other	9	9	11
Not sure	0	0	16

Source: Women of Color Resource Center 2003; National Council for Research on Women 2004; Chicago NOW 2008; Rexroat 2003.

important to them. Most felt that media coverage of these issues was inadequate. They cited gender bias, compassion fatigue, complexity of the issue, and inadequate "sexiness" of women's issues as reasons for the lack of attention to the issues. Those who felt that their issues were sensational enough (e.g., those working on violence against women) felt that media coverage was unsympathetic to women (e.g., "blaming the victim").

The vast majority of these organizations worked with other organizations on particular issues or concerns (only one said they did not). These partner organizations included a wide range of organizations—both women's organizations and non-gender-focused organizations, national and state organizations focusing on their issue or concern, and other local mainstream organizations (like the chamber of commerce or media reform organizations). This suggests that these organizations may also exert influence through these other partner organizations (Staggenborg 1995).

SUBSTANTIVE ORGANIZATIONAL FOCUS

These organizations focused on a wide variety of issues, ranging from representing particular occupational groups of women to advocating for women's health to providing services for divorced or imprisoned women (table 11). The surveyed organizations appear to be fairly representative of the population of organizations in most respects, based on evidence from the total list of organizations.

How many of these organizations focused primarily on the issues confronting women of color, that is, women of marginalized race or ethnicity? The last chapter argued that separate organization by women of color helps to highlight concerns and perspectives that such women do not have in common with white women. Chicago is a diverse city, with large African American and Hispanic communities: in the city proper, only about one-third of residents are non-Hispanic whites (Bureau of the Census 2000a). Of the respondent organizations, 2 of 23 (8 percent) organize women of marginalized race or ethnicity, about the same as the proportion for the whole population of active organizations (4 of 70, 6 percent). In terms of direct organizational focus, women of marginalized race and ethnicity are underrepresented by this set of organizations, with only a few organizations associated with specific communities (Hispanic women, Jewish women, African American women, and Korean businesswomen, although this latter organization may no longer be active).

It might seem as if this is why this set of organizations places sex equality ahead of race discrimination in determining priorities (table 12). Substantively, the issue of race discrimination on average was seen as of middling importance (between "very important" and "somewhat important"). On closer inspection, however, this seems problematic as an explanation: even organizations of women of color themselves did not identify race discrimination as being of the highest priority; they listed women's health, work and family issues, and women's poverty ahead of race discrimination. In retrospect, referring to "racial equality" rather than "racial discrimination" might have been a better phrasing to capture issues confronting people of color. However, the overriding salience of economic inequality in Chicago may be influencing the outcome here for both women's organizations in general and organizations of women of color.[4]

Interestingly, economic issues dominate the agenda of these organizations. Of the five issues ranked most important by women's organizations, work, poverty, and economic equality figured prominently. In her national survey of interest groups, Strolovitch (2004) found that women's organizations placed more emphasis on majority issues (she used violence against women as an example) than they did on issues confronting marginalized subgroups of women, such as poor women (she used welfare reform as an example). This analysis finds that this group of women's organizations ranks poverty as equally important as violence against women and places a great deal of emphasis on economic equality more generally. This is especially interesting since more organizations said they focused primarily on violence against women rather than women's poverty (table 11).

TABLE 12. Importance of Issues to Women's Organizations

Issue	Average Ranking
Economic equality	1.957
Sexual equality	2.087
Violence against women	2.261
Women's poverty	2.261
Work and family	2.348
Race discrimination	2.391
Women's health	2.478
Reproductive rights	2.957
Elderly women	2.957
Gay rights	3.348

Source: Author's analysis of original survey data.

Note: 1 = most important; 2 = very important; 3 = somewhat important; 4 = not important at all. Lower scores reflect greater importance.

Several organizations focus on other subgroups of women. One organization (the Older Women's League) focuses on older women. Census data indicates that about 10 percent of women in Chicago are older women. The set of organizations ranked older women's issues among the least important issues. The organizations we surveyed found gay rights to be the least important issue of those we asked about (see the list in the appended survey). Of course, in our survey, there were not any organizations focusing on gay women. In the overall set of organizations, we estimate that three to five organizations focus on lesbian issues. There were not any organizations focused on disabled women in our survey, nor were there any in the broader set of organizations.

Many organizations focus on business and professional women, with such organizations comprising about one-quarter of our survey group and about a third of the active organizations overall. Half as many organizations focused on poor and working-class women. Only two organizations focused on poor women, and one focused on tradeswomen. Professional workers, then, are well represented by the organizational focus of these groups, while women who are not working or who work outside of business and professional settings are underrepresented: business and professional workers comprise about 30 percent of all workers and 40 percent of women working full-time for wages and salaries (Bureau of the Census 2000a, 2000b; U.S Department of Labor 2004). This is consistent with existing research on civil society.

Since business and professional women are well represented by this set of organizations and since it appears that nonprofessional women are less represented by these organizations, we might expect that this set of organizations would not represent the interests of poor women well. But women's poverty is viewed as one of the most important issues by women's organizations. This may be because in addition to women's organizations focusing on the homeless, poor, or working-class women, organizations that aim to help incarcerated women, abused women, or divorced women see that women's poverty is an important part of dealing with each of these phenomena.

Mansbridge (2003) argues that representatives sometimes see themselves as representing a broader constituency than their mandate strictly provides, calling this *surrogate representation.* Perhaps these organizations provide such representation for poor women. Such representation may be better than no representation, but it may still be a "second-best" solution. There are good reasons to think that people are the best advocates for their own interests (Mill [1861] 1926; Pitkin 1967) and that the disadvantaged are more effective and interested than the economically advantaged in advocating for their own interests (Schlozman et al. 1999, 443). In addition, the absence of lesbian rights organizations from the survey may be the reason that such little importance is attached to gay rights by the overall set of organizations, which would support those that emphasize the importance of autonomous self-organization for advancing the perspectives of intersectionally marginalized groups.

Still, the fact that women's organizations as a whole rank women's poverty (a disadvantaged minority issue) as equally important as violence against women (a majority or universal issue) somewhat undermines the claim that women's organizations provide better representation for majority issues than minority ones, although the difference may be in the level of analysis (movement or set of organizations versus individual organizations). It certainly undermines the criticism that women-specific organizing or the women's movement in general is overly focused on "identity politics," on symbolic or cultural issues, rather than on material inequalities.

COMPARISON TO ELECTORAL REPRESENTATION

Even if this set of organizations underrepresents marginalized subgroups of women, it may provide more representation than traditional, electoral forms of representation, both descriptively and organizationally, especially for marginalized groups of women such as economically disadvantaged women or women of color. Finding the right electoral body for comparison to the local set of women's organizations can be tricky, since women's organizations engage national, state, and local issues. Some of the Chicago organizations are national in scope, others are local chapters of national organizations, and still others have a statewide or local focus.

Descriptive Representation. In terms of descriptive representation, women's movements do as well or better as local, state, or national avenues for representation for marginalized groups of women (table 13). Nationally, in 2004–5, women held only 14 percent of the seats in the Senate and 15 percent of the seats in the House, and there were no African American women in the Senate at all (although the only African American senator at the time, Barack Obama, was elected from Illinois). Women of color held 3.5 percent of overall congressional seats; 24 percent of all women holding seats were women of color (CAWP 2005b).

As in many other states, women have more of a presence in state and local elected office, but even here, women are still underrepresented. In Illinois, for example, women comprise less than a third of the state legislature, and women of color constitute about 8 percent of the state legislature (CAWP 2005a, 2005b; COWL 2008a; Illinois General Assembly 2008).[5] White women have held leadership positions in the state legislature, including majority leader in both House and Senate, lieutenant governor, and attorney general (COWL 2008a). Women of marginalized race and ethnicity have had less prominence: for example, the first Hispanic woman to be elected to the Illinois House was elected in 1997, and the first Hispanic woman was elected to the Illinois Senate as late as 2003 (COWL 2008b).

City governance would be the closest and most accessible to women in the local area. Here, too, although women are better represented in descriptive terms, they are still lacking an adequate presence. In terms of municipal government, white men are the majority in the main decision-making bodies. Of Chicago City Council members, 18 (36 percent) are women and 12 (24 percent) are women of color. Of the council's 19 committees, 5 (just under 20 percent) are headed by women. There are no official committees on women's affairs or focused on any other marginalized groups.[6]

The survey did not ask about the descriptive composition of organizations, but other data suggest that women's organizations in Chicago are at least as inclusive as elected bodies in terms of sheer numbers or descriptive representation. Looking at Web-based materials for the 22 organizations in the survey, the leadership is 97 percent female (one coleader is a man), and at least 32 percent of the leaders of these organizations are women of color. In addition to the organizations directly focusing on women of color, many other organizations include significant representation of women of color. The Older Women's League has a chapter in Chicago's South Side (Southeast Chapter) that is specifically identified as an "African American chapter"; and not only does Family Rescue report that African American women comprise a majority of their membership, but the organization is also led by women of color (Family Rescue 2007).

TABLE 13. Descriptive Representation in Women's Organization Leadership and National, State, and Local Electoral Office (2004–5)

	Women's Organizations Leadership (%)	Chicago City Council (%)	Illinois State Legislature (%)	National (Congress) (%)
Proportion women	97	36	26	14
Proportion women of color	32	24	8	3.5

Organizational Focus. Most important, however, are the substantive differences in focus between these electoral bodies and the set of women's organizations. The electoral bodies lack an institutional or organizational mechanism (as opposed to an individual) for articulating women's perspective, especially when it comes to women of color. I have argued that self-organization as women is important to the development of the distinctive perspectives of women and women of color. This argument links organizational form to substantive representation.

Although the overall state legislature or city council does not focus on women, there can be legislative caucuses. In fact, there is a women's caucus in Illinois, the Conference of Women Legislators (COWL). The conference is led by cochairs (one from each major party), both of whom are white women. COWL focuses on legislative issues concerning the welfare and advancement of women, children, and families and has won awards for its work on domestic violence, mental health, human rights, and early childhood education. The conference focuses mostly on economic issues facing family and women. COWL meets periodically with the governor to give the governor women's "perspective," although the conference does not take positions on particular policy issues. COWL serves mainly as an arena for coordination and information exchange among women legislators of different parties and does not itself publicly advance particular positions on public policy issues. There are no formal organizations of legislators focused on particular subgroups of women, such as women of color (although there are separate legislative caucuses for blacks and Latinos). Similarly, there is a women's caucus, a black caucus, and a "progressive" caucus at the national level, but there is no organization focusing specifically on women of color (interview with an Illinois state government official, 2008; COWL 2008a). At the city level, there are no formal organizations (committees or caucuses) focusing on either women or women of color.

Among the women's organizations, however, there are specific organizations focusing on and advocating for the distinctive concerns of women of color and poor women. In addition, those organizations that focus on women in general (e.g., the Chicago chapter of NOW) often have dedicated committees and engage in special projects and partnerships designed to further the interests of marginalized groups of women (Chicago NOW 2008). This is true even for organizations such as the Chicago chapter of the National Association of Women Business Owners (NAWBO): even this organization has a diversity committee and uses Black History Month and Women's History Month to highlight the accomplishments of African American businesswomen

(NAWBO (Chicago Area) 2006, 2008). No such organizations or coalitions focused on women of color coordinate elected representatives locally, statewide, or nationally.

Regarding descriptive representation, women and women of color do as well or better in terms of their presence in women's organization leadership compared to legislative presence. In terms of organizational focus, there are some organizations internal to the legislature (caucuses) that seek to represent women and other marginalized groups, but there are no organizations that focus specifically on disadvantaged groups of women. In the case of the state caucus, there is no explicit focus or agenda that highlights the concerns of marginalized women, unlike the more general women's groups outside the legislature.

This discussion suggests that women's organizations champion a wide set of issues of concern for women and that they are at least as accessible and representative (if not more so in the case of women of color) as electoral avenues of representation in descriptive terms. But does this presence of women and this organizational focus on women and women of color translate into effective representation in terms of influence on public debate? Previous chapters have shown an association between more-developed women's movements and better policies for women and have hypothesized that one major mechanism for policy change is extralegislative: women's movement activists and organizations articulate women's perspective in the public sphere, in public debate over policy issues. Women's movements introduce concepts and perspectives that would not otherwise be recognized (Mansbridge and Flaster 2007). Do these organizations affect public debate on policy issues of concern to women?

Press Coverage of Women's Policy Issues in Chicago

Are women's organizations successful in their efforts to procure attention for the issues they hold as most important? Do they have a presence in the media? Out of the 23 respondent organizations, only 5 organizations said they did not ever try to increase media coverage of women's policy issues. The majority (78 percent) of the organizations that do try to increase media coverage reported using a wide variety of methods to attract media attention, including sending out press releases, organizing protests, contacting journalists, and giving interviews (table 14).[7]

We examined newspaper coverage of the top four issues that the women's organizations collectively ranked as most important, looking for evidence of the organizations' influence on the news and comparing coverage of these issues with coverage of other selected policy issues (table 15). We searched electronically for those issues in both the *Chicago Tribune* and the *Chicago Sun-Times,* using multiple search terms. Each of these issues was mentioned in a roughly comparable number of stories over two years. The issue of women's poverty yielded the highest number of articles, producing 54 articles over two years, while the issue of economic equality for women was mentioned in 38 articles. Compared to other pressing policy issues of the day, this seems like a relatively small number of stories. For example, there were nearly ten times as many stories on social security in the *Chicago Tribune* as there were on violence against women in the same year. Even global warming and monetary policy—topics some might think of as "unsexy," technical, or dry—generated more stories in Chicago newspapers than the most-covered women's rights issue (table 15). Monetary policy attracted more press coverage than either violence against women or reparations. Perhaps marginalized communities have a harder time getting press attention for their issues than mainstream groups, regardless of the technical or controversial nature of the topic.[8]

TABLE 14. Methods of Increasing Media Coverage

Method	Organizations Using This Method ($n = 18$)
Press releases	16 (89%)
Protest/Demonstration	9 (50%)
Providing information	14 (78%)
Interviews	15 (83%)
Contacting journalists	10 (59%)
Other methods	5 (31%)

Source: Author's analysis of original survey data.

TABLE 15. Coverage of Selected Policy Issues in Chicago Newspapers, 2003–4

	Chicago Tribune	*Chicago Sun-Times*
Economic equality	28	10
Sexual equality	34	13
Violence against women	30	13
Poverty	36	18
Global warming	124	112
Reparations	24	49
Social security	298	290
Monetary policy	34	62

Source: Author's analysis of news stories.

In terms of quality, the policy issue that received the most substantive coverage in the Chicago papers was economic equality. These stories mainly discussed a state government initiative to introduce equal pay. Take, for example, the coverage of the pay equity bill that Illinois governor Rod Blagojevich had just signed. Both the *Tribune* and the *Sun-Times* had multiple articles covering the passing of this bill. A local organization was featured in the coverage, and that local organization (Women Employed) did a great deal of work to promote this piece of legislation. The articles also relied heavily on government sources, such as Governor Blagojevich and spokespeople from the Illinois Department of Labor or the Equal Employment Opportunity Commission.

Many of the articles in the Chicago papers were not such well-sourced pieces of policy analysis. In fact, more than a third of the total mentions of these policy issues occurred in the context of book and movie reviews.[9] In addition, there is an overrepresentation of conservative women's organizations in the print coverage. The large national conservative organizations (Concerned Women for America, Second Amendment Sisters, the Women's Christian Temperance Union, the National Right to Life Committee) are mentioned as often as the largest national feminist organizations, despite their smaller numbers and membership. Particularly in the *Chicago Tribune,* it seems a wider range of conservative organizations are mentioned. Thus, especially if Berry (1999) is right that conservative organizations are generally given less coverage in the news media, this overrepresentation of conservative organizations is surprising.

Are women's organizations able to represent women in this print medium, giving women's perspective, as part of a broader story on a policy issue? In all the stories on the four issues studied here, there were 293 sources cited. Nearly a third (30 percent) of these sources were women's movement organizations and activists, suggesting a considerable presence in the print media (table 16). Women's movement organizations and activists were cited as sources more frequently than government spokespeople (26 percent) or academics (16 percent), both considered high-quality, official sources by journalists. National organizations are cited very slightly more often than local organizations and chapters. But women's organizations are clearly effective in their efforts to participate in print discussions of the policy issues they deem most important.

Women's organizations emphasize the gender dimensions of policy issues. A *Chicago Tribune* article on poverty turns to discuss the growing ranks of women and children among the poor, citing a senior policy analyst for the National Women's Law Center in Washington, DC. A *Tribune* article focused on the Older Women's League is entirely focused on issues confronting elderly women and cites the local chapter of the league in highlighting issues confronting African American elderly women. An article explaining new legislative provisions to protect victims of domestic abuse from losing their jobs if they take leave to address the abuse includes interviews with the National Center on Poverty Law as well as the Chicago chapter of NOW. The interviewees provide explanations for why the law is needed, explaining that leaves are needed not only because of the health effects of abuse but also so that women may take the legal steps necessary to obtain protection.

The organizations cited in this coverage are not necessarily representative of all the local organizations that are active on a particular issue, since not all local organizations are cited in the print coverage. Still, local and national feminist organizations have a strong presence in the print media. Nine different local organizations were mentioned (one of which was a pro-life group), and nine different national organizations were mentioned (with NOW being the national women's organization most frequently cited). References to national organizations were evenly divided between feminist and antifeminist, conservative organizations, with one mention to an organization that was neither (a national association of nuns).

Even with national organizations, women's movement organizations likely offer avenues to representation that are more open to the presence of marginalized groups of women. For example, NOW (one of the most frequently cited national organizations) has developed organizational norms and laws that aim at greater inclusiveness (Barakso 2005). Nationally, one-third of the board of

TABLE 16. Distribution of Sources by Type

Academics	48 (16%)
Government officials/employees	74 (26%)
National women's organizations	35 (12%)
Local women's organizations	18 (6%)
Local chapter of national women's organizations	22 (8%)
National women's organization based in Chicago	1 (0%)
Feminists/Activists	12 (4%)
Local citizen (no organizational connection)	34 (12%)
Other	48 (16%)
Can't be ascertained	1 (0%)
Total	293

Note: "Other" includes, for example, lawyers who were asked to speak about the legality of women's policy issues and, in the case of stories about Title IX, a wrestling coach who was challenging Title IX and was cited often in a number of the stories.

NOW is comprised of women of color, and there are a wide range of caucuses and working groups focusing on issues of importance to marginalized subgroups of women. As Barakso (2005, 333) notes, "Its [NOW's] bylaws call for a minimum number of board seats in each region to be reserved for racial and ethnic minority representation and NOW also requires chapters to implement affirmative action plans. The organization subsidizes major gatherings of women of color, young women, lesbians, and poor women and actively seeks coalition with other groups representing these women. It also maintains a nominal membership fee for those with low or no income." Women of color are represented at the highest levels of leadership, including executive vice president (Barakso 2005; see also Barakso 2004).

Evidence for Hollowing Out, Outsourcing, and Diminished Participation?

As noted, some scholars have voiced concerns about a "hollowing out" of associational life and have argued that the replacement of local, more participatory organizations with large, national bureaucratic ones bodes ill for the continued vibrancy of our civil society. While this chapter has not examined trends over time and offers only a snapshot of women's organizations in one location, it does suggest that these concerns may be overdrawn. First, there appears to be a vibrant set of organizations, and more than half of them (40 of 77) are local (citywide or statewide) organizations or local chapters of national organizations. Others are national organizations based in Chicago (e.g., National Hook-up of Black Women). So the organizations spawned by the women's movement, at least in the Chicago area, are not just large, national "checkbook organizations," distant from the everyday lives of citizens. Nor is the professionalization or outsourcing of protest ubiquitous: for example, the staff of Chicago NOW is all volunteer. Photo spreads and newsletters on the Web sites of these organizations provide ample evidence of social gatherings, awards banquets, lectures and panel discussions, fund-raisers, committees and working groups, and a wide variety of other participatory activities. Last, these organizations frequently partner with each other and with other, non-women-focused organizations, to raise awareness of issues they care about.

The set of organizations in Chicago is a mix of local, state, and national organizations (and their chapters) that cover a range of foci, from networking for women publishers to women's choirs to empowering Latina lesbians. This variety in form and purpose is good, as some of these organizations are likely more effective in influencing public policy, others focus more on attracting media attention, and still others work on building social networks among women. One cross-state study (Weldon 2004) found that explicitly political organizations (as opposed to bridge clubs) had the largest direct effects on public policy but that more socially or culturally oriented organizations may help to build the counterpublics in which new ideas and perspectives can be developed. These ideas may circulate through the women's activist network as organizations work together. So even if some organizations are more locally focused and participatory and others are more professionalized, links between these types of organizations may mitigate some concerns about the alienation of citizens from large social movement organizations.

Conclusion

This chapter began with the question of how well the set of women's organizations in Chicago represented women in the public sphere, considering two key aspects of this question. First, are women differentially represented by this system of organizations? Second, how effective is the *set* of women's organizations at advancing women's perspectives in the public sphere?

The analysis suggests that women's movement organizations likely do represent privileged women (e.g., professional women) better than they do more disadvantaged women. But these organizations still represent marginalized groups of women, such as poor women, women of marginalized race and ethnicity, and lesbian women. Indeed, it seems that women's organizations are an important place where women of color and poor women find organizations and committees dedicated to their distinctive concerns and perspectives. Electoral mechanisms of representation in Chicago, Illinois, and nationally in the United States offer no formal organizational mechanisms (e.g., dedicated committees or caucuses) to advance the concerns of women of color or poor women, and marginalized women are as well or better represented in descriptive terms in the leadership of these organizations as they are in electoral contexts.

Dedicated organizations and descriptive representation are critical for the articulation of marginalized group perspectives in social movements. Women's organizations offer a site for such processes of representation—and not just for privileged women. In Chicago, there is a vibrant set of national, state, and local organizations that aim to represent women, and they work together on many issues. More general women's organizations (e.g., NOW) partner with organizations working for particular groups of women or on particular issues. This suggests that we should think of these organizations as embedded in a network or system, instead of as individual organizations, which greatly increases their capacity for information sharing and coordination. Women's organizations are not only portrayed in the print media as representatives of women; they see themselves as representing women (although they also have other aims, such as empowering women and advancing women's status). They report working on a wide array of issues, and in Chicago at least, they place as much or more importance on issues such as poverty and economic equality as they do on violence against women, sexual equality, and other issues that would seem to be of concern to a majority of women, if not all women.

On the second aspect of the question with which this chapter began, whether women's organizations are successful in inserting women's concerns in the public sphere, the analysis of print media suggests that they are. Women's organizations seem to be cited as much or more than those sources (government, academics) that journalistic norms treat as most authoritative. They offer insight into the diversity of women's lives and experiences and help to explain the importance of public policy issues for women's lives. Both national and local organizations are active and effective in this regard, and although conservative organizations seem to have an edge in attracting media attention, feminist groups also get substantial access.

Women's organizations as a set, then, better represent some privileged groups of women than they do marginalized subgroups of women, as expected. Interestingly, though, the substantive impact of this representation on the policy advocacy of women's groups may not be as dramatic as one might think. For example, although women of privileged classes clearly have many more organizational resources, issues confronting poor and working-class women were named as priorities by these organizations. In addition, despite the many differences among the women represented by these organizations, they shared many organizational and substantive goals, such as empowering women, advancing women's status, and pursuing economic equality. Finally, these organizations seem to play a unique role in providing space for marginalized subgroups of women to organize and articulate their distinctive perspectives. Thus, despite their imperfections, women's organizations provide a critical representative function, especially for the most marginalized women.

CHAPTER 6

The Advocacy State

Do social movements offer a pathway to a more inclusive democracy or toward a more polarized, fragmented, elite-dominated polity? In this conclusion, I argue that social movements do more to deepen democracy than to divide democratic publics. Indeed, under some conditions, states ought to actively support the development of social movements as a way of creating a more inclusive polity. Let me show how the research presented so far illuminates those conditions. I will also argue that a social-structural and intersectional approach reveals fundamental and otherwise obscured aspects of politics and policy. I then turn to illuminating the policy implications of this argument, drawing on concrete examples from Canada and the United States.

Favorable Conditions for Social Movement Representation

The research presented thus far suggests that social movements are the most effective avenues of representation (more influential than political parties or intralegislative descriptive representation) under the following conditions: (1) when the social group is a systematically disadvantaged one, (2) when the group is not recognized or organized through an existing institutional mechanism (e.g., an ethnic or labor party), and (3) when the policy or state action in question requires or promotes social transformation.

TYPES OF DISADVANTAGED GROUP

This research has focused on the representation of systematically disadvantaged groups (as opposed to those that are temporarily disadvantaged or disadvantaged in negligible and/or isolated ways). Recall that by referring to "systematically disadvantaged groups," I here mean social groups that have historically been subject to discrimination and continue to suffer objectively demonstrable disadvantage in multiple spheres (social, economic, political) and to whom negative meanings are ascribed by the broader society and culture (Williams 1998). Group membership is experienced as objective and immutable (Williams 1998; Young 1990, 2000). This conceptualization includes groups defined by gender, race, ethnicity, and sexuality, among other dimensions. Although class, religion, and citizenship may not seem like such immutable characteristics, they are often experienced as such by the members of such groups. Williams (1998) demonstrates that in the United States, women and African Americans are marginalized groups. In the previous chapters, I have shown that for women, women of color, and workers, civil society avenues of representation such as social movements are the best routes to policy influence. In this regard, I do not compare women to men or people of color to whites. It is possible that social movements are the best avenue of representation for everyone. But I have shown here that at least for some disadvantaged groups (women, workers, women workers, women of color), social movements offer the best avenue of representation.

An examination of policies on violence against women cross-nationally and across the U.S. states reveals that women's movements are critical to sparking policy action in this critical area of women's rights. For women of color, separate organization as part of broader social movements seems the most effective avenue of policy influence, at least in the area of violence against women. Such representation is more effective than increasing numbers of women or women of color in elective office.

Such separate organization of women or women of color does not appear to fragment or weaken social movements or to distract from material issues such as economic inequality or welfare reform. As the study of the U.S. states shows, women's movement organizations are an important source of pressure for policy development addressing women's economic concerns, for policies related to unemployment insurance, minimum wage, child care spending, and the like. Moreover, at least in the case of Chicago, it seems that even organizations focusing on what may not at first blush appear to be economic issues (domestic violence, divorced women) do make material well-being a priority. Women's organizations work as a network to achieve policy influence both through direct efforts, such as lobbying, and through indirect efforts, such as mobilizing women and raising the awareness of the general public about gender issues.

Social movements are especially important for those groups for whom group membership is more fluid at the individual level, such as class or immigration status. Although descriptive representation is not completely ineffective for such groups, the greater mutability of group membership does pose some problems. For example, electing working-class people to legislative office literally transforms their class position. This suggests that legislators from working-class backgrounds of families must rely on memory and preexisting social networks more than on reflection on current circumstances in order to translate descriptive representation into substantive representation. Not every legislator is so reflective and committed to past allegiances and relationships. Because descriptive representation by class confronts these obstacles, social movement representation is even more important for class groups than for groups defined by, say, race or gender.

INSTITUTIONAL MECHANISMS, INTERNAL MINORITIES, AND CONFLICTS OF INTEREST

In the analysis of state-level labor policies across the United States, it appears that workers in traditionally male forms of employ are better represented by unions than are women workers. In addition, in the North, where the Democratic Party has a closer relationship with labor, political parties appear to be an important avenue for workers in traditionally male fields of employ. In the South, however, where there is no political party that reliably represents labor, social movements (unions and other civil society groups representing labor) were more important. Where women's movements and unions were weak, other civil society avenues and even generalized social capital became more important. This suggests that where parties form to represent specific constituencies (women's parties, labor parties, ethnic parties) or when there are specific electoral mechanisms to represent those groups (e.g., separate electorates or the like), civil society groups become less important avenues of representation. Where group differences are institutionalized and groups have mechanisms providing a guarantee that they can speak as part of democratic policy-making processes, these civil society avenues fade in importance.

However, if an issue is perceived to affect only a disadvantaged subgroup (working-class women or women of color), institutional recognition of the broader group may not mitigate the need for social movement representation. For example, the analysis in chapter 3 showed that even in the North, when political parties aimed to represent organized labor, unions and left political parties were chiefly effective on the issues of the traditionally dominant male worker. Separate organization in women's movements still significantly improved the representation of working women. More generally, for these issues framed as internal minority ones, the separate organization of that group (whether within or outside of broader social movements) becomes important to social movement action on that issue. For example, it was through separate organization that women of color were able to identify and articulate the distinctive concerns of women of color in relation to violence. This separate organization had an indirect effect on policy outcomes (affecting the broader women's movement), and it is unlikely that these issues would have been articulated were it not for the separate organization of these women. The importance of such separate organization of marginalized constituencies is reflected in the political practice of contemporary labor movements and women's movements.[1] For issues affecting privileged minorities, however, we would not expect such separate organization to be necessary. Because privileged minorities are either adequately represented or overrepresented in these organizations and their leadership, they tend to be able to raise these issues and even frame them as universal or majority issues quite effectively (Strolovitch 2007).

Separate organization is especially important for issues where there is a conflict of interest between the dominant subgroup and the marginalized subgroup (see chapter 4 in the present study; Williams 1998). In these cases, autonomous organization of the intersectionally marginalized group may be more important. In cases where distinctive marginalized interests are compatible with dominant interests or are overlooked mainly due to oversight or insensitivity, organizational autonomy may be less important.

TYPES OF ISSUE: ISSUE FRAMES AND SOCIAL TRANSFORMATION

We learn more about when and how social movements are most effective as representatives when comparing across different policies affecting women—policies on violence against women, parental leave, minimum wage, child care, and the like. Although women's movements are critical to policy action on violence against women, they are less critical for the development of generous policies of maternity and parental leave. Moreover, it appears that patterns of class politics are more determinative of the generosity of provisions for maternity leave than are the dimensions of gender politics, such as women in government, women's bureaus, and women's movements. But further examination of the politics of leave policies finds that policies for maternity and parental leave vary widely in the degree to which they challenge gender roles. In their canonical work, Gelb and Palley (1996) distinguish between policies that change or maintain gender roles. Some family leave and workplace policies challenge gender roles, and some seek to maintain gender roles—for example, making parental leave available only to women. Women's movement activity turns out to be critical for ensuring policies that promote role change, while labor mobilization is critical for advancing generous, state-funded leave, a dimension of leave policy that poses a challenge to class hierarchies more than to gender hierarchies (in that it leaves the gender division of labor untouched). More generally, social movements are particularly important for advancing policies that seek social transformation, and social movements tend to specialize in different types of social transformation. So different social movements are likely relevant for different policies and can even determine different aspects of the same policy.

As this consideration of parental leave suggests, many policy issues are of interest to multiple constituencies. For example, spending on child care, minimum wage laws, and provisions for maternity leave are both women's issues and labor issues. As such, one would expect these issues to be of concern to both women's movements and labor movements. One can determine how movements will matter by asking which aspect of a proposed policy most challenges the prevailing policy regime. In the United States, for example, although ensuring access to unemployment insurance for pregnant women and women victims of domestic violence is an issue of greatest salience to working-class women, such a policy does not challenge the prevailing model of class relations. Ensuring access to unemployment insurance for such women does challenge the gender basis of the social policy regime, since such insurance has generally been seen as a program primarily benefiting male workers (Sapiro 1990; Nelson 1990). Increasing social spending, in the U.S. context, however, does challenge the prevailing model of class relations, and labor movements are likely to be more important here. So social movements are critical for policies requiring or advancing social transformation, and it matters which aspect of social inequality is being challenged.

Conditions Favorable to Intralegislative Descriptive Representation

Although the argument and research has emphasized the greater importance of social movements for translating descriptive representation into substantive representation, this analysis also reveals some conditions under which descriptive representation by elected officeholders is particularly effective. The research in this book shows that women in government did seem to have an important effect on the likelihood that paid pregnancy, maternity, and parental leaves would be adopted. This is consistent with emerging research on this issue (Schwindt Bayer and Mishler 2005; Kittilson 2008), but it suggests that maternity leave is different from other women's rights issues in some important way.

One important aspect of maternity leave is that such policies (which affirm the importance of women's maternal obligations) do not require women representatives to envision massive social transformation. Another important aspect is that combining work and childbirth (or care for a young infant) is an issue that confronts a majority of women, including many women who are in public office. In other words, a working mother (e.g., a legislator) does not need a feminist analysis to see that a maternity leave is in her interest. It is not only feminists who are complaining about work-family balance. So even where this is an uncrystallized interest, an issue on which there has been little social debate, women can speak from their own lives, while affirming traditional gender roles, in advocating for maternity leave. In this way, it seems, this research confirms that the ability of descriptive representatives to draw on their own experiences is especially valuable (1) when interests are uncrystallized and (2) when they are *in fact* representative of a broader group in some way (Mansbridge 1999; Phillips 1995). However, if such descriptive representatives are seeking to advance policies of social transformation, involvement with and support by a broader social movement is still critical for success.

More Democracy or More Division?

For marginalized groups seeking social transformation (especially intersectionally marginalized ones), mobilization in social movements offers a way to participate and be represented in democratic politics that is more accessible and effective than merely voting for a particular party or electing more people who "look like" they are from the group in question. Separate organizing as women or women of color does not appear to weaken social movements or distract from important issues of material conditions, nor does it seem to result in a focus on primarily "cultural" or "identity-related" concerns. Moreover, although social movements, like other avenues of representation, reflect the social dominance of particular groups to some degree, they appear to be particularly accessible and amenable to organization by intersectionally marginalized groups, making them uniquely valuable as avenues for integrating these hard-to-reach groups into our democracies. Last, the proliferation of social movement organizations need not signal a hollowing out of associational life or a lack of participation, and it improves civil society representation for systematically disadvantaged groups.

Social Structures and Intersectional Analysis

More generally, this analysis suggests that attending to the ways that social structures shape processes of representation (and political life more generally) reveals political phenomena (and, potentially, ways of deepening democracy) that are only visible at a macro level. This is even true for the intersectional analysis of policy and politics, which has often been taken to imply the study of disadvantaged social groups that are ever more narrowly defined. In contrast, this analysis supports the emerging scholarly movement toward comparing different social groups, of varying degrees and kinds of advantage and disadvantage, in their relationships with political institutions (Hancock 2007; Strolovitch 2007; Weldon 2006, 2008). Such an analysis provides concrete evidence of the value of disaggregating our analysis, revealing political dynamics that are otherwise obscured.

The Advocacy State: Implications for Public Policy

If social movements play or could play such an important role in democratic representation, especially for disadvantaged groups, this suggests that democratic states should take an active role in fostering and encouraging independent mobilization by disadvantaged groups. States that provide more openings for input from such independent groups, for example, will have more inclusive policy processes—processes that are more reflective of the diversity of opinion and experience that characterizes the population. Groups whose ideas and views would otherwise be excluded from public discussions may participate in policy deliberations. Greater inclusivity and political equality should further democracy (Young 2000; Cohen and Rogers 1992).

CAN STATES FOSTER SOCIAL MOVEMENTS WITHOUT UNDERMINING THEM?

In a study of the environmental movement in four countries, Dryzek and others (2003) argue that inclusive states—states that provide a forum for social movements within the state—actually deplete civil society and undermine democracy. State intervention, they argue, suppresses the heterogeneity that otherwise characterizes social movements, and it makes democratic authenticity and critical distance more difficult to maintain. Inclusion too often becomes co-optation, and movements are unable to maintain the critical edge that makes them so powerful. Passively exclusive states—that is, governments that provide no openings for social movements—are more conducive to the development of a burgeoning civil society than to inclusive states. The experience of the environmental movement in these four states, they argue, "pours cold water over political theorists who see the main democratic task of the state in terms of effectively organizing groups—especially disadvantaged groups—into the state" (111).[2]

Can states actively support and foster social movements of disadvantaged groups without inadvertently co-opting organizations or crowding out more critical, independent organizations? There are many tensions that arise in state efforts to promote mobilization that must be somewhat independent of the state in order to maximize the representational benefits. Indeed, it is important to recognize the dangers of state involvement in fostering such organizations. Sometimes, this can result in too much government control of these organizations, dulling their critical edge (Young 2000). At the same time, as Warren (2001, 216–17) points out, it is not as if the state can avoid shaping civil society in modern democracies: "States are deeply and inextricably involved in constituting the associational life of today's societies, not only through regulation, but through devolution of social services to associations, tax incentives, the structuring and devolving of political processes, partnerships, and alterations in the bargaining powers of social actors." States also intervene directly in civil society by supporting (and, in some cases, creating) nongovernmental associations. So the question cannot be "*whether* the state should be involved, but rather *how* it should be involved" (Warren 2001, 217). Moreover, states vary in terms of whether they are inclusive or exclusive of civil society depending on the group or issue in question (Tarrow 1998, 81–83), and every form of organization advantages some categories over others (Bachrach and Baratz 1969). So perhaps the question should not be whether the state should privilege or advantage particular groups in civil society but which ones should be so privileged.

The literature on associative democracy suggests a number of principles and measures for state action that are relevant here (though scholars are quick to note that the specific political context must be taken into account) (Warren 2001; Dryzek et al. 2003). First, states should guarantee certain "negative" freedoms or rights necessary for citizens to be able to form associations—namely, freedom of speech, conscience, assembly, and privacy (Warren 2001, 217). States may also regulate associations to some degree. Regulation in terms of guaranteeing internally democratic processes of organizations is most appropriate when organizations are compulsory and when they are imbued with statelike responsibilities, such as providing services or coordinating other organizations. States should limit interference with voluntary organizations from which exit is relatively costless. States can also promote associations conducive to greater democracy by providing support directly (in cash or kind) or indirectly (through tax exemption) (Warren 2001; Cohen and Rogers 1992). States may also encourage private associations by seeking to create public-private partnerships (Warren 2001, chap. 7). In addition, states may undertake symbolic action that powerfully motivates citizens to organize, or they may offer opportunities in reaction to which citizens form associations.

Although states should interfere less in the internal matters of voluntary organizations, it does not follow that states should not encourage or foster such organizations. Indeed, the state should use all the tools at its disposal to foster associations of various kinds, in order to produce the wide variety of democratic effects that such associations have. The democratic state can locate or help create organizations of various underrepresented groups, such as poor people, minorities, or any other group whose perspectives might enrich public discussion but whose interests and concerns tend to be marginalized or excluded in public discussions (Young 2001; Cohen and Rogers 1992).

Cohen and Rogers (1992) propose that the state should directly subsidize the formation and/or maintenance of associations for the purposes of compensating for unequal influence on public policy; the state should identify those groups who are less well represented in the current associational terrain and use public policy to facilitate their self-directed organization. The state should encourage *encompassing* organizations, and these associations, on Cohen and Rogers' view, should be involved in key areas of policy-making, particularly policies relating to the economy and welfare. Encompassingness (or completeness of representation) is determined by the proportion of the affected population that are members of the organization (Cohen and Rogers 1992, 429). In addition to this numerical measure of completeness, governments should also ask whether the full range of diversity among constituents is represented. In the case of compulsory organizations (e.g., unions), especially those that provide any statelike functions, governments must take steps to ensure fair processes internally (Warren 2001).

If we focus on the aim of representation for systematically disadvantaged groups, then, this suggests that governments can undertake a variety of measures that encourage mobilization and association. Governments can provide funding for these organizations and income support for individuals. Governments should distinguish those social groups (or subgroups) that are less well organized and specifically seek to facilitate their self-organization. As Warren (2001) notes, universal forms of income support for individuals ensure that people have some ability to choose their associational ties without regard to survival: for example, they need not attend a church or synagogue in order to obtain social services and supports they need to live. Cohen and Rogers (1992) similarly note the importance of an adequate social wage in enabling organization of workers.

To guard against the concerns of co-optation raised by Dryzek and others (2003), which are particularly salient for contexts where state functions are devolved to civil society organizations, these government-sponsored groups and processes must always be seen as potentially incomplete in terms of their representativeness. Opportunities for intervention or appeal by those who feel unrepresented by the process must always be provided. This institutionalization of dissent is critical for ensuring inclusion (Weldon 1999, 2006; Young 1997).

In terms of support for organizations, there are many concrete examples of government funding successfully catalyzing autonomous organizations in Canadian public policy. One prominent activist in the Canadian women's movement credits the community development programs of the 1960s, where the government provided funds for community development broadly construed, with creating a women's movement with significant participation by working-class women (interview with a Canadian activist, 2003). Similarly, the Secretary of State Women's Program in Canada has long funded women's organizations that undertake various activities to promote the status of women; this program is considered an important resource by feminist activists in Canada and has been critical in sparking government action on violence against women (Weldon 2002). The Court Challenges Program, which funds "equality-seeking" groups to bring court cases based on the rights enumerated in the Charter of Rights and Freedoms, has also facilitated access by disadvantaged groups to government policy-making processes. Government action can also encourage or strengthen mobilization by providing infrastructure or opportunities for organizing. Finally, in her seminal article "How the Government Built the Women's Movements," Georgia Duerst-Lahti (1989) argues that the creation of a network of state-level women's commissions was responsible for uniting the hitherto fragmented, local and disorganized U.S. women's movement into a powerful, coordinated national movement.

States may also take symbolic action that encourages mobilization. For example, government rhetoric or resolutions may name particular groups as legitimate participants in public discussion, thereby providing a positive valuation of that category of people, encouraging people to affirm that identity. An official day recognizing particular groups or issues can provide a focal point and legitimation for groups seeking to organize events drawing public attention. Local governments seeking input from particular communities or groups can have the same effect.

These examples include both nominally universal programs (like the Community Development Program) and programs targeted to disadvantaged groups. Democratic states should adopt both sorts of programs. Universal measures to support the development of a vital civil society likely improve democracy for all citizens. But if all citizens enjoy the same benefit, inequalities will be preserved, not challenged, even though the floor is raised (Cohen and Roger 1992; Bell 1987). In order to more directly attack social inequality, targeted programs to foster mobilization by disadvantaged groups are necessary. A state that works to promote self-organization of marginalized groups in both of these ways is what I am calling an *advocacy state.*

At present, the associational terrain tends to replicate inequalities in other areas of representation. This is partly because cultural and economic dominance provides some advantage in civil society as in other areas of political life. Adopting only universal programs to facilitate organizing will do little to alleviate these inequalities as advantaged groups as well as disadvantaged groups seek to avail themselves of these resources. In order to correct for these existing inequalities, public policy must undertake specific efforts both to encourage disadvantaged groups to mobilize and to support their efforts at self-organization.

Williams (1998) notes that where groups lack a sense of group consciousness, government efforts directed at representing these groups can smack of vanguardism. But this presents a particular problem for disadvantaged groups, who face more barriers in attempting the kind of mobilization and organization that creates and depends on group consciousness (Weldon 2006; Cohen and Rogers 1992). One way of addressing this issue is to provide resources specifically for mobilizing and organizing disadvantaged constituencies, without prejudging what those specific constituencies are.

DEFINING GROUP DISADVANTAGE IN PUBLIC POLICY

The major practical question that arises in thinking about how to design policies that support only systematically disadvantaged groups is how best to identify such groups. In democratic theory, the debate over how to identify systematically disadvantaged groups (which has mostly focused on distinguishing groups with a claim to special political representation) seems to have developed a consensus that distinguishing such groups in public policy is too difficult and fraught with peril to risk the attempt. Even the strongest proponents of efforts to improve representation for marginalized groups have backed away from recommending *institutionalized* political representation for specific groups, because of three problems that seem particularly pressing: (1) how to distinguish genuinely disadvantaged groups in practice without freezing social relations or essentializing social groups, (2) determining who would apply such criteria if they could be developed, and (3) how powerful groups could be persuaded to adopt measures to remedy inequality where those measures are likely to undermine their own power.

No proponent of group rights suggests that they should be extended to any group that claims to be disadvantaged, so groups must do more than just *claim* to be disadvantaged. Although some scholars have proposed criteria for distinguishing disadvantaged groups from other groups (Williams 1998; Young 1990, 2000), other scholars of group rights view these criteria as impractically broad or vague (Kymlicka 1995; Glazer 1983). In addition, difficulty in establishing who belongs to the group will make such group-specific measures difficult to implement (Young 2002).

Still more troubling is the question of who applies these criteria and decides when they are met. As Williams (1998, 214) notes (in a discussion of consociationalism):

> There is also the troubling question of who will have the power to decide which groups will be included . . . It seems likely that this power will be wielded by those groups that are already relatively powerful compared to other groups that may have an equally defensible moral claim to inclusion, so that the resulting institutions may contribute little to the political equality of the historically marginalized groups about which we should be most concerned.

Moreover, institutionalization (e.g., legal recognition of disadvantaged groups) can freeze social relations (Young 2000). Institutions are relatively stable entities, while social group politics are fluid and constantly changing. What happens when groups fade or become less disadvantaged over time? Further, does recognizing groups in institutions exacerbate and perpetuate tensions among them, leading to "balkanization" (Phillips 1992, 294–95)?

These practical political problems lead noted proponents of group representation to eschew measures to ensure the representation of disadvantaged groups, except under the direst circumstances. For example, Phillips (1992, 298) concludes, "My reservations refer exclusively to that more ambitious step of institutionalising group representation, for in exploring the possible extension of feminist arguments into a case for formal and substantial group representation, I have come to the conclusion that the potential risks outweigh the gains" (cf. Young 2000, 150; Williams 1998, 212).

The fluidity of social groups and the ease with which disadvantage may be ameliorated seem to me to be overdrawn in this discussion. For example, in Norway, where women are more than a third of the legislature (36.1 percent) and have been for two decades, where there are state agencies aimed at improving equality, and where there is an active women's movement, the main institutions of society nevertheless remain male-dominated, and we would still consider women a disadvantaged group (Skeije and Teigen 2005). So although we want to recognize the dynamic, iterative relationship between state and society here and although we want to think about how easily state structures can adopt to changing social contexts, we should be careful not to overstate the likelihood of total, lasting social transformation in a short period of time (Eckstein 1988).

ACTUAL POLICIES DISTINGUISHING DISADVANTAGE: LESSONS FROM POLITICAL PRACTICE

Perhaps this is a case where practice may guide theory. Some government policies have been effectively distinguishing disadvantaged groups using general criteria for some time. For example, take the Disadvantaged Business Enterprise Program adopted by the federal Department of Transportation in the United States (a similar program exists in Texas, called the Historically Underutilized Business [HUB] Program). The Court Challenges Program in Canada also successfully distinguished disadvantaged groups. Indeed, in some ways, this now-discontinued policy can serve as a model for the sort of measure envisioned here. Government-funded organizations represent the disadvantaged in challenging the government itself. Despite government funding, organizations have been able to maintain their independence and autonomy from government.

The Court Challenges Program of Canada. The Court Challenges Program in Canada was a program aimed at improving access to the Canadian legal system for members of historically disadvantaged groups who have a grievance with federal law or policy. Specifically, the program provided funding to defray the cost of undertaking a lawsuit against the federal government. The case had to have the potential to be an important test case that would advance the substantive equality rights of disadvantaged groups. The substantive equality standard requires that a law be examined in terms of its differential impact, rather than in terms of achieving formal equality. Applicants must demonstrate that they have financial need for such funding, and for-profit entities are not eligible to apply. In their application, the organization or individual purporting to represent a group must aim for inclusiveness and accessibility: the diversity of interests in the community must be taken into account, and any meetings or consultations undertaken in preparation for the case must be as accessible as possible (e.g., held in handicapped-accessible buildings). The program also undertakes efforts to inform various communities about the existence of the program and to help them to apply for funding (Court Challenges Program 2003).

For the purposes of the Court Challenges Program, historically disadvantaged groups are defined as those groups specifically named in the Charter of Rights and Freedoms provisions for equality rights (see the discussion of section 15 that follows) or those groups that are analogously situated. In practice, this definition has included women; racial, ethnic, religious, and linguistic minorities; mentally and physically disabled people; and gays and lesbians. The program has funded many of the important Canadian Supreme Court cases advancing equality rights and is considered a very important program by a wide range of equality-seeking organizations, including women's groups, groups representing the disabled, First Nations people (Aboriginal Canadians), visible minorities, and the like.[3] In 2001–2, cases funded included two cases seeking judicial recognition of societal racism, two regarding social and economic rights, two regarding immigration law, one case regarding the treatment of same-sex couples, one regarding a divorced spouse's rights to her husband's pension, one advocating voting rights for prisoners, one regarding children's rights, a case of discrimination based on religion, and one case based on deafness, among others. Many of these cases were Supreme Court cases (Court Challenges Program 2002).

Officially, the Court Challenges Program was originally established in 1978 to cover the costs incurred by those wishing to apply to the courts to clarify the extent of the minority language rights specified in the Constitution Act, 1867 (Court Challenges Program 1994). The program was probably also created as a way for the federal government under Pierre Trudeau to undermine the Parti

Québécois efforts to advance Bill 101, their signature language legislation for the province of Quebec (Brodie 2001). At the outset, the federal government made all decisions about which cases to fund (Court Challenges Program 1994). The program was broadened in response to the adoption of the Canadian Charter of Rights and Freedoms. When section 15, which governs equality rights, took effect in 1985, it was decided to broaden the mandate of the Court Challenges Program to allow disadvantaged groups to assert the equality rights they were guaranteed under the Constitution of Canada. Section 15 reads:

> (1) Every individual is equal before and under the law and has the right to the equal protection and equal benefit of the law without discrimination and, in particular, without discrimination based on race, national or ethnic origin, colour, religion, sex, age or mental or physical disability.
>
> (2) Subsection (1) does not preclude any law, program or activity that has as its object the amelioration of conditions of disadvantaged individuals or groups including those that are disadvantaged because of race, national or ethnic origin, colour, religion, sex, age or mental or physical disability.

The decision to add challenges under the equality provisions of the Charter of Rights and Freedoms (section 15) to the Program mandate was a response to pressure by organizations representing women; the disabled, cultural, and racial minority communities; gays and lesbians; and other groups. These groups argued that without funding, the newly acquired rights would have a more limited impact, since they would remain inaccessible to the people they were supposed to protect. It was also an effort on the part of the Progressive Conservative Party to attract progressive voters (Brodie 2001).

Since the Court Challenges Program involved challenges to the federal government, it was important that funding decisions were made by a body that was independent of government. To this end, the Canadian Council on Social Development (CCSD) was given the task of administering the Court Challenges Program. Two independent panels were set up, one to study applications for assistance relating to language rights and the other to study applications relating to equality rights. These panels became the only bodies that could decide which cases were to be funded by the program. Between 1985 and 1992, the equality component of the program financed 178 cases at all levels of the legal system, including 24 cases in the Supreme Court. The government briefly eliminated the program's financing from 1992 to 1994 (Epp 1996, 770).

The program was reinstated in 1994 in response to public pressure. In 1993, the Canadian prime minister announced the government's intention to reestablish the program (Court Challenges Program 1995). Price Waterhouse was charged with supervising consultations with concerned groups (Court Challenges Program 1995). As a result of these consultations, the government basically adopted the same mandate that the former program had had. In addition, it was agreed that the reinstated program would be given the resources to enable it to approach various communities and groups. Participating organizations of women, Native Canadians, racial and ethnic minorities, the disabled, and other groups also agreed to create a new nonprofit organization that would be completely independent of the federal government. Language groups and equality-seeking groups were to be equally represented on the board of directors. Two separate panels were to be set up to decide which applications for funding would be accepted. An Equality Rights Panel, comprised of seven members in order to reflect the different membership of the various groups involved and to promote equality of representation, was established. At least one of the members of the Equality Rights Panel was to come from a racial minority, and another was to come from the groups representing disabled persons. A Language Rights Panel would also be created (Court Challenges Program 1995).

In late December 1994, more than 1,000 letters were sent to all the groups involved in the promotion of language rights, equality-seeking groups, institutions, associations of lawyers, human rights commissions, and other organizations. The letter informed groups that the program was in the process of reinstatement and sought applications for the program's two rights panels. Two selection committees were struck to choose the members of the panels. Panel members are appointed for up to three years. Each panel is responsible for independently selecting the cases to be funded and establishing the amount of this funding. Panel members are given a per diem honorarium and are reimbursed for travel and lodging (Court Challenges Program 2002; interview with a senior Canadian bureaucrat, 2003).

There are three categories of Court Challenges Program members: equality members, language members, and director members. The membership meets at the annual general meeting to conduct the program's business, including the election of board members. The membership groups have established an Equality Advisory Committee and a Language Advisory Committee. These committees serve as forums on program-related issues of interest to their members and provide advice to the board on policy issues throughout the course of the year. The work of these committees and panels is supported by a staff located at the Court Challenges Program office in Winnipeg, Manitoba. On April 1, 2000, the Court Challenges Program's membership was composed of 108 equality members and 19 language members. The membership was quite active: over 90 individuals participated in annual meetings (Court Challenges Program 2002; interview with a senior Canadian bureaucrat, 2003). The program was once again shut down, with little fanfare, in 2006, by the newly elected Conservative government. There has been widespread criticism and opposition to this move but, so far, no move to reconsider the decision.

The Disadvantaged Business Enterprise Program. The current procurement policies adopted by the U.S. Department of Transportation require that business owners belonging to disadvantaged groups have access to the competition for government contracts. Under a policy first introduced by President Reagan, the federal Department of Transportation sets goals for the inclusion of minority- and women-owned businesses in its procurement policy. States and primary contractors receiving federal money must demonstrate that they have made a good faith effort to include disadvantaged business enterprises as part of the bidding processes. If contractors fail to employ a representative number of subcontractors from Disadvantaged Business Enterprise (DBE) groups, the federal government requires evidence that they made a good faith effort to involve such groups.

The program was first conceived under the Carter administration, but the original DBE statute was passed under the Reagan administration. The original statute received little attention when it was added by a House representative. It did not specify women as a disadvantaged group. Women were designated as presumptively disadvantaged under a little-discussed rider on the 1987 reauthorization of the act. It seems that the move to add women was a response to women's concerted lobbying efforts. The proposal came out of the Environment and Public Works Committee and was championed by Idaho Republican senator Steve Simms. The senator's logic was reportedly that if minorities were to be so designated, women ought also to be designated (interview with a senior U.S. bureaucrat, 2003).

The Reagan and first Bush administrations were strangely silent on these programs. Under the second Clinton administration, however, there was much debate on the topic of how disadvantaged groups ought to be designated. Opponents attacked the process as illogical and capricious. The program also came under legal attack in the recent Supreme Court decision *Adarand II.*

However, it appears that the program has survived these attacks. Interestingly, despite the general discussion of affirmative action programs in universities, there has been little public discussion of these procurement programs.

Disadvantaged groups are defined as including socially and economically disadvantaged groups. The Department of Transportation defines these terms using the conditions laid out in the Small Business Act (15 U.S.C. 637(d)), which defines socially disadvantaged individuals as "those who have been subjected to racial or ethnic prejudice or cultural bias because of their identity as a member of a group without regard to their individual qualities." Economically disadvantaged people are there defined as "those socially disadvantaged individuals whose ability to compete in the free enterprise system has been impaired due to diminished capital and credit opportunities as compared to others in the same business area who are not socially disadvantaged." As the act stipulates, this general definition is translated into a list of specific groups through an administrative rule-making process: "All determinations made . . . with respect to whether a group has been subjected to prejudice or bias shall be made by the Administrator after consultation with the Associate Administrator for Minority Small Business and Capital Ownership Development."

Those groups who have been denied are entitled to a hearing. Groups may also petition the relevant administrator in the small business administration in order to receive a designation as a disadvantaged group. For example, South Asian Americans successfully petitioned the administration for inclusion, while a group of Hasidic Jews who petitioned to receive such a designation were denied (interview with a senior U.S. bureaucrat, 2003). The administration is also mandated actively to seek out disadvantaged groups and inform them of the program and to recruit participants.

Federally, the categories of "disadvantage" are established based on aggregate statistics about how women and minorities fare in contracting procedures. When the Disadvantaged Business Enterprise Program was established in 1978 to 1996, the percentage of women- and minority-owned construction firms that receive federal contracts increased from 1.9 percent to 14.8 percent (OSDBU 2003a). But women and minorities are still dramatically underrepresented in terms of both the percentage receiving contracts and the amount of money received. This is true even when the proportion of available and qualified women- or minority-owned businesses is taken as the baseline. Non-DBEs still control over 85 percent of highway construction funds provided through federal aid (OSDBU 2003a). Where state DBE programs have been canceled (as in Michigan), the proportion of contracts awarded to women and minorities has dropped dramatically to nearly zero. There is much evidence that "old boys' networks" persist, particularly in the area of construction, and that without these affirmative measures, DBEs would not have a chance to compete with non-DBEs on an equal playing field (OSDBU 2003a, 2003b).[4] Note that the disadvantage that is documented (lack of access to government contracts) is closely related to the targeted measure in question (targeted policies in government procurement). This disadvantage is documented for the group in general and is presumed to be relevant for each enterprise owned by an individual from that group. Currently, groups presumed to be disadvantaged include citizens of the United States (or lawfully admitted permanent residents) who are women, African Americans, Hispanic Americans, Native Americans, Asian Pacific Americans, and Subcontinent Asian Americans. Applicants must submit a signed, notarized certification that each "presumptively disadvantaged" owner is, in fact, socially and economically disadvantaged.

The federal Department of Transportation maintains that since it is a federal body, it can use aggregate national statistics to evaluate its procurement practices and need not evaluate local variations in disadvantaged groups. Moreover, given recent legal challenges, the department now permits individuals to petition to be certified as DBEs even if they are not members of a disadvantaged group. Firms owned and controlled by individuals who are not presumed to be socially and economically disadvantaged (including individuals whose presumed disadvantage has been rebutted) may apply for DBE certification. They must make a case-by-case determination of whether each individual whose ownership is relied on for DBE certification is socially and economically disadvantaged. The applicant firm has the burden of demonstrating that the individuals who own and control it are socially and economically disadvantaged. An individual whose personal net worth exceeds $750,000 is not economically disadvantaged, according to the Code of Federal Regulations (49 CFR 26.67, 280–82).

Lessons from the Court Challenges Program and the Disadvantaged Business Enterprise Program. These two programs demonstrate that is it practically possible to design and implement policies that provide targeted benefits to disadvantaged groups without freezing social relations or essentializing social groups. Although these programs are subject to political struggle, the outcome of political decisions does not inescapably favor the powerful or dominant groups. It is possible, then, to deepen democracy by using similar criteria to provide support to organizational efforts of systematically disadvantaged groups. Organizing these groups into the state has not, in these instances, depleted civil society or weakened social movements: in Canada and the United States, organizations of the disadvantaged groups that benefit from these policies (e.g., women and African Americans) continue to flourish and push for social justice for these groups. I say more about this in the section that follows.

CONCERNS ABOUT CO-OPTATION: THE WOMEN'S MOVEMENT IN CANADA

The concern about co-optation or crowding out of grassroots organizations is a recurrent one and is important to address at slightly greater length.[5] The concern about co-optation is that inclusion in the state is superficial inclusion (e.g., inclusion on the margins of state activity, or symbolic inclusion) that nevertheless dulls the capacity for criticism, moderating activist language and claims as they seek to preserve their limited access, mistaking it for signs of real change. While there is a much broader discussion about these issues,[6] I want to focus specifically on the question of whether state funding for movement activities necessarily weakens an organizations' ability to continue its work advocating for a disadvantaged constituency and publicly criticizing government. While individuals vary in terms of their willingness to sacrifice their ideals for personal gain, social movements as a whole are notorious for being overly vigilant about such "sellouts," making necessary compromise and moderation on the part of movement leaders difficult to combine with continued movement support. This means social movements (as opposed to particular activists) are not so easily co-opted (cf. Beckwith 2007).

It is not clear that state support for social movements necessarily weakens them and makes them dependent on the state. As noted, the Canadian women's movement has enjoyed a wide variety of different kinds of state support but continues to flourish as one of the strongest and most vital women's movements in the world. The federal government has provided funding to women's organizations through the Women's Program since the 1970s, yet Canada today has one of the largest numbers of women's organizations per capita of any country in the world.[7] Efforts to completely withdraw such funding were unsuccessful, as activists were able to mobilize considerable opposition to funding cuts.

Seasoned women's movement activists are quite circumspect about relying entirely on government funding. Most organizations seek to maintain a diverse set of funding sources, even while drawing extensively on government support (interviews with Canadian antiviolence activists, 2003). Even if state support has catalyzed a social movement, this should not be taken as implying that the state can permanently or ultimately control the result of this mobilization. Activists may ultimately capitulate to state demands for moderation and adjustment, or they may not, instead resisting these demands and developing "protective responses" (Coy and Hedeen 2005). One review of the Canadian government's citizenship programs, which foster participation and organization by women and minorities, concludes that the state was never able to use these programs to manipulate civil society groups to its own strategic ends (Pal 1993). One cannot always easily put the genie back in the bottle (Brodie 2001).

As these examples suggest, maintaining support for these programs and maintaining sufficient independence to operate or survive when support is periodically canceled or reduced requires considerable effort. But this is not the same as being impossible. Dryzek (2000; cf. Dryzek et al. 2005) argues that policies to benefit disadvantaged groups will only be adopted when they coincide with a core state imperative. It is difficult to see what imperative is served by funding women's organizations that criticize the government's inaction on violence against women or that sue the government itself. But even if a political imperative motivates policymakers at the outset, that does not suggest that the policy will be ineffective. Certainly, when movement goals coincide with a core state imperative, cooperation with the state should be less fraught. But this does not imply that governments do not fund those organizations who criticize or challenge the state (Brodie 2001). In sum, these examples suggest that government programs that offer targeted subsidies and other forms of support to disadvantaged groups' efforts to mobilize may be more feasible than is often presumed in the literature.

An advocacy state adopts both universal measures to foster voluntary associations, such as provisions requiring public consultation and openness on the part of government, and measures aimed to encourage and support self-organization by marginalized groups. Such measures can include funding for lawsuits (like the Court Challenges Program), for more specific program activities (like the Women's Program), and for developing organizations and community services (like the community development programs of the 1960s), as well as providing administrative infrastructure and research support (like the women's commissions in the United States and the Secretary of State citizenship programs—for example, the Women's Program—in Canada). Such measures encourage groups to mobilize, articulate their views, and press them in the public sphere and on the government agenda itself. For organizations that are compulsory or difficult to exit (like unions), the state should combine support with measures regulating the internal procedures of these groups.

Conclusion

Social movements are an important avenue of representation for systematically disadvantaged groups. Particularly for those groups who fall through the cracks of the system of institutionally recognized interests, social movements offer a more fluid and accessible channel of policy influence. In fact, social movements offer a solution to the deepest, most persistent problems of representation. On issues that affect only disadvantaged subgroups, social movements offer a mode of political mobilization that is effective and within reach for citizens seeking self-determination. Poor people and people who are not citizens can and do organize social movements. Political parties, interest groups, and electoral politics all fail to reach these segments of the population who vote and organize less frequently than citizens in other groups. Social movements constitute a critical avenue of policy influence for women, workers, and women of color, often more important than political parties, interest groups, or electing group members to government office (descriptive representation). Indeed, they are so important that we ought to further such mobilization wherever we can.

Appendix

TABLE A1. **Summary Table for Three Variables, 36 Countries, 1994**

Country	Women in the Legislature (%)	Strong and Autonomous Women's Movement	Scope of Government Response to Violence against Women
Australia	9.5	Yes	7
Canada	18	Yes	7
United States	10.9	Yes	6
Costa Rica	14	Yes	5
France	6.4	Yes until 1985; no after	5
Ireland	12.7	Yes	5
Israel	9.2	Yes	5
New Zealand	21.2	Yes	5
Belgium	12	Yes	4
India	8	Yes	4
Norway	39.4	Yes	4
Sweden	40.4	No	4
United Kingdom	9.5	Yes	4
Austria	23.5	No	3
Bahamas	8.2	No	3
Barbados	10.7	Yes	3
Colombia	10.8	Yes	3
Luxembourg	20	No	3
Netherlands	31.3	Yes	3
Spain	16	No	3
Denmark	33	Yes until 1983; no after	2
Finland	33.5	No	2
Germany	26.2	No	2
Iceland	25.4	No	2
Portugal	8.7	No	2
Switzerland	18	No	2
Trinidad and Tobago	18.9	Yes (since 1989)	2
Greece	6	No	1
Jamaica	11.7	Yes (since 1994)	1
Japan	2.7	No	1
Mauritius	2.9	No	1
Papua New Guinea	0	No	0
Botswana	10	No	0
Italy	15.1	No	0
Nauru	5.6[a]	No	0
Venezuela	5.9	No	0

Source: Interparliamentary Union 1995; Weldon 2002a.

[a]This figure is for 1986–89, but the Interparliamentary Union does not include updated data for the 1992 election.

TABLE A2. Family Policies in 34 Stable Democracies, 1994

County	Number of Leaves	Paid Leaves	Leave Time (in weeks)	Source of Pay (1 = public)	Non-discrimination Policy	Gender Role Change Policies
Australia	3	0	58	0	0	1
Austria	2	2	36	1	0	0.67
Bahamas	1	1	8	0.6	0.5	0.83
Barbados	1	1	12	1	0.5	0.83
Belgium	3	2.3	30	1	1	2
Botswana	1	0.3	12	0	0.5	0.83
Canada	2	1.6	23	1	1	1.67
Colombia	1	1	12	1	0.5	0.83
Costa Rica	1	1	16	0.5	0.5	0.83
Denmark	3	3	45	1	1	2
Finland	3	2.8	27	1	1	2
France	3	2.3	55	1	1	2
Germany	2	2	46	1	0.5	1.17
Greece	2	0.8	19	1	1	1.67
Iceland	2	2	12	1	0	0.67
India	1	1	12	1	1	1.33
Ireland	1	0.7	14	1	1	1.33
Israel	2	0.8	24	1	0.5	1.17
Italy	2	1.1	26	1	1	1.67
Jamaica	1	1	12	0	0.5	0.83
Japan	2	0.6	23.5	1	1	1.67
Luxembourg	2	1.5	18	1	0.5	1.17
Mauritius	1	1	12	0	0	0.33
Netherlands	3	1.5	27	1	1	2
New Zealand	3	0	28	0	1	2
Norway	3	3	42	1	0.5	1.5
Portugal	2	1	19	1	0	0.67
Spain	3	0.8	54	1	0	1
Sweden	3	2.9	40	1	0.5	1.5
Switzerland	1	1	8	0	0.5	0.83
Trinidad and Tobago	1	0.6	13	1	0	0.33
United Kingdom	1	0.9	14	1	0.5	0.83
United States	1.5	0	12	0	1	1.5
Venezuela	1	1	18	1	1	1.33
Average	2	1.3	25.1	0.8	0.6	1.3
Highest value	3	3	58	1	1	2
Lowest value	1	0	8	0	0	0.33
Range	2	3	50	1	1	1.66

Source: ILO 1994.

TABLE A3. **Independent Variables, 34 Stable Democracies, 1994**

Country	Women in Parliament		Women's Movement		Women's Policy Machinery	Unions	Strikes and Lockouts	Government Seats Left Parties (%)
	Number	Percent	Strength	Autonomy				
Australia	13	8.8	1	1	1	35	4,770	54
Austria	40	22	0	0	0	41	25	42
Bahamas	4	8.2	1	0	0	25	0	
Barbados	3	11	1	1	0	32	54	
Belgium	20	9.4	1	1	1	52	248	30
Botswana	4	10	0	0	0	19	13	
Canada	53	18	1	1	1	38	2,528	0
Colombia	18	11	1	1	0	26	1,678	
Costa Rica	8	14	1	1	1	17	127	
Denmark	60	34	0	0	0	92	1,468	38
Finland	78	39	0	0	0	79	1,293	0
France	37	6.4	1	0	0	31	7,199	0
Germany	176	26	1	0	1	29		0
Greece	18	6	1	1	0	24	2,386	57
Iceland	15	24	0	0	0	85	41	
India	42	7	1	1	0	21	7,804	
Ireland	21	13	1	1	0	47	249	20
Israel	11	9.2	1	1	0	23	456	
Italy	95	15	1	1	0	44	5,248	4
Jamaica	7	12	0	1	0	24	65	
Japan	14	2.7	1	0	0	24	1,339	12
Luxembourg	12	20	0	0	0	43	1	
Mauritius	2	2.8	0	0	0	37	43	
Netherlands	47	31	1	1	1	28	123	27
New Zealand	21	21	1	1	0	23	413	0
Norway	65	39	1	1	0	73	78	41
Portugal	20	8.7	0	0	1	26	1,472	0
Spain	56	16	1	0	0	19	7,317	45
Sweden	141	40	0	0	0	113	202	12
Switzerland	35	18	0	0	0	32	16	20
Trinidad and Tobago	7	19	1	1	0	22	98	
United Kingdom	60	9.2	1	0	0	34	440	0
United States	48	11	1	1	0	16	230	0
Venezuela	12	5.9	0	0	1	17		
Average	38	17	1	1	0	38	1,482	19

TABLE A4. **Measure of Policy Regimes by State**

State	Labor Overall	Women's Labor	Traditional Labor
Alabama	1	0	1
Alaska	4	2	4
Arizona	2	1	1
Arkansas	5	2	1
California	9	5	3
Colorado	7	3	2
Connecticut	4	3	3
Delaware	8	3	3
Florida	6	3	2
Georgia	1	0	1
Hawaii	6	2	3
Idaho	1	1	1
Illinois	5	2	4
Indiana	4	1	3
Iowa	5	1	2
Kansas	7	2	2
Kentucky	2	0	2
Louisiana	4	1	1
Maine	9	3	5
Maryland	4	0	4
Massachusetts	7	4	4
Michigan	2	0	2
Minnesota	9	4	4
Mississippi	2	1	1
Missouri	4	2	2
Montana	4	1	2
Nebraska	6	3	1
Nevada	1	0	1
New Hampshire	3	1	2
New Jersey	8	3	3
New Mexico	7	2	2
New York	9	3	5
North Carolina	5	2	1
North Dakota	1	0	1
Ohio	2	0	2
Oklahoma	6	2	2
Oregon	5	2	4
Pennsylvania	6	1	1
Rhode Island	7	3	4
South Carolina	1	0	1
South Dakota	6	2	1
Tennessee	1	0	1
Texas	4	3	1
Utah	1	0	1
Vermont	9	3	5
Virginia	1	0	1
Washington	6	4	3
Washington, DC	7	3	5
West Virginia	2	0	2
Wisconsin	5	3	4
Wyoming	6	2	1

Text of Questionnaire

Women's Organizing, Representation, and the Public Sphere: Questionnaire

Please provide the name of the organization:

____

Q1. Is this a women's organization? *A "women's organization" is one whose membership or focus is predominantly on women in general or any subgroup of women (i.e., African American women, Hispanic lesbians, etc.) (circle one below)*

1. Yes
2. No
3. Don't know

If a subgroup, which one(s)? ______________________________

____

(i.e., African American women, elderly women, women violinists)

Q2. Is this a feminist organization? (A feminist organization is one that promotes sexual equality and/or the empowerment of women.) (circle one)

1. Yes
2. No
3. Don't Know/Not applicable

Q3. Below we list a series of purposes. For each purpose tell me how high a priority it is for your organization:

A. Providing Networking Opportunities for Women?
   1. The highest priority for this organization
   2. A high priority
   3. A moderate priority
   4. A low priority
   5. Not a priority at all
   6. Don't know

B. Providing Women-Centered Socializing Opportunities?
   1. The highest priority for this organization
   2. A high priority
   3. A moderate priority
   4. A low priority
   5. Not a priority at all
   6. Don't know

C. Advancing Women's Status?
   1. The highest priority for this organization
   2. A high priority
   3. A moderate priority
   4. A low priority
   5. Not a priority at all
   6. Don't know
D. Providing Information/Creating Awareness about Women/Gender Issues?
   1. The highest priority for this organization
   2. A high priority
   3. A moderate priority
   4. A low priority
   5. Not a priority at all
   6. Don't know
E. Influencing Public Policy/Law Generally?
   1. The highest priority for this organization
   2. A high priority
   3. A moderate priority
   4. A low priority
   5. Not a priority at all
   6. Don't know
F. Giving Women a Voice/Representing Women?
   1. The highest priority for this organization
   2. A high priority
   3. A moderate priority
   4. A low priority
   5. Not a priority at all
   6. Don't know
G. Empowering Women?
   1. The highest priority for this organization
   2. A high priority
   3. A moderate priority
   4. A low priority
   5. Not a priority at all
   6. Don't know
H. Influencing Public Decision Making on Specific Topics?
   1. The highest priority for this organization
   2. A high priority
   3. A moderate priority
   4. A low priority
   5. Not a priority at all
   6. Don't know
   (Specify ____)

I. Are there any other purposes that I have not mentioned that are a priority for your organization? What are they? (If more than one, give me the most important)
(Specify ________________________________)

Q4. I am now going to name a series of policy issues or areas. For each one, please tell me whether it is most important, very important, somewhat important, or not at all important for your organization.

A. Reproductive Rights (Abortion, Sterilization Abuse, etc.) ______
Is this issue:
1. Most important
2. Very important
3. Somewhat important
4. Not at all important
5. Don't know

B. Violence against Women (Domestic Violence/Rape/Sexual Harassment, etc.)
____
Is this issue:
1. Most important
2. Very important
3. Somewhat important
4. Not at all important
5. Don't know

C. Work and Family (Maternity/Parental Leave, Child Care) ________
Is this issue:
1. Most important
2. Very important
3. Somewhat important
4. Not at all important
5. Don't know

D. Economic Equality (Equal Pay for Equal Work/Comparable Worth) _______
Is this issue:
1. Most important
2. Very important
3. Somewhat important
4. Not at all important
5. Don't know

E. Women's Health (Breast Cancer, etc.) ________
Is this issue:
1. Most important
2. Very important

3. Somewhat important
4. Not at all important
5. Don't know

F. Women's Poverty (Welfare/HousingAssistance/Homelessness) ________
Is this issue:
1. Most important
2. Very important
3. Somewhat important
4. Not at all important
5. Don't know

G. Gay Rights ________
Is this issue:
1. Most important
2. Very important
3. Somewhat important
4. Not at all important
5. Don't know

H. Elderly Women (Social Security/Elder Abuse/Age Discrimination) ________
Is this issue:
1. Most important
2. Very important
3. Somewhat important
4. Not at all important
5. Don't know

I. Sexual Equality Generally (Equal Opportunity/Sex Discrimination) _______
Is this issue:
1. Most important
2. Very important
3. Somewhat important
4. Not at all important
5. Don't know

J. Race Discrimination ________
Is this issue:
1. Most important
2. Very important
3. Somewhat important
4. Not at all important
5. Don't know

K. Is there some other policy issue I have not mentioned that is important to your organization?
(Specify ____)
(If there is more than one, give me the most important, please.)

Q5. Considering this list of topics again, please indicate, of all these issues, which ONE issue is the MOST important issue for your organization (circle one):

Reproductive Rights
Violence against Women
Work and Family
Economic Equality
Women's Health
Woman's Poverty
Gay Rights
Elderly Women
Sexual Equality
Race Discrimination

Of all these issues I have read, which is the most important to your organization?
Or other I did not mention: ______________________
None of the above
Not appropriate (explain) ______________________

Q6. Does the issue you just mentioned as the most important to your organization (see Q5 above) receive an adequate amount of coverage in the media?
Yes (If Yes go to Q8)
No (If No to Q6, ask Q7)

Q7. (If No) why do you think the issue does not receive an adequate amount of media coverage? Go to Q9.

Q8. If Yes to Q6, ask: Do you think the media coverage given to the issue you specified as most important to your organization is adequate? Yes (go to Q9) No
(If No) Please elaborate ______________________

Q9. How important is it to your organization to gain media coverage for the issue you have distinguished as most important?

1. Not important at all
2. Not very important
3. Somewhat important
4. Very important

Q10. Does your organization ever try to increase media coverage of women's policy issues?

1. Yes (If Yes, go to Q11)
2. No (If No, go to Q12)

Q11. (If Yes) Which methods are used to increase coverage? Do you use:
Press releases? Yes No
Protests/Demonstrations? Yes No
Providing information/research to media? Yes No
Interviews with media? Yes No
Contacting sympathetic journalists? Yes No
Other methods we have not mentioned? Yes No (If Yes, please specify
____)

Q12. Do you ever partner with other women's groups? If so, which ones?
1. No
2. Yes—specify ____________________________________

Q13. What percent of your budget would you estimate is spent on media coverage?
If you don't know exactly, can you give me your best estimate? __________
If you still can't say, would it be better to call back at another time to get an answer? Yes No
If yes:
The number I should call? _______________________
The best time to call? __________________________
Other relevant info.: ______________________________

Notes

Introduction

1. For examples of activists claiming to represent broader constituencies, see Chuang 2002; Davila 2002; Shepard 2003; Curtin 2003; Hays 2004; Levy 2005; Duff-Brown 2006.

2. Reed 1986; Cohen and Arato 1992, especially 565–66; Epstein 2001; Fisher 2006; Richards 2006; Banaszak, Beckwith, and Rucht 2003; Tarrow 1998; Skocpol 1999, 2003; Putnam 2000; Strolovitch 2004; Verba et al. 1995.

3. For further discussion, see Gitlin 1995; Dudas 2005; Dobrowolsky 1998; Peters 1991; Dryzek 1990; Young 2003; Costain 2005.

4. I use the term *disadvantaged groups* here to refer to social groups that have been systematically and historically disadvantaged, or what Williams (1998) calls "marginalized groups." Marginalized groups are those that have historically been subject to discrimination; that continue to suffer demonstrable disadvantage in multiple spheres (social, economic, political); that identify themselves as being a disadvantaged group, to whom negative meanings are ascribed by the broader society and culture; and who are defined by some immutable characteristic (or a characteristic that is most often experienced as immutable) such as race, ethnicity, gender, sexual orientation, and the like (see Williams 1998; Young 1990, 2000).

5. In earlier work (Weldon 2002b), I argued that the empirical literature on group representation has focused on proving or disproving that *individual* members of marginalized groups (especially in the United States) in the legislature (or other decision-making body) make a positive impact on the representation of those groups. This is still true even of the best recent empirical work on this topic (Swers 2002; Gay 2002; Whitby and Krause 2001; Tate 2001; Sanbonmatsu 2003). For exceptions, see Strolovitch 2003; Wolbrecht and Hero 2005. Even though the theoretical literature is broader, it has still mostly focused on debates about descriptive representation (Dovi 2002; Mansbridge 1999; Williams 1998; Young 1990, 2000; Phillips 1995).

6. For work suggesting that social movements or government agencies can be representatives, see Weldon 2002; Mazur 2002; Meyer 2003. For work on the politically significant links between feminist organizations and legislators, see Carroll 2003; Sawer 2004; Costain 1998.

7. Exceptions include Bollen and Jackman 1989; Lipset 1994; Markoff 1999; Meyer et al. 2005; Paxton 2002; Poletta 2002; Muller 1995. Even these works tend to focus on social movements as outlets for participation rather than representation. Vickers,

Rankin, and Appel (1993) consider the representative role of a major Canadian women's organization (the National Action Committee on the Status of Women) as part of a general analysis of the political significance of that organization.

8. Cohen and Arato (1992, 19) see social movements as "a form of citizen participation in public life" but do not explicitly consider social movements to be a form of democratic representation. Della Porta (2005) and Dryzek (1990) see social movements as instantiations or real-world examples (to some degree and in some cases) of deliberative democracy. Dryzek and others (2003, especially chap. 5) focus on whether the relationship between social movements and the state promotes or undermines citizen participation. Polletta (2002) examines social movement organizations as efforts to embody participatory democracy. In a cross-national study, Norris (2002) treats social movements as forms of participation.

9. Specific sets of interviews or surveys used are described in the relevant chapter. Specific dates and descriptions of interviewees are provided when the specific interview is cited, as much as is possible given guidelines for the protection of human subjects. Interviews were undertaken with Norwegian activists, legislators, and bureaucrats in 1995; with Canadian activists, police, and bureaucrats in 2002–3; with state and local legislators, activists, and bureaucrats in the United States in 2007–9; and with federal bureaucrats in the United States in 1998–99 and 2002–3. These interviews do not include the research used to develop data about violence against women and women's commissions, described in chapter 4.

10. Of course, any analysis necessarily oversimplifies the ongoing, iterative relationship between state and social movement, because analysts must start somewhere. See Meyer 2005 on what Meyer calls the "chicken-and-egg issue" in theorizing social movements and democracy.

11. Although Dryzek and others (2003) acknowledge the possibility of a dual strategy (combining autonomous or outside action with integration into the state) being successful under some conditions, these conditions are extremely circumscribed, and the thrust of the overall argument is that some kinds of exclusion from the state are preferable to inclusion for social movements in most cases.

12. On gender differences, see Klein 1984; Mueller 1988; CAWP 1997, 2006; Inglehart and Norris 2003. On race/ethnicity in the United States, see Welch and Hibbing 1988; Hero and Tolbert 1995; Claasan 2004. For cross-national evidence, see the *Public Opinion Quarterly* special issue "Race, Public Opinion, and the Social Sphere" (Bobo 1997). On class, see Hill and Leighley 1994; Shapiro and Young 1989; Inglehart and Norris 2003. For evidence on how political attitudes vary across subgroups, see Whitaker 1999, 79; CAWP 2000, 2004; Bedolla and Scola 2006.

13. For example, theorists of gender, race, and class politics predominantly argue that gender, race, class, and other aspects of group domination cannot be understood separately from one another. Such axes of disadvantage intersect one another, mutually modifying each other. Indeed, in the strong version of this idea, race, class, and gender have no meaning and cannot be understood apart from one another. They are not autonomous categories. See Zinn and Dill 1996; Ferber 1998; Collins 1990, 1998; Brewer

1999; Crenshaw 1994. Others argue that gender itself is an unstable category (e.g., Butler 1993).

14. Some scholars argue that civil society cannot simultaneously be a transmission belt for dominant social values and an arena where a diversity of ideas flourish (Mosher 2003). But civil society provides a process for sorting through diverse ideas, and although some ideas may become dominant as a result of this process, they are not always the same ideas. So there is no contradiction in seeing civil society as a competitive context for ideas at the same time as one sees congruence between state and the dominant norms of civil society as important for functioning democracy. Discussions in civil society transform not only civil society itself but social norms and the state more generally.

15. This is not to suggest, of course, that marginalized groups or counterpublics do not exclude anyone. Of course, such publics are themselves riven by societal inequalities. But these groupings respond to some specific exclusions—including *internal exclusion* (Young 2000)—in the dominant public sphere.

16. This is not to suggest that having a group perspective represented exhausts representation for group members. Group members may wish to have particular interests or policies adopted, but it is unlikely that these are shared across the whole group. So representation for the group as a whole (as opposed to some subgroup or particular organization) can only be measured more broadly. (I thank Carol Gould for raising this issue.)

17. This is not to dispute Rehfeld's provocative but persuasive argument that there are indeed nondemocratic forms of representation for which we need a better theoretical account. Here I focus on the limits of overly formal criteria for democratic representation.

Chapter 1

1. I am arguing for a consideration of movements and institutions as sources, not determinants, of representation. Many studies have examined the relationship between institutions or movements and the number of women elected. I am arguing for a conceptualization of institutions and movements as representative in themselves.

2. I follow Williams (1998, 16) here in defining marginalized groups as those groups for which social and political inequality is structured along the lines of group membership, for which group membership is not experienced as voluntary or mutable, and for which negative meanings are assigned to group identity. Williams emphasizes that patterns of social and political inequality persist over time and continue into the present. For a discussion of why women and African Americans in the United States are marginalized groups, see Williams 1998.

3. This literature includes a wide array of studies, covering many types of policy issues and groups. See Bullock and MacManus 1987; Darcy, Welch, and Clark 1987; Darden 1984, 109; Gay 2001, 2002; Grofman et al. 1992; Hill 1981; Jones 1996; Kittilson 2008; Matland 1993; Matland and Studlar 1996; Meier et al. 1999; Nixon and Darcy

1996; Rule and Zimmerman 1994; Sanbonmatsu 2003; Schwindt-Bayer and Mishler 2005; Selden, Brudney, and Kellough 1998; Shugart 1994; Singh 1998; Swers 2002; Welch 1990a, 1990b; Welch and Studlar 1990; Zimmerman 1994.

4. For examples of this trend, see Celis 2008; Childs 2006; Krook et al. 2008; Weldon 2002; Wolbrecht and Hero 2005; See also articles in the special issue of *Politics & Gender* (vol. 2, no. 4 [December 2006]) focusing on the concept of critical mass.

5. Lublin 1999; Cameron, Epstein, and O'Halloran 1996; Epstein and O'Halloran 1999; Fraga et al. 1986; Gigendil 1996; Gigendil and Vengroff 1997; Hero and Tolbert 1995; Kerr and Miller 1997; Kittilson 2008; Meier et al. 1999; Tremblay 1998; Schwindt-Bayer and Mishler 2005; Swers 2002;Welch and Studlar 1990.

6. Sometimes, descriptive representation is defined as the extent to which the legislature reflects or mirrors the makeup of the population: better representation is indicated by a larger number or proportion of candidates or legislators that are female (i.e., Matland and Studlar 1996; Welch and Studlar 1990) or by the proportion of legislators of the marginalized group in relation to the population (Grofman et al. 1992). Note that this operationalization still rests on the assumption that individuals "stand for" their group(s), since it suggests that each additional legislator adds an increment of "better representation" for the group or groups in question.

7. This is still true even of the best recent empirical work on this topic (see Swers 2002; Gay 2002; Whitby and Krause 2001; Tate 2001; Sanbonmatsu 2003). For exceptions, see Strolovitch 2003; Wolbrecht and Hero 2005.

8. In a more recent article, Mansbridge (2005) also discusses this theoretical problem of essentialism in arguments for descriptive representation, and I agree with her argument there that the connection between personal and group experiences or perspectives can be conceptualized in a way that avoids some of these problems, but I think it takes more work to show how, for example, Young's (2004) account of group perspective avoids these problems. I aim to fill that gap here.

9. At best, an individual member of the group, without interacting with others from the social group, can articulate a truncated version of the group perspective, *if* she is so inclined. This is a weak version of the argument that in cases where group perspectives are uncrystallized, the reactions of members of marginalized groups in legislatures can help to define the interests of marginalized groups (Phillips 1995; Mansbridge 1999). The argument is that because a group perspective has not been clearly defined, the reactions of individuals from marginalized groups to particular situations can help to draw attention to differences in group perspective. Because I see individuals as more limited in relation to the group perspective, I see their contribution as being more muted.

10. Readers may wonder why I do not draw on social choice theory, since that approach has produced so much sophisticated theorizing of the relation between individual and group preferences. Space does not permit an extended treatment of the issue, but I would suggest that methodological individualist tools are relatively poorly suited to a theorization of social group perspective. Social group perspectives are not achieved by aggregating individual preferences. Indeed, the preferences of individuals (even the

very self-understandings and identities that influence preferences) are transformed in the course of interaction with others. Moreover, without intragroup interaction, individual members' views may not even include the categories or ideas that would otherwise emerge, so adding up individual preferences will not reveal group perspective. Finally, group perspective, as I understand it, is much less determinative than a specific preference. This makes social choice theory a poor tool for conceptualizing the relation between the perspectives of social groups and the experiences of their members.

11. Activism around the issues of violence against women began in the 1970s and 1980s and was discussed at international women's conferences in the 1980s. In 1995, women's groups from 180 countries signed an agreement stating that violence against women is a problem demanding top priority (U.S. Department of Labor 1996). Other international agreements prohibiting violence against women preceded this particular agreement.

12. Responsiveness, as defined here, should not necessarily be understood to imply effectiveness. A government that responds to violence sooner (attempting to take immediate action to address a policy) but does so ineffectively is still more responsive than one that does nothing (Weldon 2002). Indeed, some scholars have examined the question of whether responsiveness conflicts with effectiveness (see Rodrik and Zeckhauer 1988).

13. Elman (1996) and Weldon (2002) do consider the impact of the number of women in public office, but the impact is considered in terms of policy effectiveness or responsiveness, not in terms of political representation.

14. The dependent variable has eight categories (0 to 7) and so can be used in an OLS regression equation. Note that the dependent variable is not an event count (sometimes multiple areas are addressed in a single piece of legislation and are therefore not independent). Thus, a Poisson regression function is not appropriate (Winkelmann 1997).

15. Governments sometimes obtain the same score by enacting different policies. This is generally considered a problem with this sort of indicator, but for our purposes, this feature of the indicator is of little interest. Policy experts and activists argue that there is no single policy solution and that an appropriate policy response is one that attacks the problem on all fronts (Busch 1992; CEDAW 1998; Chalk and King 1998; Elman 1996). For this reason, the dependent variable is measured in terms of the number of different sorts of things that governments are doing (scope) rather than by which of the seven policy areas they address. On this measure, a government that undertook only a criminal response or only public education initiatives would receive a lower score than one that undertook both a criminal justice response and public education initiatives.

16. Unfortunately, the usual criteria for assessing composite dependent variables are inappropriate for this measure of scope and for my research question more generally. For example, a common mode of assessing a composite indicator is to examine correlations among the items. The items in this indicator (policy areas) are conceptually related to the problem of violence against women and are widely considered important

elements of comprehensive response to the problem. But they need not be correlated with each other in order to indicate the breadth of government response. For example, funding for battered women's shelters is often distinct from funding for rape crisis centers: governments often fund one, but not the other, even though both are important elements of any government response to violence against women. If the adoption of these two different types of policies is only weakly correlated, should I conclude that one of them is unnecessary or unrelated to the underlying concept, the scope of government response to violence against women? I think the answer is no, since we can see that they are both clearly related to government response to violence against women. Eliminating one of these items would weaken, not strengthen, the measure, because the very concept of the scope of government action suggests that policy will range across distinct areas. One would not necessarily expect government provision of public education programs to be related to government funding for rape crisis centers.

17. Also, a study on effectiveness would require cross-nationally comparable data that is of higher quality and that covers a longer period of time (probably at least 20 years) than the data currently available. For example, official statistics should not be used for a study of effectiveness in even a single national context because of problems with underreporting to police and changing legal definitions. For a discussion of data sources on violence in the United States, see Greenfeld 1997; Chalk and King 1998. For a discussion of the problems with cross-national comparisons in this area, see Timmerman and Bajema 1999.

18. A very thin definition of democracy is employed here. I am examining countries in which basic civil liberties are respected and in which free and fair elections are regularly held based on the Comparative Survey of Freedom (Freedom House 1997). States that were continuously democratic from 1974 to 1994 were judged to be stable democracies. The total number of countries in the study is 36.

19. Women's movements are not equivalent to women's organizations. The idea that organized interests provide a form of representation has a long history and is one of the core ideas of pluralism (see Williams 1998 for a discussion). I am arguing here that women's movements, which include but are not limited to women's organizations, provide such a representative function. Women's movement activities such as protests, cultural productions, and "personal politics" are important in changing public opinion and giving women a public voice. Indeed, these broader activities of protest may be necessary before traditional lobbying activities by formal groups can have any effect (Costain 1998).

20. This means that women's movement strength is logically separable from policy influence, thus avoiding what would otherwise be a tautological claim: that women's movements influence policy-making when they are influential in policy-making.

21. I compared these expert assessments with data on the number and membership of women's organizations drawn from historical accounts and encyclopedias of women's organizations. I found that coding strength according to the number and membership of organizations would have produced the same comparative assessments in most cases where data permitted an assessment.

22. Note that a women's movement is never coded as strong simply because it appears to have influenced policies on violence against women. The codings are taken from Weldon 2002 and are summarized in the appendix.

23. The machinery is coded 1 only if both conditions are met, because neither condition alone is theoretically sufficient for political influence. Examination of the interactions between these two dimensions supports this coding.

24. Some scholars have used the logged number of women to capture the critical mass effect (cf. Berkman and O'Connor 1993; Hansen 1992). This operationalization does not change the conclusion (results not shown).

25. Unfortunately, the cross-national data on levels of violence are not of sufficient quality to warrant inclusion in a regression analysis. The data that do exist and are somewhat comparable suggest that level of violence bears little relationship to government response. For example, the level of violence against intimate female partners appears to be roughly similar in Norway, Sweden, the United States, and Canada, but government responsiveness to domestic violence varies widely across these governments.

26. Absolute numbers of women also do not have a linear relationship with government responsiveness (results not shown). Of course, one might suspect that the effect of additional women will be visible where they have more influence. But the presence of women in more influential positions, such as the proportion of women in cabinet, still has no association with responsiveness to violence against women (not shown).

Chapter 2

1. For exceptions, see the chapter on reconciliation policy in Mazur 2002; Morgan 2006; Kittilson 2008; Schwindt-Bayer and Mishler 2005.

2. I discuss Gelb and Palley's (1987) categorization of policies a bit later in this chapter, as it pertains to policies in general and is not primarily aimed at categorizing welfare states.

3. Some feminist scholars and activists (e.g., social feminists) have argued that the goal is not to change gender roles but to revalue them. There is not space here to adequately review and critique these arguments. Here, I acknowledge these disagreements but assert that gender role change (and not just revaluation) is critical for ensuring that women have the full range of personal and professional opportunities that are presented to men, and this seems to me to be a core element of sexual equality.

4. Concerns about comparing cases with extreme values (Collier and Mahoney 1996) are less salient here since I pair the comparison with a quantitative cross-national analysis to test the generalizability of the findings.

5. This means, for example, that I do not discuss the paid parental leave offered in California, since the determinants of such laws are likely to operate at a state level and since these policies vary across the 50 states. Such state-level leave policies in the United States are discussed in chapter 3.

6. *Cleveland Board of Education v. Lafleur* (1973) was favorable to pregnant workers, while *Geduldig v. Aiello* (1974) undermined the rights of pregnant workers.

7. The final bill allows employers to exempt elective abortion from insurance coverage except to save the life of the mother.

8. Working women in early twentieth-century Norway were mostly very poor and/or unmarried and constituted a small proportion of the adult female population, so these policies did not affect most women (Leira 1993). Two other acts adopted soon afterward (1915) guaranteed maternal health care regardless of employment status, and the child welfare act provided welfare benefits to single mothers. The first of these later measures was backed by a cross-class coalition of women's groups, the second was backed by a cross-gender coalition of leftists (Sainsbury 2001).

9. Norwegian feminists emphasized the importance of organizing to elect more women to government. They were very successful at exploiting particular features of the Norwegian electoral system (organizing campaigns to cross out the names of men and write in the names of women), and the large number of women elected in the 1971 local/county elections has come to be called the 'Women's Coup" (Bystydzienski 1995, 45).

10. The "daddy leave," which had been discussed publicly earlier, was not part of these reforms.

11. President Clinton did ease rules permitting states to offer unemployment insurance for pregnant women in 2000, creating so-called Baby UI (but this was a measure passed by Congress). President Bush eliminated these provisions soon after his election and blocked states from offering such benefits (Marquis 2002). These were not acts of Congress, and the number of women in the legislature has little effect here. Rather, as in the cases discussed in this chapter, changes in the partisan control of Congress, business opposition, and support from unions made the difference.

Chapter 3

1. For example, the major 2005 budget bill contained provisions allowing states "to impose new fees on Medicaid recipients, cut federal child-support enforcement funds, impose new work requirements on state welfare programs and squeeze student lenders—all for the purpose of slowing the growth of federal entitlement programs" (Murray and Weisman 2005).

2. For an excellent discussion of current issues in state theory, see Aronowitz and Bratsis 2002.

3. In the aggregate, lawyers, doctors, professional politicians, and businesspeople are the largest occupational groups among both state and national legislators. This is also true for some state populations, but a complete state-by-state occupational breakdown is not available (National Council of State Legislators 2008; Texas Politics 2006; Watchke 2001).

4. The self-reported affiliation with business may reflect a desire to associate oneself with business and so must be interpreted with caution.

5. The same occupational groups that perceived stronger support from business (business, farmers, sales) were also those that perceived less support from women's groups. Otherwise, occupation did not seem to have any clear relationship to perceived

support from women's groups. I mention this because women's groups turn out to be important for the representation of labor.

6. Indeed, the better paid a state legislative position is, the more likely it is that lower-income groups could afford to be state legislators: otherwise, they might not be able to afford to combine running for state legislator with their current occupation. Alternatively, we know that more professionalized legislatures may be less accessible (e.g., to women).

7. I thank Suzie Parker for raising this point.

8. The Department of Justice created a model antitrafficking policy as a guide for the states. The department tracks which states have adopted or are in the process of adopting this model policy. See U.S. Department of Justice Civil Rights Division 2004.

9. Although some may be skeptical of the inclusion of cultural or social organizations among women's movement organizations, it is important to note that social movement scholars identify such social and cultural networks as critical for enabling mobilization, as the "connective tissue" of social organizations (Tarrow 1998). In addition, such organizations are often important sites for the development of women's perspective (Weldon 2004).

Chapter 4

1. I use the term *women of color* to refer to women belonging to marginalized race and/or ethnic groups (Burnham 2001). For a definition of marginalized groups, see Williams 1998, 16.

2. A social movement is a network of activists who attempt to change society, employing a wide range of tactics in *sustained* confrontation with powerful opponents (Klandermans 1986; Johnson 1999; Meyer 2000; Tarrow 1998).

3. Others express concern about identity-based organizations but acknowledge that such organizations sometimes facilitate mobilization (see Skocpol 1999, 2003; Snow and McAdam 2000). For theoretical discussions of whether identity politics undermine democracy, see Gutmann 2003; Young 2000.

4. See, for example, Gamson 1991; Bernstein 1997; Downton and Wehr 1998; Taylor 1999.

5. Some may wonder whether the effects of separate organization vary across states with different histories and political contexts. Of course, there may be some such variation, but what does not vary across states is the existence of groups of women who are disadvantaged relative to women of the dominant race/ethnicity. To the extent that such women are disadvantaged in each state, we can see if separate organizing of such women affects social movements and policies in systematic ways, without arguing that we are capturing all the relevant effects of such organizing or every relevant aspect of the state political context.

6. A policy may be rendered ineffective for many reasons (design flaws, lack of political will, incompetence, etc.), but an *unresponsive* government would not have adopted a policy at all (Rodrik and Zeckhaur 1988; Weldon 2002a).

7. I refer to survey data because criminal justice data (e.g., reports to police) is less reliable for examining rates of violence against women (especially variation across racial, ethnic, and income groups), since the majority of incidents are not reported to police, there are big differences in reporting rates across groups, and the likelihood of having contact with the criminal justice system varies across groups (Tjaden and Thoennes 2000; Crenshaw 1994).

8. These examples are drawn from interviews conducted in 2000 and 2001 with domestic violence coalitions in the 50 states.

9. The total number of women's organizations and the number of organizations focusing on women of color is derived from the Electrapages database. This database includes over 10,000 U.S. women's organizations self-identifying as feminist organizations. The self-identified nature of the listing may raise concerns about overcounting or undercounting. But in comparing the Electrapages with other directories of women's groups (e.g., National Council for Research on Women 1992; Women of Color Resource Center 2003; Barrett 1993), the Electrapages seems to be more comprehensive, including most of the feminist groups listed by other key directories and many not listed there. Overcounting could occur if some organizations that were not actually feminist organizations or not organizations of women of color were counted. Indeed, some directories (e.g., Barrett 1993) seem to include many organizations that are not really women's organizations. However, a perusal of the organizations included in the Electrapages does not reveal any obviously wrongly included organizations. The indicator of women's movement strength provided here is positively correlated with standard measures of movement strength. Although the Electrapages are no longer online, a print version of the directory may be obtained for a fee from the Women's Information Exchange (wie@pon.net). For raw data, see Weldon 2004. Copies of original search results are available from the author on request.

10. The measure does not reflect variation in the structure or size of organizations. Unfortunately, high-quality data on associations is difficult to come by, and detailed data on the size and composition of these organizations is even more difficult to obtain, especially for a cross-state comparison. These difficulties are magnified when one aims to include local and less formal kinds of organizations, common forms of organizing for women of color and women in general. The measurement strategy proposed here makes the best use of the available data. Note that the measure developed here is positively correlated with standard measures of movement strength.

11. Because the measure includes action across many different types of government action, one would not necessarily expect a high rate of correlation among the elements, and traditional measures of the degree of relationship among the elements of a scale do not apply. The relationship between the elements is conceptual (i.e., relationship to the problem of violence against women) rather than empirical (see Weldon 2002a, 2002b). Nevertheless, readers should note that the elements load onto a single dimension that accounts for 85 percent of the variance.

12. Although the data includes policies adopted in 2000, it is possible that some policy advances were made earlier. This raises some questions about temporal order, since

some of the dependent variables are measured for the year 2000 or more recent years. Still, the variable does accurately reflect the state of government policy at the end of 2000. Since many legislative measures, especially those involving spending, require frequent reauthorization, and because state governments have reversed previous policies, continued funding for domestic violence shelters, for example, is an important policy outcome in the year in question, even if the policy is not initiated in that year.

13. This is a rough measure of responsiveness to violence against women of color, but it is meaningful as a "first cut" at a previously unexamined empirical question. A lack of baseline data and difficulties in constructing a measure that was comparable across states with markedly different minority populations prevented a better measure.

14. In interviews with commission representatives, access to the legislature and executive was determined by asking about whether commission representatives met with representatives of the legislature and executive, the rank of officials with whom they met, and the regularity of meetings. Women's organizations were judged as having access to those commissions reporting regular meetings between the commission and women's groups. Data are for 1999.

15. Although political parties are often important in analyses of state politics, for policies on violence against women, cross-national studies show that women's movements are generally more important (Weldon 2002a). At a national level, antiviolence legislation has enjoyed unanimous, bipartisan support since the late 1990s. Thus, degree of liberalism and partisanship more generally provide little explanatory leverage in this policy issue area.

16. I use data from Berry and others (1993) since it is more complete and recent than data from Wright, Erickson, and McIver (1985, 1993). Using Wright, Erickson, and McIver's data set does not change the conclusion.

17. Strolovitch (2006) shows that organizations that are not focused on women tend to view women's issues (e.g., violence) as irrelevant to their mission.

18. Similarly, education, another common control variable, had no effect (not shown).

19. The term *forcible rape,* which seems redundant, is the FBI's term and excludes statutory rape.

20. Since the 50 states constitute a population, sampling was not employed. I discuss significance as a shorthand way of discussing the importance of the predictors, although, strictly speaking, significance is not relevant (Gill 2001).

21. Murphy (1998) finds that the number of women in the legislature had a small but significant effect on the adoption of police reforms concerning domestic violence. This seemingly contradictory result may be explained by the narrower focus of the dependent variable and by the absence of controls for women's movement impact.

Chapter 5

1. For example, the excellent collection of essays in Ferree and Martin (1995) examines some important organizations in detail (e.g., *Ms.* magazine) but also includes

chapters that systematically investigate changes in the internal structure of women's organizations over time. None of these chapters, however, examines the representativeness of all women's organizations as a set.

2. In one exception, Staggenborg (1995) delineates different types of women's organizations and considers their differing goals and effectiveness. Maryann Barakso's interesting work on democratic procedures in women's organizations (e.g., Barakso 2007) also comes close to what I have in mind here but still considers the degree of (participatory) democracy exhibited by each organization rather than the representativeness and effectiveness of women's organizations as a set.

3. Sources for listings of women's organizations included Women of Color Resource Center 2003, National Council for Research on Women 2004, Chicago NOW 2004, and Rexroat 2003.

4. In a comparison survey we did in Boston, it appeared that economic inequality had less importance to women's movements there, while race equality had more importance, but this was true for both general women's organizations and those focused on women of color.

5. This figure is based on an analysis of the member information on the Senate and the House available on the Illinois General Assembly home page at http://www.ilga.gov/.

6. These figures are based on an analysis of the list of standing committees provided by the city clerk at http://www.chicityclerk.com/standingcommittee.php.

7. Earl and others (2004) have pointed out that scholars should be aware of the biases that stem from using newspapers as sources of data on protest, because not all organizations are equally likely to be covered. Of course, this analysis does not do that, since it involves comparing the activities reported by women's organizations with press coverage of those activities. Indeed, the data here suggest that the print media do not necessarily accurately reflect the activities, numbers, or scope of activities of women's groups.

8. Indeed, Rohlinger (2002, 2006) shows that social movement organizations get differential degrees of coverage based on their tactics, identity, and political opportunities. Comparing one very similar set of organizations at the same time in the same place, we are focusing on whether women's organizations try to get media coverage at all and, if they do, whether they are successful in attracting media attention for the issues they say are important. The narrow question we ask in this section of this chapter is whether the set of women's groups in Chicago are effective representatives in the sense that they are attracting public attention for the issues they say are important.

9. These counts do not include duplicate or irrelevant articles.

Chapter 6

1. Women's organizations increasingly encourage separate organization by marginalized subgroups of women (Weldon 2006; Barakso 2005). Trade unions are also in-

creasingly adopting formal rules about gender representativeness (see McBride 1999; AFL-CIO 2009).

2. Dryzek and others (2005) do recognize that social movements sometimes can be integrated without depleting civil society, but their discussion makes clear that they view this as unlikely in most cases, and the overall thrust of the argument of their book is that passive exclusion is better than inclusion and that those who argue for actively including marginalized groups in the state ought to think about the dangers of co-optation and depletion of civil society more carefully.

3. For an excellent critical review of the program's impact, see Brodie 2001, especially 371–74.

4. For example, in Michigan, within nine months of ending the state DBE program in 1989, there were no minority-owned businesses participating in state highway construction projects. Seven years later, in 1996, DBEs received only 1.1 percent of state highway contract dollars. Similarly, in Louisiana, there are approximately 165 qualified DBEs available. In 1996, those DBEs performed approximately 160 prime contracts and subcontracts, worth 12.4 percent of federal aid dollars. On state construction projects, however, where there is no similar program, those same firms performed 2 prime contracts and 12 subcontracts, or only 0.4 percent of state highway construction dollars.

5. For an excellent discussion of how to conceptualize and weigh the advantages of institutional access versus the potential costs of demobilization/deradicalization stemming from co-optation, see Coy and Hedeen 2007.

6. Meyer (2007, 130–31), for example, defines co-optation in a more refined way as the necessary adjustments to language and the like that come with political inclusion. The consequences of co-optation, though, are part of what is at issue here, so for purposes of discussion, I focus on the meaning of co-optation as advanced by critics of social movement engagement with the state.

7. For a listing of organizations by country, see Denise Osted's online directory of women's organizations (http://www.distel.ca/womlist/womlist.html). The number of Canadian women's organizations is second or third in the world, despite the fact that there are many more populous countries with active women's movements.

References

Abramovitz, Mimi. 1992. *Regulating the Lives of Women: Social Welfare Policy from Colonial Times to the Present.* Boston: South End Press.

Acker, Joan. 1995. "Feminist Goals and Organizing Processes." In *Feminist Organizations: Harvest of the New Women's Movement,* ed. Myra Marx Ferree and Patricia Yancey Martin, 137–44. Philadelphia: Temple University Press.

ACORN. 2005. *Living Wage Resource Center.* http://www.acorn.org (accessed October 20, 2005).

AFL-CIO. *See* American Federation of Labor and Congress of Industrial Organizations.

Agnew, Vijay. 1998. *In Search of a Safe Place: Abused Women and Culturally Sensitive Services.* Toronto: University of Toronto Press.

Alesina, A., E. Glaeser, and B. Sacerdote. 2001. "Why Doesn't the United States Have a European-Style Welfare State?" *Brookings Papers on Economic Activity* 2 (Fall): 187–277.

American Federation of Labor and Congress of Industrial Organizations (AFL-CIO). 2004. *Overcoming Barriers to Women in Organization and Leadership: Report to the AFL-CIO Executive Council.* Washington, DC: AFL-CIO. http://www.aflcio.org/issues/civilrights/upload/overcomingbarrierswomen.pdf (accessed 2008).

Aronowitz, Stanley, and Peter Bratsis, eds. 2002. *Paradigm Lost: State Theory Reconsidered.* Minneapolis: University of Minnesota Press.

Associated Press. 2002. "Poll: Majority Don't Think Right-to-Work Helps." Associated Press State and Local Wire, BC cycle, September 3.

Associated Press. 2005. "Unions Say Labor Bill Won't End Nevada Right-to-Work Law." Associated Press State and Local Wire, BC cycle, May 18.

Ashford, D. 1978. *Comparative Public Policies.* Beverly Hills: Sage.

Avdeyeva, Olga. 2007. "When Do States Comply with International Treaties? Policies on Violence against Women in Post-Communist Countries." *International Studies Quarterly* 51 (December): 877–900.

Babbie, Earl. 2001. *The Practice of Social Research.* 9th ed. Belmont, CA: Wadsworth.

Bachrach, Peter, and Morton S. Baratz. 1962. "Two Faces of Power." *American Political Science Review* 5:947–52.

Banaszak, Lee Ann, Karen Beckwith, and Dieter Rucht, eds. 2003. *Women's Movements Facing the Reconfigured State.* New York: Cambridge University Press.

Barakso, Maryann. 2004. *Governing NOW.* Ithaca: Cornell University Press.

Barakso, Maryann. 2005. "Civic Engagement and Voluntary Associations: Reconsidering the Role of the Governance Structures of Advocacy Groups." *Polity* 37:315–34.

Barakso, Maryann. 2007. "Is There a 'Woman's Way' of Governing? Assessing the Organizational Structures of Women's Membership Associations." *Politics & Gender* 3 (2007): 201–27.

Barrett, Jacqueline, ed. 1993. *Encyclopedia of Women's Associations Worldwide.* Farmington Hills, MI: Gale Group.

Bashevkin, Sylvia. 1996. "Interest Groups and Social Movements." In *Comparing Democracies: Elections and Voting in Global Perspective,* ed. Lawrence LeDuc, Richard G. Niemi, and Pippa Norris. Thousand Oaks, CA: Sage.

Baumgartner, Frank R., and Bryan D. Jones. 1993. *Agendas and Instability in American Politics.* Chicago: University of Chicago Press.

Beck, Juliette. 2000. "Why We Are Protesting." *Washington Post,* April 16, final edition, Op-ed, B07.

Beckwith, Karen. 2000. "Beyond Compare? Women's Movements in Comparative Perspective." *European Journal of Political Research* 37:431–68.

Beckwith, Karen. 2005a. "A Common Language of Gender." *Politics & Gender* 1 (1): 128–37.

Beckwith, Karen. 2005b. "The Comparative Politics of Women's Movements: Teaching Comparatively, Learning Democracy." *Perspectives on Politics* 3 (3): 583–96.

Beckwith, Karen. 2007. "Mapping Strategic Engagements of Women's Movements." *International Feminist Journal of Politics* 9 (3): 312–39.

Bell, Derrick A. 1987. *And We Are Not Saved: The Elusive Quest for Racial Justice.* New York: Basic Books.

Bergman, S. 2004. "Collective Organizing and Claim Making on Child Care in Norden: Blurring the Boundaries between the Inside and the Outside." *Social Politics* 11 (2): 217–46.

Bergqvist, Christina, A. Borchorst, A. Christensen, V. Ramstedt-Silén, N. C. Raaum, and A. Styrkársdóttir, eds. 1999. *Equal Democracies? Gender and Politics in the Nordic Countries.* Oslo: Scandinavian University Press.

Berkman, Michael B., and Robert E. O'Connor. 1993. "Do Women Legislators Matter? Female Legislators and State Abortion Policy." *American Politics Quarterly* 21 (1): 102–24.

Bernstein, Mary. 1997. "Celebration and Suppression: The Strategic Uses of Identity by the Lesbian and Gay Movement." *American Journal of Sociology* 103 (3): 531–65.

Bernstein, Nina. 2000. "Council Readies Unique Sex Bias Measure." *New York Times,* December 1, late edition—final, B-3.

Berry, Jeffrey. 1999. "The Rise of Citizen Groups." In *Civic Engagement in American Democracy,* ed. Theda Skocpol and Morris Fiorina, 367–94. Washington, DC: Brookings Institution.

Berry, William D., Evan J. Ringquist, Richard C. Fording, and Russell L. Hanson. 1998. "Measuring Citizen and Government Ideology in the American States, 1960–93." *American Journal of Political Science* 42 (1): 327–28.

Blau, Peter M. 1977. "A Macrosociological Theory of Social Structure." *American Journal of Sociology* 83 (1): 26–54.

Block, Fred. 1987. *Revising State Theory.* Philadelphia: Temple University Press.

BLS. *See* U.S. Bureau of Labor Statistics.

Bobo, Lawrence. 1997. "Race, Public Opinion and the Social Sphere." In Special issue on race, *Public Opinion Quarterly* 61:1–15.

Bobrow, Davis B., and John Dryzek. 1987. *Policy Analysis by Design.* Pittsburgh: University of Pittsburgh Press.

Bollen, Kenneth A., and Robert W. Jackman. 1989. "Democracy, Stability, and Dichotomies." *American Sociological Review* 54 (4): 612–21.

Brady, David. 2003. "The Politics of Poverty: Left Political Institutions, the Welfare State and Poverty." Luxembourg Income Study Working Paper 352, June. http://www.lisproject.org/publications/liswps/352.pdf.

Brandth, Berit, and Elin Kvande. 2009. "Gendered or Gender-Neutral Care Politics for Fathers?" *Annals of the American Academy of Political and Social Science* 624:177–89.

Bourdieu, Pierre. 1986. "The Forms of Capital." In *Handbook of Theory and Research for the Sociology of Education,* ed. John G. Richardson, 241–58. New York: Greenwood Press.

Brewer, Rose. 1999. "Theorizing Race, Class and Gender: The New Scholarship of Black Feminist Intellectuals and Black Women's Labor." *Race, Gender and Class* 6 (2): 29–47.

British Columbia Ministry for Women's Equality. 1995. *A Gender Lens for Program Evaluation.* Victoria: B.C. Ministry for Women's Equality, Research and Evaluation Branch.

Brodie, Ian. 2001. "Interest Group Litigation and the Embedded State: Canada's Court Challenges Program." *Canadian Journal of Political Science/Revue canadienne de science politique* 34 (2): 357–76.

Bullock, Charles, III, and Susan MacManus. 1987. "The Impact of Staggered Terms on Minority Representation." *Journal of Politics* 49:543–52.

Burnham, Linda. 2001. Introduction to *Time to Rise: U.S. Women of Color—Issues and Strategies,* ed. Maylei Blackwell, Linda Burnham, and Jung Hee Choi, 7–16. Berkeley, CA: Women of Color Resource Center.

Burtless, Gary, and Christopher Jencks. 2002. "American Inequality and Its Consequences." Luxembourg Income Study Working Paper 339, March. http://www.lisproject.org/publications/liswps/339.pdf.

Busch, Diane Mitsch. 1992. "Women's Movements and State Policy Reform Aimed at Domestic Violence against Women: A Comparison of the Consequences of Movement Mobilization in the United States and India." *Gender and Society* 6:587–608.

Butler, Judith. 1993. *Bodies That Matter: On the Discursive Limits of "Sex."* New York: Routledge.

Bystydzienski, Jill, ed. 1992. *Women Transforming Politics: Worldwide Strategies for Empowerment.* Bloomington: Indiana University Press.

Bystydzienski, Jill. 1995. *Women in Electoral Politics: Lessons from Norway.* Westport, CT: Praeger.

Caiazza, Amy. 2007. *I Knew I Could Do This Work: Seven Strategies That Promote Women's Activism and Leadership in Unions.* Washington, DC: IWPR.

Caiazza, Amy, and Robert D. Putnam. 2002. "Women's Status and Social Capital across the States." Institute for Women's Policy Research Briefing Paper, IWPR Publication I911.

Call, Jack, David Nice, and Susette Talarico. 1991. "An Analysis of State Rape Shield Laws." *Social Science Quarterly* 72 (4): 774–88.

Cameron, Charles, David Epstein, and Sharyn O'Halloran. 1996. "Do Majority-Minority Districts Maximize Substantive Representation in Congress?" *American Political Science Review* 90 (4): 794–812.

Canadian Charter of Rights and Freedoms. 1982. Constitution Act 1982 (79). Enacted as Schedule B to the Canada Act 1982 (U.K.) 1982, c. 11.

Canadian International Development Agency. 2000. *CIDA Evaluation Guide.* Ottawa: CIDA.

Carey, John M., Richard G. Niemi, and Lynda W. Powell. 2000. State Legislative Survey and Contextual Data, 1995 (United States) (computer file). ICPSR03021-v1. Producer, Kathleen Carr, Ohio State University, Polimetrics Lab, 1995. Distributor, Inter-university Consortium for Political and Social Research, Ann Arbor, MI.

Carroll, Susan J. 2003. "Are U.S. Women State Legislators Accountable to Women? The Complementary Roles of Feminist Identity and Women's Organizations." Paper presented at the Gender and Social Capital Conference, St. John's College, University of Manitoba, Winnipeg, Manitoba, May 2–3.

CEDAW. *See* United Nations Convention on the Elimination of All Forms of Discrimination against Women.

Celis, Karen. 2008. "Gendering Representation." In *Politics, Gender, and Concepts,* ed. Gary Goertz and Amy G. Mazur. Cambridge: Cambridge University Press.

Center for American Women and Politics (CAWP). 1997. *The Gender Gap: Attitudes on Public Policy Issues.* http://www.cawp.rutgers.edu/fast_facts/index.php (accessed September 2000).

Center for American Women and Politics (CAWP). 2005a. Fact sheet on women office-holders. http://www.cawp.rutgers.edu/fast_facts/index.php (accessed March 2005).

Center for American Women and Politics (CAWP). 2005b. Fact sheet on women of color in public office. http://www.cawp.rutgers.edu/fast_facts/index.php (accessed March 2005).

Center for American Women and Politics (CAWP). 2006. *Facts and Findings: Gender Gap and Voting Behavior.* http://www.cawp.rutgers.edu/fast_facts/index.php (accessed November 18, 2006).

Center for American Women and Politics (CAWP). 2009. Fact sheet on women in Congress 2009. http://www.cawp.rutgers.edu/fast_facts/levels_of_office/documents/cong.pdf (accessed September 2009).

Chalk, Rosemary, and Patricia King, eds. 1998. *Violence in Families.* National Research Council and Institute of Medicine. Washington, DC: National Academy Press.

Chambers, Simone, and Will Kymlicka, eds. 2002. *Alternative Conceptions of Civil Society.* Princeton: Princeton University Press.

Chhibber, Pradeep, and Irfan Nooruddin. 2004. "Do Party Systems Matter? The Number of Parties and Government Performance in the Indian States." *Comparative Political Studies* 37 (2): 152–87.

Chicago NOW. 2008. Home page. http://www.chicagonow.org/aboutus.php (accessed 2008).

Childs, Sarah. 2006. "The Complicated Relationship between Women's Descriptive and Substantive Representation." *European Journal of Women's Studies* 13 (1): 7–21.

Chuang, Angie. 2002. "Activist Will Speak for Internment Survivors at Manzanar." *Oregonian,* April 26, D02.

CIA. *See* U.S. Central Intelligence Agency.

CIDA. *See* Canadian International Development Agency.

Claasen, Ryan L. 2004. "Political Opinion and Distinctiveness: The Case of Hispanic Ethnicity." *Political Research Quarterly* 57 (4): 609–20.

Clawson, Rosalee A., and Ryan Tom. 1999. "Invisible Lawmakers: Media Coverage of Black and Female State Legislators." Paper presented at the Annual Meeting of the Midwest Political Science Association, Chicago, IL, April 15–17.

Code of Federal Regulations. 2001. Title 49 (Transportation), secs. 23 and 26, vol. 1, pp. 280–82. Revised as of October 1, 2001. U.S. Government Printing Office.

Cohen, Cathy J. 1999. *The Boundaries of Blackness: AIDS and the Breakdown of Black Politics.* Chicago: University of Chicago Press.

Cohen, Jean, and Andrew Arato. 1992. *Civil Society and Political Theory.* Cambridge, MA: MIT Press.

Cohen, Joshua, and Joel Rogers. 1992. "Secondary Associations and Democratic Governance." *Politics & Society* 20:393–472.

Cohen, Joshua, and Joel Rogers. 1995. *Associations and Democracy.* London: Verso.

Coleman, James S. 1988. "Social Capital in the Creation of Human Capital." *American Journal of Sociology* (Supplement, Organizations and Institutions: Sociological and Economic Approaches to the Analysis of Social Structure) 94:S95–S120.

Collier, David, and James Mahoney. 1996. "Insights and Pitfalls: Selection Bias in Qualitative Research" (in Research Note). *World Politics* 49 (1): 56–59.

Collins, Patricia Hill. 1990. *Black Feminist Thought: Knowledge, Consciousness, and the Politics of Empowerment.* New York: Routledge.

Collins, Patricia Hill. 1998. "It's All in the Family: Intersections of Gender, Race and Nation." *Hypatia* 13 (3): 62–82.

Conference of Women Legislators (COWL) (Illinois). 2008a. Home page. http://www.cowlil.com/index.html (accessed June 2008).

Conference of Women Legislators (COWL) (Illinois). 2008b. Women Firsts in Illinois Government (Fact Sheet). http://www.cowlil.com/women_firsts.htm.

Connors, Jane Frances. 1989. *Violence against Women in the Family.* Vienna: United Nations Centre for Social Development and Humanitarian Affairs. ST/CSDHA/2.

Cool, Julie. 2008. "Women in Parliament." Revised October 9, 2008. Political and Social

Affairs Division, PRB 0562E. http://www.parl.gc.ca/information/library/PRBpubs/prb0562-e.htm#awomen.

Costain, Anne N. 1998. "Women Lobby Congress." In *Social Movements and American Political Institutions,* ed. Anne N. Costain and Andrew S. McFarland, 171–84. Lanham, MD: Rowman and Littlefield.

Costain, Anne N. 2005. "Social Movements as Mechanisms for Political Inclusion." In *The Politics of Democratic Inclusion,* ed. Christina Wolbrecht and Rodney Hero, 108–21. Philadelphia: Temple University Press.

Court Challenges Program. 1995. *Court Challenges Program Annual Report, 1994–1995.* Winnipeg: Court Challenges Program.

Court Challenges Program. 2002a. *Court Challenges Program Annual Report, 2001–2002.* Winnipeg: Court Challenges Program.

Court Challenges Program. 2002b. *A Guide to the Court Challenges Program of Canada.* Winnpeg: Court Challenges Program.

COWL. *See* Conference of Women Legislators.

Coy, Patrick G., and Timothy Hedeen. 2005. "A Stage Model of Social Movement Cooptation: Community Mediation in the United States." *Sociological Quarterly* 46 (3): 405–35.

Crenshaw, Kimberlé Williams. 1994. "Mapping the Margins: Intersectionality, Identity Politics, and Violence against Women of Color." In *The Public Nature of Private Violence,* ed. Martha Albertson Fineman and Rixanne Mykitiuk, 93–118. New York: Routledge.

Curtin, Dave. 2003. "'Silent Majority' Favoring Invasion of Iraq Finds Its Voice and Shouts." *Denver Post,* March 6, A-01.

Dahl, Robert. 1962. *Who Governs?* New Haven: Yale University Press.

Danziger, Sheldon, and Peter Gottschalk. 1995. *America Unequal.* Cambridge, MA: Harvard University Press.

Darcy, R., Susan Welch, and Janet Clark. 1987. *Women, Elections and Representation.* New York: Longman.

Darden, Joe T. 1984. "Black Political Underrepresentation in Majority Black Places." *Journal of Black Studies* 15:101–6.

Davidson, Chandler, and George Korbel. 1981. "At-Large Elections and Minority-Group Representation: A Re-Examination of Historical and Contemporary Evidence." *Journal of Politics* 43:982–1005.

Davies, Miranda, ed. 1994. *Women and Violence: Realities and Responses Worldwide.* Atlantic Highlands, NJ: Zed Books.

Davila, Florangela. 2002. "Activist in Bid to Oust Veteran NAACP Leader." *Seattle Times,* November 24, 4th edition, local news, B1.

Davis, Angela Y. 1998. Interview. In *The Angela Y. Davis Reader,* ed. James Joy, 297–328. Oxford: Blackwell.

Dawson, Michael. 1994. *Behind the Mule: Race and Class in African American Politics.* Princeton: Princeton University Press.

Dawson, Michael, and Cathy Cohen. 1993. "Neighborhood Poverty and African American Politics." *American Political Science Review* 87 (2): 286–302.

DBE. *See* Transportation Equity Act for the 21st Century.

Della Porta, Donatella. 2005. "Deliberation in Movement: Why and How to Study Deliberative Democracy and Social Movements." *Acta Politica* 40 (3): 336–50.

Djupe, Paul A., Anand E. Sokhey, and Christopher P. Gilbert. 2007. "Present but Not Accounted For: Gender Difference in Civic Resource Acquisition." *American Journal of Political Science* 51 (4): 906–20.

Dobrowolsky, Alexandra. 1998. "Of 'Special Interest': Interest, Identity and Feminist Constitutional Activism in Canada." *Canadian Journal of Political Science/Revue canadienne de science politique* 31:707–42.

Dodson, Debra L., ed. 1991. *Gender and Policymaking. Studies of Women in Office*. The Impact of Women in Public Office Project. Rutgers: Center for American Women in Politics.

Dovi, Suzanne. 2002. "Preferable Descriptive Representatives: Will Just Any Woman, Black, or Latino Do?" *American Political Science Review* 96 (4): 729–43.

Downton, James, Jr., and Paul Wehr. 1998. "Persistent Pacifism: How Activist Commitment Is Developed and Sustained." *Journal of Peace Research* 35 (5): 531–50.

Dryzek, John. 1990. *Discursive Democracy: Politics, Policy and Political Science*. Cambridge: Cambridge University Press.

Dryzek, John. 1996. *Democracy in Capitalist Times: Ideals, Limits, and Struggles*. New York: Oxford University Press.

Dryzek, John. 2000. *Deliberative Democracy and Beyond: Liberals, Critics, Contestations*. Oxford: Oxford University Press.

Dryzek, John, David Downes, Christian Hunold, and David Sclosberg, with Hans-Kristian Hernes. 2003. *Green States and Social Movements: Environmentalism in the United States, United Kingdom, Germany, and Norway*. Oxford: Oxford University Press.

Dudas, Jeffrey R. 2005. "In the Name of Equal Rights: 'Special' Rights and the Politics of Resentment in Post-Civil Rights America." *Law & Society Review* 39 (4): 723–57.

Duerst-Lahti, Georgia. 1989. "The Government's Role in Building the Women's Movement." *Political Science Quarterly* 104 (3): 249–68.

Duff-Brown, Beth. 2006. "Cultural Issues, Funding on Table at AIDS Event." *Houston Chronicle*, August 13, 2006, A-26.

Duncan, Simon. 1995. "Theorizing European Gender Systems." *Journal of European Social Policy* 5 (4): 263–84.

Duthu, N. Bruce. 2008. "Broken Justice in Indian Country." *New York Times*, August 11, national edition.

Earl, Jennifer, Andrew Martin, John D. McCarthy, and Sarah A. Soule. 2004. "The Use of Newspaper Data in the Study of Collective Action." *Annual Review of Sociology* 30:65–80.

Echols, Alice. 1989. *Daring to Be Bad: Radical Feminism in America, 1967–1975*. Minneapolis: University of Minnesota Press.

Eckstein, Harry. 1988. "A Culturalist Model of Political Change." *American Political Science Review* 82 (3): 789–804.

Edwards, Bob, Michael W. Foley, and Mario Diani. 2001. *Beyond Tocqueville: Civil Society and the Social Capital Debate in Comparative Perspective.* Hanover, NH: Tufts/University Press of New England.

Electrapages Directory. An On-Line Directory of Women's Organizations. 2000. Now available only in hard copy (accessed July 28, 2000). Data available free at http://web.ics.purdue.edu/~weldons/ or for a fee from Women's Information Exchange (wie@pon.net).

Elman, R. Amy. 1996. *Sexual Subordination and State Intervention: Comparing Sweden and the United States.* Providence: Berghahn Books.

Elman, R. Amy. 2003. "Refuge in Reconfigured States: Shelter Movements in the United States, Britain, and Sweden." In *Women's Movements Facing the Reconfigured State,* ed. Lee Ann Banaszak, Karen Beckwith, and Dieter Rucht. New York: Cambridge University Press.

Endersby, James W., and Charles E. Menifeld. 1998. "Representation, Ethnicity and Congress: Black and Hispanic Representatives and Constituencies." Paper presented at the Annual Meeting of the American Political Science Association, Boston, MA, September 3–6.

Engels, Friedrich. [1884] 1978. "The Origin of the Family, Private Property, and the State." In *The Marx-Engels Reader,* ed. Robert Tucker. New York: Norton.

Epp, Charles R. 1996. "Do Bills of Rights Matter? The Canadian Charter of Rights and Freedoms." *American Political Science Review* 90 (4): 765–79.

Epstein, Barbara. 2001."What Happened to the Women's Movement?" *Monthly Review* 53 (1). http://www.monthlyreview.org/0501epstein.htm.

Epstein, David, and Sharyn O'Halloran. 1999. "Social Science Approach to Race, Redistricting and Representation." *American Political Science Review* 93 (2): 187–91.

Esping-Andersen, Gøsta. 1990. *The Three Worlds of Welfare Capitalism.* Princeton: Princeton University Press.

Esping-Andersen, Gøsta. 1999. *Social Foundations of Postindustrial Economies.* New York: Oxford University Press.

Family Rescue. 2007. *2007 Annual Report.* http://www.familyrescueinc.org/pdf/FamilyRescue07AnnualRpt.pdf.

Fatton, Robert, Jr. 1988. "Bringing the Ruling Class Back In: Class, State, and Hegemony in Africa." *Comparative Politics* 20 (3): 253–64.

Ferber, Abby. 1998. "Deconstructing Whiteness: The Intersections of Race and Gender in White Supremacist Thought." *Ethnic and Racial Studies* 21 (1): 48–62.

Ferree, Myra Marx, and Patricia Yancey Martin. 1995. *Feminist Organizations: Harvest of the New Women's Movement.* Philadelphia: Temple University Press.

Ferree, Myra Marx, and Silke Roth. 1998. "Gender, Class, and the Interaction between Social Movements: A Strike of West Berlin Day Care Workers." *Gender and Society* 12 (6): 626–48.

Fisher, Dana. 2006. *Activism, Inc.: How the Outsourcing of Grassroots Campaigns Is Strangling Progressive Politics in America.* Stanford, CA: Stanford University Press.

Fix, Michael, and Raymond J. Struyk. 1993. *Clear and Convincing Evidence: Measurement of Discrimination in America.* Washington, DC: Urban Institute Press.

Fraga, Luis Ricardo, Kenneth J. Meier, and Robert E. England. 1986. "Hispanic Americans and Educational Policy: Limits to Equal Access." *Journal of Politics* 48 (4): 850–76.

Fraser, Nancy. 1992. "Rethinking the Public Sphere: A Contribution to the Critique of Actually Existing Democracy." In *Habermas and the Public Sphere,* ed. Craig Calhoun, 109–42. Cambridge, MA: MIT Press.

Fraser, Nancy. 1995. "Politics, Culture, and the Public Sphere: Toward a Postmodern Conception." In *Social Postmodernism: Beyond Identity Politics,* ed. Linda Nicholson and Steven Seidman. Cambridge: Cambridge University Press.

Freedom House. 1997. *The Comparative Survey of Freedom 1995–1996: Survey Methodology.* http://www.freedomhouse.org/template.cfm?page=351&ana_page=341&year=2008.

Freeman, Jo, and Victoria Johnson, eds. 1999. *Waves of Protest: Social Movements since the Sixties.* New York: Rowman and Littlefield.

Frye, Marilyn. 1983. "Oppression." In *The Politics of Reality.* Trumansburg, NY: Crossing Press.

Frymer, Paul. 2005. "Race, Parties and Democratic Inclusion." In *The Politics of Democratic Inclusion,* ed. Christina Wolbrecht and Rodney E. Hero. Philadelphia: Temple University Press.

Frymer, Paul. 2008. *Black and Blue: African Americans, the Labor Movement, and the Decline of the Democratic Party.* Princeton: Princeton University Press.

Fuentes, M., and A. Gunder Frank. 1989. "Ten Theses on Social Movements." *World Development* 17 (2): 179–91.

Gamson, William A. 1991. "Commitment and Agency in Social Movements." *Sociological Forum* 6:27–50.

Ganesan, A.V. 1999. "The Battle in Seattle; What Was That All About?" *Washington Post,* December 5, final edition, Outlook, B01.

García Bedolla, Lisa, and Becki Scola. 2006. "Finding Intersection: Race, Class, and Gender in the California Recall Vote." *Politics and Gender* 2:5–27.

Gauthier, Anne Hélène. 1996. *The State and the Family: A Comparative Analysis of Family Policies in Industrialized Countries.* Oxford: Clarendon Press.

Gay, Claudine. 2001. "The Effect of Black Congressional Representation on Political Participation." *American Political Science Review* 95 (3): 589–602.

Gay, Claudine. 2002. "Spirals of Trust? The Effect of Descriptive Representation on the Relationship between Citizens and Their Government." *American Journal of Political Science* 46 (4): 717–32.

Gelb, Joyce. 1989. *Feminism and Politics: A Comparative Perspective.* Berkeley: University of California Press.

Gelb, Joyce. 2003. *Gender Policies in Japan and the United States: Comparing Women's Movements, Rights, and Politics.* New York: Palgrave.

Gelb, Joyce, and Marian Lief Palley. 1987. *Women and Public Policies.* Rev. and expanded edition. Princeton: Princeton University Press.

Gelb, Joyce, and Marian Lief Palley. 1996. *Women and Public Policies: Reassessing Gender Politics.* Charlottesville: University Press of Virginia.

Geller-Schwartz, Linda. 1995. "An Array of Agencies: Feminism and State Institutions in Canada." In *Comparative State Feminism,* ed. Dorothy McBride Stetson and Amy G. Mazur. Newbury Park, CA: Sage.

Giddens, Anthony. 1982. "Action, Structure, Power." In *Profiles and Critiques in Social Theory.* Berkeley: University of California Press.

Gigendil, Elisabeth. 1996. "Gender and Attitudes towards Quotas for Women Candidates in Canada." *Women and Politics* 16 (4): 21–43.

Gigendil, Elisabeth, and Richard Vengroff. 1997. "Representational Gains of Canadian Women or Token Growth? The Case of Quebec's Municipal Politics." *Canadian Journal of Political Science/Revue canadienne de science politique* 30 (3): 513–37.

Gill, Jeff. 2001. "Whose Variance Is It Anyway? Interpreting Empirical Models with State-Level Data." *State Politics and Policy Quarterly* 1 (3): 318–38.

Gitlin, Todd. 1995. *The Twilight of Common Dreams: Why America Is Wracked by Culture Wars.* New York: Metropolitan Books.

Glazer, Nathan. 1983. "Individual Rights against Group Rights." In *Ethnic Dilemmas: 1964–1982,* 254–73. Cambridge, MA: Harvard University Press.

Goodin, Robert E. 2003. "Democratic Accountability: The Third Sector and All." Working paper 19, Hauser Center, Harvard. http://www.hks.harvard.edu/hauser/PDF_XLS/workingpapers/workingpaper_19.pdf (accessed September 2005).

Gornick, Janet, and Marcia Meyers. 2007. "Institutions That Support Gender Egalitarianism in Parenthood and Employment." A core essay for the Real Utopias Project. http://www.ssc.wisc.edu/~mscaglio/2006documents/Gornick_Meyers_2007_Institutions_Gender_Egalitarianism.pdf (accessed June 2008).

Gray, Virginia, and David Lowery. 1993. "The Diversity of State Interest Group Systems." *Political Research Quarterly* 46 (1): 81–97.

Grey, Sandra. 2006. "Numbers and Beyond: The Relevance of Critical Mass Research." *Politics & Gender* 2 (4): 492–501.

Green, Leslie. 1994. "Internal Minorities and Their Rights." In *Group Rights,* ed. Judith Baker, 101–17. Toronto: University of Toronto Press.

Greenfeld, Lawrence A. 1997. *Sex Offenses and Offenders: An Analysis of Data on Rape and Sexual Assault.* U.S. Department of Justice, Office of Justice Programs, Bureau of Justice Statistics.

Greenhouse, Steven. 1998. "Unions Unite in a Campaign for Child Care." *New York Times,* March 2, late edition—final, B-1.

Grofman, Bernard, Lisa Handley, and Richard G. Niemi. 1992. *Minority Representation and the Quest for Voting Equality.* Cambridge: Cambridge University Press.

Gutmann, Amy. 2003. *Identity in Democracy.* Princeton: Princeton University Press.

Haider-Markel, Donald P., Mark R. Joslyn, and Chad J. Kniss. 2000. "Minority Group Interests and Political Representation: Gay Elected Officials in the Policy Process." *Journal of Politics* 62 (2): 568–77.

Hancock, Ange-Marie. 2007a. "Intersectionality as a Normative and Empirical Paradigm." *Politics & Gender* 3 (2): 248–54.

Hancock, Ange-Marie. 2007b. "When Multiplication Doesn't Equal Quick Addition: Examining Intersectionality as a Research Paradigm." *Perspectives on Politics* 5 (1): 63–79.

Hansen, Susan B. 1993. "Differences in Public Policy towards Abortion." *Understanding the New Politics of Abortion,* ed. Malcolm Goggin, 222–48. Newbury Park, CA: Sage.

Harris, Angela. 1990. "Race and Essentialism in Feminist Legal Theory." *Stanford Law Review* 42 (February): 581–616.

Harvey, David. 1996. *Justice, Nature and the Geography of Difference.* Oxford: Blackwell.

Hays, Elizabeth. 2004. "Union Rallies against Plan to Shut Clinic." *Daily News,* September 29, 3.

Heise, Lori, with Jacqueline Pitanguy and Adrienne Germain. 1994. *Violence against Women: The Hidden Health Burden.* World Bank Discussion Paper. Washington, DC: World Bank.

Hero, Rodney E. 2007. *Racial Diversity and Social Capital: Equality and Community in America.* New York: Cambridge University Press.

Hero, Rodney, and Caroline J. Tolbert. 1995. "Latinos and Substantive Representation in the U.S. House of Representatives: Direct, Indirect, or Non-Existent?" *American Journal of Political Science* 39:640–52.

High-Pippert, Angela, and John Comer. 1998. "Female Empowerment: The Influence of Women Representing Women." *Women and Politics* 19 (4): 53–66.

Hill, David B. 1981. "Political Culture and Female Representation." *Journal of Politics* 43:159–68.

Hill, Kim Quaile, and Jan E. Leighley. 1994. "Mobilizing Institutions and Class Representation in U.S. State Electorates." *Political Research Quarterly* 47 (1): 137–50.

Hines, Revathi I. 2001. "African Americans' Struggle for Environmental Justice and the Case of the Shintech Plant: Lessons Learned from a War Waged." *Journal of Black Studies* 31 (6): 777–89.

hooks, bell. 2000. *Feminist Theory: From Margin to Center.* Boston: South End Press.

Hooks, Gregory. 1991. "The Variable Autonomy of the State: A Comment on 'Steel and the State.'" *American Sociological Review* 56 (5): 690–93.

Howard, Judith A. 1994. "A Social Cognitive Conception of Social Structure." In "Conceptualizing Structure in Social Psychology," special issue, *Social Psychology Quarterly* 57 (3): 210–27.

Howell, Jude, and Diane Mulligan. 2005. *Gender and Civil Society: Transcending Boundaries.* New York: Routledge.

Htun, Mala. 2003. *Sex and the State: Abortion, Divorce, and the Family under Latin American Dictatorships and Democracies.* New York: Cambridge University Press.

Htun, Mala. 2004. "Is Gender Like Ethnicity? The Political Representation of Identity Groups." *Perspectives on Politics* 2 (3): 439–58.

Htun, Mala. Forthcoming. *Sex, Race, and Representation.* New York: Cambridge University Press.

Htun, Mala, and S. Laurel Weldon. 2010a. "When and Why Do Governments Promote Women's Rights?" *Perspectives on Politics* 8 (2): 207–16.

Htun, Mala, and S. Laurel Weldon. 2010b. "When and Why Do Governments Promote Sex Equality? Violence against Women, Reproductive Rights, and Parental Leave on Cross-National Perspective." Paper presented at the Annual Meeting of the Midwest Political Science Association, Chicago, April.

Human Rights Watch. 1995. *The Human Rights Watch Global Report on Women's Human Rights.* New York: Human Rights Watch Women's Project.

ILJ. *See* Institute for Law and Justice.

Illinois General Assembly. 2007. Home page. http://www.ilga.gov/.

ILO. *See* International Labour Organization.

Inglehart, Ron, and Pippa Norris. 2003. *Rising Tide: Gender Equality and Cultural Change around the World.* Cambridge: Cambridge University Press.

Ingram, Helen, and Anne Schneider. 1993. "Social Construction of Target Populations: Implications for Politics and Policy." *American Political Science Review* 87 (2): 334–47.

Institute for Law and Justice (ILJ). 1998a. *Review of State Sexual Assault Legislation.* Alexandria, VA: ILJ. www.ilj.org.

Institute for Law and Justice (ILJ). 1998b. *Review of State Domestic Violence Legislation.* Alexandria, VA: ILJ. www.ilj.org.

Institute for Law and Justice (ILJ). 2001a. *2000 Legislative Session: Violence against Women Legislation.* Alexandria, VA: ILJ. www.ilj.org.

Institute for Law and Justice (ILJ). 2001b. *1999 Domestic Violence, Stalking, and Sexual Assault Legislation.* Alexandria, VA: ILJ. www.ilj.org.

Institute for Women's Policy Research (IWPR). 1996. *The Status of Women in the States.* Washington, DC: IWPR.

International Labour Organization (ILO). 1994. *Conditions of Work Digest.* Vol. 13. Geneva: ILO.

International Labour Organization (ILO). 1995. *Guidelines for the Integration of Gender Issues into the Design, Monitoring, and Evaluation of ILO Programmes and Projects.* Geneva: ILO. http://www.ilo.org/public/english/bureau/program/eval/guides/gender/.

International Labour Organization (ILO). 1997. *World Labour Report.* Geneva: ILO.

International Labour Organization (ILO). 2004. *Global Employment Trends for Women 2004.* March. http://www.ilo.org/public/english/employment/strat/download/trendsw.pdf (accessed August 2006).

Interparliamentary Union (IPU). 1995. *Women in Parliaments: 1945–1995.* Reports and Documents 23. Geneva.

IPU. *See* Interparliamentary Union.

IWPR. *See* Institute for Women's Policy Research.

Jacobs, Lawrence R., and Robert Y. Shapiro. 1994. "Studying Substantive Democracy: Public Opinion, Institutions, and Policymaking." *PS: Political Science and Politics* 27 (March): 9–16.

Jacoby, William G. 1991. *Data Theory and Dimensional Analysis.* Quantitative Applications in the Social Sciences 07-078. Newbury Park, CA: Sage.

Japanese International Cooperation Agency (JICA). 1999. *A Milestone in Gender Mainstreaming of JICA's Cooperation.* Evaluation bulletin, November. Tokyo: JICA.

Jaquette, Jane. 1997. "Women in Power: From Tokenism to Critical Mass." *Foreign Policy* 108:23–37.

Jencks, Christopher. 1992. *Rethinking Social Policy: Race, Poverty and the Underclass.* New York: Basic Books.

Jenkins, Ron. 2001. "Iowa Debate Spills over into Oklahoma." Associated Press, July 23.

JICA. *See* Japanese International Cooperation Agency.

Johnson, Janet Elise. 2007. "Domestic Violence Politics in Post-Soviet States." *Social Politics: International Studies in Gender, State & Society* 14 (3): 380–405.

Johnson, Victoria. 1999. "The Strategic Determinants of a Countermovement: The Emergence and Impact of Operation Rescue Blockades." In *Waves of Protest: Social Movements since the Sixties,* ed. Jo Freeman and Victoria Johnson, 241–66. New York: Rowman and Littlefield.

Johnston, Darlene. 1989. "Native Rights as Collective Rights: A Question of Group Self-Preservation." *Canadian Journal of Law and Jurisprudence* 2 (1): 19–34.

Jones, Bryan, and Frank R. Baumgartner. 2005. *The Politics of Attention: How Government Prioritizes Problems.* Chicago: University of Chicago Press.

Jones, Mark P. 1996. "Increasing Women's Representation via Gender Quotas: The Argentine Ley de Cupos." *Women and Politics* 16 (4): 75–98.

Joseph, Antoine. 1994. "Pathways to Capitalist Democracy: What Prevents Social Democracy?" *British Journal of Sociology* 45 (2): 211–34.

Kaplan, Gisela. 1992. *Contemporary Western European Feminism.* New York: New York University Press.

Kathlene, Lyn. 1995. "Position Power versus Gender Power: Who Holds the Floor?" In *Gender Power, Leadership and Governance,* ed. Georgia Duerst-Lahti and Rita Mae Kelly, 167–93. Ann Arbor: University of Michigan Press.

Katzenstein, Mary Fainsod. 1989. "Organizing against Violence: Strategies of the Indian Women's Movement." *Pacific Affairs* 62:53–71.

Katzenstein, Mary Fainsod. 1995. "Discursive Politics and Feminist Activism in the Catholic Church." In *Feminist Organizations: Harvest of the New Women's Move-*

ment, ed. Myra Marx Ferree and Patricia Yancey Martin. Philadelphia: Temple University Press.

Katzenstein, Mary Fainsod. 1998. *Faithful and Fearless.* Ithaca: Cornell University Press.

Katznelson, Ira. 2005. *When Affirmative Action Was White: An Untold History of Racial Inequality in Twentieth Century America.* New York: W. W. Norton.

Keeter, Scott, Carolyn Miller, Andrew Kohut, Robert M. Groves, and Stanley Presser. 2000. "Consequences of Reducing Nonresponse in a National Telephone Survey." *Public Opinion Quarterly* 64 (2): 125–48.

Keiser, Lael. 1999. "The Influence of Women's Political Power on Bureaucratic Output: The Case of Child Support Enforcement." *British Journal of Political Science* 27 (1): 136–48.

Kerr, Brinck, and Will Miller. 1997. "Latino Representation, It's Direct and Indirect." *American Journal of Political Science* 41:1066–71.

Key, V. O. 1949. *Southern Politics in State and Nation.* New York: Vintage.

Kingdon, John W. 1984. *Agendas, Alternatives, and Public Policies.* Boston: Little, Brown.

Kitschelt, Herbert. 1993. "Social Movements, Political Parties, and Democratic Theory." *Annals of the American Academy of Political and Social Science* 528 (July): 13–29.

Kittilson, Miki Caul. 2008. "Representing Women: The Adoption of Family Leave in Comparative Perspective." *Journal of Politics* 70 (2): 323–34.

Kittilson, Miki Caul, and Katherine Tate. 2005. "Political Parties, Minorities and Elected Office." In *The Politics of Democratic Inclusion,* ed. Christina Wolbrecht and Rodney E. Hero. Philadelphia: Temple University Press.

Klandermans, Bert. 1986. "New Social Movements and Resource Mobilization: The European and American Approach." *Journal of Mass Emergencies and Disasters* 4:13–37.

Klein, Ethel. 1984. *Gender Politics: From Consciousness to Mass Politics.* Cambridge, MA: Harvard University Press

Korpi, Walter, and Joakim Palme. 2003. "New Politics and Class Politics in the Context of Austerity and Globalization: Welfare State Regress in 18 Countries, 1975–1995." *American Journal of Political Science* 48 (3): 496–512.

Krook, Mon Lena, Karen Celis, Sarah Childs, and Johanna Kantola. 2008. "Rethinking Women's Substantive Representation." *Representation: The Journal of Representative Democracy* 44 (2): 99–110.

Kymlicka, Will. 1991. *Liberalism, Community, and Culture.* Oxford: Oxford University Press.

Kymlicka, Will. 1995. *Multicultural Citizenship: A Liberal Theory of Minority Rights.* Oxford: Oxford University Press.

Lawless, Jennifer L. 2004. "Politics of Presence? Congresswomen and Symbolic Representation." *Political Research Quarterly* 57 (1): 81–99.

LeDuc, Lawrence, Richard G. Niemi, and Pippa Norris. 1996. *Comparing Democracies: Elections and Voting in Global Perspective.* Thousand Oaks, CA: Sage.

Leighley, Jan. 2005. "Race, Ethnicity and Electoral Mobilization: Where's the Party?" In

The Politics of Democratic Inclusion, ed. Christina Wolbrecht and Rodney E. Hero. Philadelphia: Temple University Press.

Leira, Arnaug. 1993. "The 'Women-Friendly' Welfare State? The Case of Norway and Sweden." In *Women and Social Policies in Europe: Work, Family, and the State*, ed. Jane Lewis, 49–71. Brookfield, VT: Edward Elgar.

Leira, Arnaug. 2002. *Working Parents and the Welfare State: Family Change and Policy Reform in Scandinavia*. New York: Cambridge University Press.

Levinson, David. 1989. *Family Violence in Cross-Cultural Perspective*. Newbury Park, CA: Sage.

Levy, Paul. 2005. "Clyde Bellecourt Day in Minneapolis." *Minneapolis Star Tribune*, May 1, metro edition, 1B.

Lewis, Jane, ed. 1993. *Women and Social Policies in Europe: Work, Family, and the State*. Brookfield, VT: Edward Elgar.

Lewis, Jane, ed. 1998. *Gender, Social Care, and Welfare State Restructuring in Europe*. Brookfield, VT: Ashgate.

Lindblom, Charles, and Edward Woodhouse. 1993. *The Policy-Making Process*. Englewood Cliffs, NJ: Prentice-Hall.

Lipset, Seymour Martin. 1994. "The Social Requisites of Democracy Revisited: 1993 Presidential Address." *American Sociological Review* 59 (1): 1–22.

Lorde, Audre. 1984. "The Master's Tools Will Never Dismantle the Master's House." In *Sister Outsider: Essays and Speeches*. Berkeley: The Crossing Press.

Los, M. 1994. "The Struggle to Redefine Rape in the Early 1980s." In *Confronting Sexual Assault: A Decade of Legal and Social Change*, ed. J. V. Roberts and R. M. Mohr, 20–56. Toronto: University of Toronto Press.

Lublin, David. 1997. *The Paradox of Representation: Racial Gerrymandering and Minority Interests in Congress*. Princeton: Princeton University Press.

Lublin, David. 1999. "Racial Redistricting and African-American Representation: A Critique of 'Do Majority-Minority Districts Maximize Substantive Black Representation in Congress?'" *American Political Science Review* 93:183–86.

Lugones, Maria. 1994. "Purity, Impurity and Separation." *Signs* 19 (2): 458–79.

MacKinnon, Catharine. 1989. *Toward a Feminist Theory of the State*. Cambridge, MA: Harvard University Press.

Mandel, Hadas, and Moshe Semyonov. 2005. "Family Policies, Wage Structures and Gender Gaps: Sources of Earnings Inequality in 20 Countries." *American Sociological Review* 70 (6): 949–68.

Mansbridge, Jane. 1995. "What Is the Feminist Movement?" In *Feminist Organizations: Harvest of the New Women's Movement*, ed. Myra Marx Ferree and Patricia Yancey Martin, 27–34. Philadelphia: Temple University Press.

Mansbridge, Jane. 1999. "Should Blacks Represent Blacks and Women Represent Women? A Contingent 'Yes.'" *Journal of Politics* 61 (3): 628–57.

Mansbridge, Jane. 2001. "The Making of Oppositional Consciousness." In *Oppositional*

Consciousness: The Subjective Roots of Social Protest, ed. Jane Mansbridge and Aldon Morris. Chicago: University of Chicago Press.

Mansbridge, Jane. 2003. "Rethinking Representation." *American Political Science Review* 97 (4): 515–28.

Mansbridge, Jane. 2005. "Quota Problems: Combating the Dangers of Essentialism." *Politics & Gender* 1 (4): 622–37.

Mansbridge, Jane, and Katherine Flaster. 2007. "The Cultural Politics of Everyday Discourse: The Case of the 'Male Chauvinist.'" *Critical Sociology* 33:627–60.

March, James, and Johan Olsen. 1989. *Rediscovering Institutions: The Organizational Basis of Politics.* New York: Free Press.

Markoff, John. 1999. "Where and When Was Democracy Invented?" *Comparative Studies in Society and History* 41 (4): 660–90.

Marquis, Christopher. 2002. "Bush to End Rule Allowing Jobless Money for New Parents." *New York Times,* U.S. sec., September 24.

Marx, Anthony. 1998, *Making Race and Nation.* Cambridge: Cambridge University Press.

Matland, Richard. 1993. "Institutional Variables Affecting Female Representation in National Legislatures: The Case of Norway." *Journal of Politics* 55:737–55.

Matland, Richard, and Donley T. Studlar. 1996. "The Contagion of Women Candidates in Single-Member District and Proportional Representation Electoral Systems: Canada and Norway." *Journal of Politics* 58:707–33.

Matthews, Nancy. 1993. "Surmounting a Legacy: The Expansion of Racial Diversity in a Local Anti-Rape Movement." In *Violence against Women: The Bloody Footprints,* ed. Pauline B. Bart and Eileen Gail Moran. Newbury Park, CA: Sage.

Mazur, Amy G. 1995. "Strong State and Symbolic Reform: The *Ministere des Droits de la Femmes* in France." In *Comparative State Feminism,* ed. Dorothy McBride Stetson and Amy G. Mazur. Newbury Park, CA: Sage.

Mazur, Amy G. 2002. *Theorizing Feminist Policy.* Oxford: Oxford University Press.

McAdam, Doug, Sidney Tarrow, and Charles Tilly. 2001. *Dynamics of Contention.* New York: Cambridge University Press.

McBride, Anne. 1999. *More Women Elected to Representative Positions in Unions.* European Foundation for the Improvement of Living and Working Conditions UK9908124F, 28-08-1999. http://www.eurofound.europa.eu/eiro/1999/08/feature/uk9908124f.htm.

McBride, Dorothy, and Amy G. Mazur. 2008. "Women's Movements, Feminism, and Feminist Movements." In *Politics, Gender, and Concepts,* ed. Gary Goertz and Amy G. Mazur, 219–43. Cambridge: Cambridge University Press.

McCall, Leslie. 2005. "The Complexity of Intersectionality." *Signs: Journal of Women in Culture and Society* 30 (3): 1771–1800.

McCarthy, John. 1987. "Pro-Choice and Pro-Life Mobilization: Infrastructure Deficits and New Technologies." In *Social Movements in an Organizational Society: Collected Essays,* ed. Mayer Zald and John D. McCarthy. New Brunswick, NJ: Transaction Books.

McCarthy, John. 2007. Inaugural Lecture: McCarthy Award for the Study of Social Movements. Notre Dame, South Bend, IN, May.

McGrory, Mary. 1999. "Labor's Battle in Seattle." *Washington Post,* December 2, final edition, A03.

McIver, John P., and Edward Carmines. 1981. *Unidimensional Scaling.* Quantitative Applications in the Social Sciences 07-024. Newbury Park, CA: Sage.

McLaren, J. 2000. *Evaluating Programs for Women: A Gender-Specific Framework.* Winnipeg: Health Canada Prairie Women's Health Centre of Excellence.

Meier, Kenneth, Robert D. Wrinkle, and J. L. Polinard. 1999. "Representative Bureaucracy and Distributional Equity: Addressing the Hard Question." *Journal of Politics* 61 (4): 1025–39.

Melkas, Helina, and Richard Anker. 1997. "Occupational Segregation by Sex in Nordic Countries: An Empirical Investigation." *International Labour Review* 136 (3): 341–63.

Meyer, David S. 2000. "Social Movements." In *Conscious Acts and the Politics of Change,* ed. Robin L. Teske and Mary Ann Tetreault, 35–55. Columbia: University of South Carolina Press.

Meyer, David S. 2003. "Restating the Woman Question: Women's Movements and State Restructuring." In *Women's Movements Facing the Reconfigured State,* ed. Lee Ann Banaszak, Karen Beckwith, and Dieter Rucht, 275–94. New York: Cambridge University Press.

Meyer, David S. 2006. *The Politics of Protest: Social Movements in America.* New York: Oxford University Press.

Meyer, David S., Valerie Jenness, and Helen Ingram, eds. 2005. *Routing the Opposition: Social Movements, Public Policy, and Democracy.* Minneapolis: University of Minnesota Press.

Mezey, Susan Gluck. 1994. "Increasing the Number of Women in Office: Does It Matter?" In *The Year of the Woman: Myths and Realities,* ed. Elizabeth Adell Cook, Sue Thomas, and Clyde Wilcox, 255–70. Boulder: Westview Press.

Mill, J. S. [1861] 1926. *Considerations on Representative Government.* London: Longmans, Green.

Minkoff, Debra C. 1995. "Interorganizational Influences on the Founding of African American Organizations, 1955–1985." *Sociological Forum* 10 (1): 51–79.

Minkoff, Debra C. 1997. "Organizational Mobilizations, Institutional Access, and Institutional Change." In *Women Transforming Politics,* ed. Cathy C. Cohen, Kathleen B. Jones, and Joan C. Tronto, 477–96. New York: New York University Press.

Mladenka, Kenneth R. 1989. "Blacks and Hispanics in Urban Politics." *American Political Science Review* 83:165–91.

Molyneux, Maxine. 1998. "Analyzing Women's Movements." In *Feminist Visions of Development: Gender Analysis and Policy,* ed. Cecile Jackson and Ruth Pearson. London: Routledge.

Morgan, Kimberly J. 2006. *Working Mothers and the Welfare State: Religion and the Pol-*

itics of Work-Family Policies in Western Europe and the United States. Stanford, CA: Stanford University Press.

Morris, Aldon, and Naomi Braine. 2001. "Social Movements and Oppositional Consciousness." In *Oppositional Consciousness: The Subjective Roots of Social Protest*, ed. Jane Mansbridge and Aldon Morris, 20–37. Chicago: University of Chicago Press.

Mosher, Michael. 2002. "Conclusion: Are Civil Societies the Transmission Belts of Ethical Transmission?" In *Alternative Conceptions of Civil Society*, ed. Simone Chambers and Will Kymlicka, 207–30. Princeton: Princeton University Press.

Mueller, Carol. 1995. "The Organizational Basis of Conflict in Contemporary Feminism." In *Feminist Organizations: Harvest of the New Women's Movement*, ed. Myra Marx Ferree and Patricia Yancey Martin, 263–75. Philadelphia: Temple University Press.

Muller, Edward N. 1988. "Democracy, Economic Development, and Income Inequality." *American Sociological Review* 53:50–68.

Muller, Edward N. 1995. "Economic Determinants of Democracy." *American Sociological Review* 60 (6): 966–82.

Murphy, Patricia. 1997. "Domestic Violence Legislation and the Police." *Women and Politics* 18 (2): 27–53.

Murray, Shailagh, and Jonathon Weisman. 2005. "Senate Approves Cuts, but Not Drilling." *Washington Post*, December 22, A01.

National Association of Women Business Owners (NAWBO) Chicago Area. 2006. *Bulletin* (January). http://www.nawbochicago.org/BulletinJan06.htm.

National Association of Women Business Owners (NAWBO) Chicago Area. 2008. Committees. http://nawbochicago.org/involvement/committees.php (accessed May 2008).

National Council for Research on Women (NCRW). 2004. *NOW: A Directory of National Women's Organizations*. New York: National Council for Research on Women.

National Council of State Legislatures (NCSL). 2008. Overview of demographic information about state legislatures. http://www.ncsl.org/programs/legismgt/about/demographic_overview.htm.

NAWBO. *See* National Association of Women Business Owners.

NCRW. *See* National Council for Research on Women.

NCSL. *See* National Council of State Legislatures.

Nelson, Barbara. 1990. "The Origins of the Two-Channel Welfare State." In *Women, the State, and Welfare*, ed. Linda Gordon. Madison: University of Wisconsin Press.

Nelson, Barbara J., and Kathryn A. Carver. 1994. "Many Voices but Few Vehicles: The Consequences for Women of Weak Political Infrastructure in the United States." In *Women and Politics Worldwide*, ed. Barbara J. Nelson and Najma Chowdhury. New Haven: Yale University Press.

Niezgodski, David L. 2009. (Indiana state representative) Home page. http://www.in.gov/legislative/house_democrats/niezgodski_index.html (accessed August 2009).

Nixon, David L., and R. Darcy. 1996. "Special Election and the Growth of Women's

Representation in the U.S. House of Representatives." *Women and Politics* 16 (4): 99–107.

Norris, Pippa. 1987. *Politics and Sexual Equality: The Comparative Position of Women in Western Democracies.* Boulder: Lynne Rienner.

Norris, Pippa. 2002. *Democratic Phoenix: Reinventing Political Activism.* Cambridge: Cambridge University Press.

Oakley, Maureen Rand, and Gertrude A. Steuernagel. 2000. "Explaining Fetal Rights Policy: Competing Rights?" Paper presented to the Annual Meeting of the Midwest Political Science Association, Chicago.

O'Connor, Julia S., Ann Shola Orloff, and Sheila Shaver. 1999. *States, Markets, Families: Gender, Liberalism, and Social Policy in Australia, Canada, Great Britain, and the United States.* Cambridge: Cambridge University Press.

Odame, H. 2000. *Engendering the Logical Framework.* Netherlands: International Service for National Agricultural Research (ISNAR).

Odell, Larry. 2005. "Democrat Denounces Right-to-Work." Associated Press State and Local Wire, BC cycle, August 11.

Office of the City Clerk (Chicago). 2008. "Committee Members and Jurisdictions." http://www.chicityclerk.com/standingcommettee.php.

Office of Small and Disadvantaged Business Utilization (OSDBU), U.S. Department of Transportation. 2003a. *Paving the Road to Equal Opportunity: The Need for DOT's Disadvantaged Business Enterprise Program.* http://www.osdbu.dot.gov/DBEProgram/dbe_archive.cfmo.

Office of Small and Disadvantaged Business Utilization (OSDBU), U.S. Department of Transportation. 2003b. *Myths and Facts: DOT's Disadvantaged Business Enterprise Program.* http://www.osdbu.dot.gov/DBEProgram/dbe_archive.cfm.

Office of Small and Disadvantaged Business Utilization (OSDBU), U.S. Department of Transportation. 2003c. *Memorandum of Understanding between the U.S. Small Business Administration and the U.S. Department of Transportation.* http://www.osdbu.dot.gov/DBEProgram/memofunder.cfm.

OSDBU. *See* Office of Small and Disadvantaged Business Utilization.

Pal, Leslie. 1993. *Interests of State.* Montreal: McGill-Queens University Press.

Parmley, Suzette. 2001. "Hopes and Fear Greet NJ Paid-Leave Bill." *Philadelphia Inquirer,* February 19, New Jersey edition, local sec., A01.

Paxton, Pamela. 2002. "Social Capital and Democracy: An Interdependent Relationship." *American Sociological Review* 67 (2): 254–77.

Peck, L. 1998. *Evaluating Gender Equality—Policy and Practise: An Assessment of Sida's Evaluations in 1997–1998.* Stockholm: Swedish Agency for Development Cooperation (SIDA).

Perrucci, Robert, and Earl Wysong. 1999. *The New Class Society.* New York: Rowman and Littlefield.

Peters, B. Guy. 1991. *European Politics Reconsidered.* New York: Holmes and Meier.

Phillips, Anne. 1992. "Democracy and Difference: Some Problems for Feminist Theory." *Political Quarterly* 63 (1): 79–90.

Phillips, Anne. 1995. *The Politics of Presence.* Oxford: Clarendon Press.

Pitkin, Hannah Fenichel. 1967. *The Concept of Representation.* Berkeley: University of California Press.

Piven, Frances, and Richard Cloward. [1971] 1993. *Regulating the Poor: The Functions of Public Welfare.* Rev. ed. New York: Vintage.

Poggione, Sarah. 2004. "Exploring Gender Differences in State Legislators' Policy Preferences." *Political Research Quarterly* 57 (2): 305–14.

Polletta, Francesca. 2002. *Freedom Is an Endless Meeting: Democracy in American Social Movements.* Chicago: University of Chicago Press.

Porta, Donatella della. 2005. "Deliberation in Movement: Why and How to Study Deliberative Democracy and Social Movements." *Acta Politica* 40 (3): 336–50.

Poulantzas, Nicos. [1968] 1973. *Political Power and Social Classes.* London: New Left Books.

Powell, G. Bingham. 1982. *Contemporary Democracies: Participation, Stability, and Violence.* Cambridge, MA: Harvard University Press.

Preston, Julia. 2007. "Illegal Immigrants in U.S. Face Increased Deportations." *New York Times,* May 1.

Putnam, Robert D. 1993. *Making Democracy Work: Civic Traditions in Modern Italy.* Princeton: Princeton University Press.

Putnam, Robert D. 2000. *Bowling Alone: The Collapse and Revival of American Community.* New York: Touchstone.

Raaum, Nina. 2005. "Gender Equality and Political Representation: A Nordic Comparison." *Western European Politics* 28 (4): 872–97.

Rae, Nicole C. 1994. *Southern Democrats.* New York: Oxford University Press.

Raghunathan, Abhi. 2001. "A Feud Brewing over Family Leave." *New York Times,* February 4.

Randall, Vicki. 1987. W*omen and Politics: An International Perspective.* 2nd ed. Chicago: University of Chicago Press.

Raphael, Jody. 1996. "Domestic Violence and Welfare Receipt." *Harvard Women's Law Journal* 19:201–27.

Raphael, Jody. 1997. "Domestic Violence as a Barrier to Employment." *Poverty & Race* 6 (4): 11–12.

Reed, Adolph. 1986. *The Jesse Jackson Phenomenon: The Crisis of Purpose in Afro-American Politics.* New Haven: Yale University Press.

Rehfeld, Andrew. 2006. "Towards a General Theory of Political Representation." *Journal of Politics* 68 (1): 1–21.

Rennison, Callie Marie, and Sarah Welchans. 2002. *Intimate Partner Violence.* BJS Special Report, May, 178247, U.S. Department of Justice, Office of Justice Programs.

Rexroat, Jennifer. 2003. "List of Women's Organizations." Unpublished women's studies syllabus. University of Illinois, Chicago.

Richards, Patricia. 2006. "The Politics of Difference and Women's Rights: Lessons from Pobladoras and Mapuche Women in Chile." *Social Politics* 13 (1): 1–29.

Richie, Beth E., and Valli Kanuha. 2000. "Battered Women of Color." In *Gender Basics:*

Feminist Perspectives on Women and Men, ed. Anne Minas, 2nd ed., 213–20. Belmont, CA: Wadsworth.

Roberts, Julian V., and Robert J. Gebotys. 1992. "Reforming Rape Laws: Effects of Legislative Change in Canada." *Law and Human Behavior* 16 (5): 555–73.

Roby, P. A. 1995. "Becoming Shop Stewards: Perspectives on Gender and Race in Ten Trade Unions." *Labor Studies Journal* 20 (3): 65–82.

Rochon, Thomas R. 1998. *Culture Moves: Ideas, Activism, and Changing Values.* Princeton: Princeton University Press.

Rochon, Thomas R., and Daniel A. Mazmanian. 1993. "Social Movements and the Policy Process." *Annals of the American Academy of Political and Social Science* 528 (July): 75–87.

Rodrik, Dani, and Richard Zeckhauser. 1988. "The Dilemma of Government Responsiveness." *Journal of Policy Analysis and Management* 7:601–20.

Rohlinger, Deana A. 2002. "Framing the Abortion Debate." *Sociological Quarterly* 43 (4): 479–507.

Rohlinger, Deana A. 2006. "Friends and Foes: Media, Politics, and Tactics in the Abortion War." *Social Problems* 53 (4): 537–61.

Romanelli, Elaine. 1991. "The Evolution of New Organizational Forms." *Annual Review of Sociology* 17:79–103.

Rule, Wilma, and Joseph S. Zimmerman, eds. 1994. *Electoral Systems in Comparative Perspective: Their Impact on Women and Minorities.* Westport, CT: Greenwood Press.

Rupp, Leila J., and Verta Taylor. 1999. "Forging Feminist Identity in an International Movement: A Collective Identity Approach to Twentieth Century Feminism." *Signs* 24 (2): 363–86.

Sainsbury, Diane. 2001. "Gender and the Making of Welfare States: Norway and Sweden." *Social Politics* 8 (1): 113–43.

Sanbonmatsu, Kira. 2002. *Democrats, Republicans, and the Politics of Women's Place.* Ann Arbor: University of Michigan Press.

Sanbonmatsu, Kira. 2003. "Gender-Related Political Knowledge and the Descriptive Representation of Women." *Political Behavior* 25 (4): 367–88.

Sanday, Peggy Reeves. 1981. *Female Power and Male Dominance: On the Origins of Sexual Inequality.* New York: Cambridge University Press.

Sapiro, Virginia. 1990. "The Gender Basis of American Social Policy." In *Women, the State, and Welfare,* ed. Linda Gordon. Madison: University of Wisconsin Press.

Sawer, Marian. 2004. "'When Women Support Women . . .' EMILY's List and the Substantive Representation of Women in Australia." Refereed paper presented to the Australasian Political Studies Association Conference, University of Adelaide, September 29–October 1.

SBA. *See* U.S. Small Business Act.

Schlozman, K. L., S. Verba, and H. E. Brady. 1999. "Civic Participation and the Equality Problem." In *Civic Engagement in American Democracy,* ed. Theda Skocpol and Morris Fiorina. Washington, DC: Brookings Institution.

Schram, Sanford, Joe Soss, and Richard Fording. 2003. *Race and the Politics of Welfare Reform.* Ann Arbor: University of Michigan Press.

Schwartzman, Kathleen C. 1998. "Globalization and Democracy." *Annual Review of Sociology* 24:159–81.

Schwindt-Bayer, Leslie A., and William Mishler. 2005. "An Integrated Model of Women's Representation." *Journal of Politics* 67 (2): 407–28.

Scott, Dean. 2002. "Is California a Bellwether on Paid Family Leave?" *Kiplinger Business Forecasts,* no. 1108.

Selden, Sally Coleman, Jeffrey L. Brudney, and J. Edward Kellough. 1998. "Bureaucracy as a Representative Institution: Toward a Reconciliation of Bureaucratic Government and Democratic Theory." *American Journal of Political Science* 42:717–44.

Shapiro, R., and J. T. Young. 1989. "Public Opinion and the Welfare State: The United States in Comparative Perspective." *Political Science Quarterly* 104:59–89.

Sheahan, J. 1987. *Patterns of Development in Latin America: Poverty, Repression, and Economic Strategy.* Princeton: Princeton University Press.

Shepard, Scott. 2003. "Sharpton Launches Run for President." *Atlanta Journal-Constitution,* January 22, home edition, news, 3A.

Shugart, Matthew S. 1994. "Minorities Represented and Underrepresented." In *Electoral Systems in Comparative Perspective: Their Impact on Women and Minorities,* ed. Wilma Rule and Joseph S. Zimmerman. Westport, CT: Greenwood Press.

Singh, Robert. 1998. *The Congressional Black Caucus: Racial Politics in the U.S. Congress.* Thousand Oaks, CA: Sage.

Skjeie, Hege, and Mari Teigen. 2005. "Political Constructions of Gender Equality: Travelling Towards . . . a Gender Balanced Society?" *NORA: Nordic Journal of Women's Studies* 13 (3): 187–97.

Skocpol, Theda. 1999. "Advocates without Members: The Recent Transformation of American Civic Life." In *Civic Engagement in American Democracy,* ed. Theda Skocpol and Morris P. Fiorina, 461–510. Washington, DC: Brookings Institute Press.

Skocpol, Theda. 2003. "Voice and Inequality: The Transformation of American Civic Democracy." American Political Science Association presidential address. http://www.apsanet.org/skocpol.cfm.

Smeeding, Timothy. 2003. "Public Policy and Economic Inequality: US In Comparative Perspective." Luxembourg Income Study working paper. http://www.lisproject.org/publications/wpapers.htm.

Smith, Andrea. 2001. "Violence against Women of Color." In *Time to Rise: U.S. Women of Color—Issues and Strategies,* ed. Maylei Blackwell, Linda Burnham, and Jung Hee Choi, 89–102. Berkeley, CA: Women of Color Resource Center.

Snow, David, and Doug McAdam. 2000. "Identity Work Processes in the Context of Social Movements." In *Self, Identity, and Social Movements,* ed. Sheldon Stryker, Timothy J. Owens, and Robert W. White, 41–67. Minneapolis: University of Minnesota Press.

Spill, Rorie L., Michael J. Licari, and Leonard Ray. 2001. "Taking on Tobacco: Policy Entrepreneurship and the Tobacco Litigation." *Political Research Quarterly* 54 (3): 605–22.

Staggenborg, Suzanne. 1995. "Can Feminist Organizations Be Effective?" In *Feminist Organizations: Harvest of the New Women's Movement,* ed. Myra Marx Ferree and Patricia Yancey Martin, 339–55. Philadelphia: Temple University Press.

StateNet. 2005a. "Legislative Reporting." http://www.legislate.com/resources/ (accessed October 20, 2005).

StateNet. 2005b. "Partisanship Chart." http://www.statenet.com/resources/ (accessed October 2005).

Staudt, Kathleen, ed. 1997. *Women, International Development, and Politics: The Bureaucratic Mire.* Philadelphia: Temple University Press.

Stepan-Norris, Judith. 1997. "The Making of Union Democracy." *Social Forces* 76 (2): 475–510.

Stepan-Norris, Judith, and Maurice Zeitlin. 2003. *Left Out: Reds and America's Industrial Unions.* Cambridge: Cambridge University Press.

Stetson, Dorothy McBride. 1995. "The Oldest Women's Policy Agency: The Women's Bureau in the United States." In *Comparative State Feminism,* ed. Dorothy McBride Stetson and Amy G. Mazur. Newbury Park, CA: Sage.

Stetson, Dorothy McBride. 1997. *Women's Rights in the USA.* 2nd ed. New York: Garland.

Stetson, Dorothy McBride, and Amy G. Mazur, eds. 1995. *Comparative State Feminism.* Newbury Park, CA: Sage.

Stetson, Dorothy McBride, and Amy G. Mazur. 2000. "Women's Movements and the State: Job-Training Policy in France and the U.S." *Political Research Quarterly* 53 (3): 597–623.

Stetson, Dorothy McBride, and Amy G. Mazur. 2006. "Measuring Feminist Mobilization: Cross-National Convergences and Feminist Networks in Western Europe." In *Global Feminism: Transnational Women's Activism, Organizing and Human Rights,* ed. Myra Marx Ferree and Aili Mari Tripp, 219–46. New York: New York University Press.

Strolovitch, Dara Z. 2004. "Affirmative Representation." *Democracy and Society* 1 (1): 3–5.

Strolovitch, Dara Z. 2006. "Do Interest Groups Represent the Disadvantaged? Advocacy at the Intersections of Race, Class, and Gender." *Journal of Politics* 68 (4): 893–908.

Strolovitch, Dara Z. 2007. *Affirmative Advocacy: Race, Class, and Gender in Interest Group Politics.* Chicago: University of Chicago Press.

Swain, Carol M. 1993. *Black Faces, Black Interests: The Representation of African Americans in Congress.* Cambridge: Harvard University Press.

Swank, Duane. 2006. *Comparative Parties Dataset* and *Comparative Parties Codebook.* http://www.marquette.edu/polisci/faculty_swank.shtml (on Duane Swank's home page) (accessed June 2006).

Swarns, Rachel L. 1998. "Pataki's Veto of Day Care Spending Rallies Democrats and Labor Unions." *New York Times,* May 8, late Edition—final, B-5.

Swers, Michele L. 2002. *The Difference Women Make: The Policy Impact of Women in Congress.* Chicago: University of Chicago Press.

Tamerius, Karen L. 1995. "Sex, Gender, and Leadership in the Representation of Women." In *Gender Power, Leadership, and Governance,* ed. Georgia Duerst-Lahti and Rita Mae Kelly, 93–112. Ann Arbor: University of Michigan Press.

Tang, Kwong-leung. 1998. "Rape Law Reform in Canada: The Success and Limits of Legislation." *International Journal of Offender Therapy and Comparative Criminology* 42 (3): 258–70.

Tarrow, Sidney. 1998. *Power in Movement.* 2nd ed. Cambridge: Cambridge University Press.

Tate, Katherine. 2001. "The Political Representation of Blacks in Congress: Does Race Matter?" *Legislative Studies Quarterly* 26 (4): 623–38.

Taylor, John, and Eleanor Burt. 2005. "Voluntary Organisations as e-Democratic Actors: Political Identity, Legitimacy and Accountability and the Need for New Research." *Policy & Politics* 33 (4): 601–16.

Taylor, Verta. 1999. "Gender and Social Movements." *Gender and Society* 13 (1): 8–33.

Taylor, Verta, and Nancy Whittier. 1999. "Collective Identity in Social Movement Communities." In *Waves of Protest: Social Movements since the Sixties,* ed. Jo Freeman and Victoria Johnson. New York: Rowman and Littlefield.

Texas Building and Procurement Commission (State of Texas). 2003. *Historically Underutilized Business.* http://www.window.state.tx.us/procurement/prog/hub/.

Texas Politics. 2006. The Legislative Branch. http://texaspolitics.laits.utexas.edu, Liberal Arts Instructional Technology Services, University of Texas at Austin.

Thomas, Sue. 1994. *How Women Legislate.* Oxford: Oxford University Press.

Timmerman, Greetje, and Cristien Bajema. 1999. "Sexual Harassment in Northwest Europe: A Cross-Cultural Comparison." *European Journal of Women's Studies* 6:419–39.

Tjaden, Patricia, and Nancy Thoennes. 1998. *Prevalence, Incidence, and Consequences of Violence against Women.* Research in Brief. National Institute of Justice, United States.

Tjaden, Patricia, and Nancy Thoennes. 2000. *Extent, Nature, and Consequences of Intimate Partner Violence.* Research Report. National Institute of Justice, United States.

Transportation Equity Act for the 21st Century (TEA-21). 1998. SEC. 1101.(b), Disadvantaged Business Enterprises, June 9.

Tremblay, Manon. 1998. "Do Female MPs Substantively Represent Women? A Study of Legislative Behaviour in Canada's 35th Parliament." *Canadian Journal of Political Science/Revue canadianne de science politique* 31:435–65.

Tripp, Aili Mari, and Alice Kang. 2008. "The Global Impact of Quotas: On the Fast Track to Female Representation." *Comparative Political Studies* 41 (5): 338–61.

Trotter, Joe, and Eric Ledell Smith. 1997. *African Americans in Pennsylvania Shifting Historical Perspectives.* University Park: Penn State University Press.

Truman, David. 1951. *The Governmental Process.* New York: Knopf.

United Nations Commission on the Elimination of All Forms of Discrimination against Women. 1998. *Report of the Special Rapporteur on Violence against Women, Its Causes and Consequences.* New York: United Nations. http://www.un.org/womenwatch/daw/csw.

United Nations Convention on the Elimination of All Forms of Discrimination against Women (CEDAW). 1998. http://www.un.org/womenwatch/daw/cedaw/.

U.S. Bureau of Labor Statistics (BLS). 2005a. *Characteristics of Minimum Wage Workers: 2005.* http://www.bls.gov/cps/minwage2005.htm.

U.S. Bureau of Labor Statistics (BLS). 2005b. Division of Labor Force Statistics. *Union Membership.* Table 5, "Union Affiliation of Employed Wage and Salary Workers by State." http://www.bls.gov/news.release/union2.t05.htm (accessed September 23, 2005).

U.S. Bureau of the Census. 2000a. *DP-1. Profile of General Demographic Characteristics: 2000 Data Set: Census 2000 Summary File 1 (SF 1) 100-Percent Data Geographic Area: Chicago city, Illinois.* http://factfinder.census.gov (accessed March 21, 2005).

U.S. Bureau of the Census. 2000b. *Statistical Abstract of the United States.* http://www.census.gov/prod/www/statistical-abstract-us.html.

U.S. Bureau of the Census. 2003. Table 4, "Poverty Status Status of Families, by Type of Family, Presence of Related Children, Race, and Hispanic Origin: 1959 to 2001." http://www.census.gov/hhes/www/poverty/histpov/hstpov4.html (accessed July 10, 2003).

U.S. Central Intelligence Agency. 1993. *CIA World Factbook 1993–1994.* Washington, DC: Brassey's.

U.S. Central Intelligence Agency. 2009. *The World Factbook 2009.* Washington, DC: Central Intelligence Agency. https://www.cia.gov/library/publications/the-world-factbook/index.html.

U.S. Department of Justice, Civil Rights Division. 2004. http://www.usdoj.gov/crt/crim/trafficking_newsletter/ antitraffnews_novdec04.pdf (accessed October 20, 2005).

U.S. Department of Labor. 2004. *Highlights of Women's Earnings in 2003.* Bureau of Labor Statistics, U.S. Department of Labor. Report 978. http://www.bls.gov/cps/cpswom2003.pdf.

U.S. Department of Labor, Wage and Hour Division. www.dol.gov/esa/minwage/america.htm (accessed September 23, 2005).

U.S. Department of Labor, Women's Bureau and the President's Interagency Council on Women, the White House. 1996. *Bringing Beijing Home: The Fourth World Conference—A Success for the World's Women.* January.

U.S. Disadvantaged Business Enterprise (DBE). *See* Transportation Equity Act for the 21st Century.

U.S. Small Business Act (15 U.S.C. 637(d)). 1953. http://www.sba.gov/regulations/sbaact/sbaact.html.

Van Der Ros, Janneke. 1994. "Norway: The State and Women: A Troubled Relationship in Norway." In *Women and Politics Worldwide,* ed. Barbara J. Nelson and Najma Chowdhury, 527–44. New Haven: Yale University Press.

Verba, Sidney, Kay Lehman Schlozman, and Henry Brady. 1995. *Voice and Equality: Civic Voluntarism in American Politics.* Cambridge, MA: Harvard University Press.

Verloo, Mieke, and Connie Roggeband. 1996. "Gender Impact Assessment: The Development of a New Instrument in the Netherlands." *Impact Assessment* 14 (1): 3–20.

Vickers, Jill, Pauline Rankin, and Christine Appel. 1993. *Politics as If Women Mattered.* Toronto: University of Toronto Press.

Walby, Sylvia. 1990. *Theorizing Patriarchy.* Oxford: Basil Blackwell.

Walker, Gillian. 1990. *Family Violence and the Women's Movement: The Conceptual Politics of Struggle.* Toronto: University of Toronto Press.

Walker, Jack L. 1991. *Mobilizing Interest Groups in America: Patrons, Professions, and Social Movements.* Ann Arbor: University of Michigan Press.

Warren, Mark. 2001. *Democracy and Association.* Princeton, NJ: Princeton University Press.

Watchke, Gary. 2001. Profile of the 2001 Wisconsin Legislature: Jan. 3, 2001, Brief 01-3. *Wisconsin Briefs.* Legislative Reference Bureau.

Weir, Margaret. 1992. "Ideas and the Politics of Bounded Innovation." In *Structuring Politics: Historical Institutionalism in Comparative Analysis,* ed. Sven Steinmo, Kathleen Thelen, and Frank Longstreth. Cambridge: Cambridge University Press.

Welch, Susan. 1990. "The Impact of At-Large Elections on the Representation of Blacks and Hispanics." *Journal of Politics* 52 (4): 1050–76.

Welch, Susan, and John Hibbing. 1992. "Financial Conditions, Gender, and Voting in American National Elections." *Journal of Politics* 54 (1): 197–213.

Welch, Susan, and Donley T. Studlar. 1990. "Multi-Member Districts and the Representation of Women: Evidence from Britain and the United States." *Journal of Politics* 52:391–412.

Weldon, S. Laurel. 1999. "The Political Representation of Women: The Impact of a Critical Mass." In *Stand! Contending Ideas and Issues: Comparative Politics,* ed. Rebecca Davis. Boston: Houghton Mifflin.

Weldon. S. Laurel. 2001. "Review of *Voice, Trust and Memory.*" *Constellations* 8 (2): 272–79.

Weldon, S. Laurel. 2002a. *Protest, Policy and the Problem of Violence against Women: A Cross-National Comparison.* Pittsburgh: University of Pittsburgh Press.

Weldon, S. Laurel. 2002b. "Beyond Bodies: Institutional Sources of Representation for Women in Democratic Policymaking." *Journal of Politics* 64 (4): 1153–74.

Weldon, S. Laurel. 2004a. "The Dimensions and Policy Impact of Feminist Civil Society: Democratic Policymaking on Violence against Women in the Fifty U.S. States." *International Feminist Journal of Politics,* 6 (1): 1–28.

Weldon, S. Laurel. 2004b. "Citizens, Victims, Deviants: Restructuring Government Policies on Violence Against Women in Canada." Paper presented to the Midwest Political Science Association meeting, April, Chicago.

Weldon, S. Laurel. 2006a. "The Structure of Intersectionality: A Comparative Politics of

Gender." Symposium on the Comparative Politics of Gender, *Politics and Gender* 2 (2): 235–48.

Weldon, S. Laurel. 2006b. "Inclusion, Solidarity and Social Movements: The Global Movement on Gender Violence." *Perspectives on Politics* 4 (1): 55–74.

Weldon, S. Laurel. 2006c. "Women's Movements, Identity Politics, and Policy Inputs: A Study of Policies on Violence Against Women in the 50 United States." *Political Research Quarterly* 59 (1): 111–22.

Weldon, S. Laurel. 2008. "The Concept of Intersectionality." In *Politics, Gender, and Concepts,* ed. Gary Goertz and Amy G. Mazur. Cambridge: Cambridge University Press.

Weldon, S. Laurel. 2010. Home page: Identity Politics Data. http://web.ics.purdue.edu/~weldons/.

Whitaker, Lois Duke, ed. 1999. *Women in Politics: Outsiders or Insiders?* 3rd ed. Upper Saddle River, NJ: Prentice-Hall.

Whitby, Kenny J. 1997. *The Color of Representation.* Ann Arbor: University of Michigan Press.

Whitby, Kenny J., and George A. Krause. 2001. "Race, Issue Heterogeneity and Public Policy: The Republican Revolution in the 104th US Congress and the Representation of African-American Policy Interests." *British Journal of Political Science* 31 (3): 555–72.

Whittier, Nancy. 1995. *Feminist Generations.* Philadelphia: Temple University Press.

Williams, Melissa. 1998. *Voice, Trust, and Memory: Marginalized Groups and the Failings of Liberal Representation.* Princeton: Princeton University Press.

Wilson, Graham K. 1990. *Interest Groups.* Oxford: Blackwell.

Winkelmann, Rainer. 1997. *Econometric Analysis of Count Data.* 2nd ed. New York: Springer.

Wolbrecht, Christina. 2000. *The Politics of Women's Rights: Parties, Position, and Change.* Princeton: Princeton University Press.

Wolbrecht, Christina, Karen Beckwith, and Lisa Baldez. 2008. *Political Women and American Democracy.* New York: Cambridge University Press.

Wolbrecht, Christina, and Rodney Hero, eds. 2005. *The Politics of Democratic Inclusion.* Philadelphia: Temple University Press.

Women of Color Resource Center. 2003. *National Directory of Women of Color Organizations and Projects.* Oakland, CA: Women of Color Resource Center.

World Bank, Operations Evaluation Department. 1999. "An Evaluation of the Gender Impact of Bank Assistance." Approach paper. Washington, DC: World Bank.

Wright, Erik Olin. 1997. *Class Counts: Comparative Studies in Class Analysis.* Cambridge: Cambridge University Press.

Wright, Gerald C., Robert S. Erickson, and John McIver. 1985. "Measuring State Political Ideology with Survey Data." *Journal of Politics* 47:469–89.

Wright, Gerald C., Robert S. Erickson, and John McIver. N.d. http://socsci.colorado.edu/~mciverj/wip.html (accessed October 20, 2005).

Young, Iris Marion. 1990. *Justice and the Politics of Difference.* Princeton: Princeton University Press.

Young, Iris Marion. 1994. "Gender as Seriality: Thinking about Women as a Social Collective." *Signs* 19:713–38.

Young, Iris Marion. 1997. "Deferring Group Representation." In *Nomos: Group Rights,* ed. Will Kymlicka and Ian Shapiro. New York: New York University Press.

Young, Iris Marion. 2000. *Inclusion and Democracy.* Oxford Series in Political Theory. Oxford: Oxford University Press.

Young, Iris Marion. 2001. "Activist Challenges to Deliberative Democracy." *Political Theory* 29 (5): 670–90.

Young, Iris Marion. 2005. *On Female Body Experience: "Throwing Like a Girl" and Other Essays.* New York: Oxford University Press.

Zimmerman, Joseph S. 1994. "Equity in Representation for Women and Minorities." In *Electoral Systems in Comparative Perspective: Their Impact on Women and Minorities,* ed. Wilma Rule and Joseph S. Zimmerman. Westport, CT: Greenwood Press.

Zinn, Maxine Baca, and Bonnie Thornton Dill. 1996. "Theorizing Difference from Multiracial Feminism." *Feminist Studies* 22 (92): 321–31.

Zippel, Kathrin. 2007. "The Missing Link for Promoting Gender Equality: Family-Work & Antidiscrimination Policies." Paper prepared for Janet Gornick and Marcia Meyers' Real Utopian Vision, "Institutions that Support Gender Egalitarianism in Parenthood and Employment." http://www.ssc.wisc.edu/~mscaglio/2006documents/Zippel_2007_Gender_Equality.pdf (accessed June 2008).

Index

Printed and bound by CPI Group (UK) Ltd, Croydon, CR0 4YY

09/06/2025

14686099-0002